VICTORIA

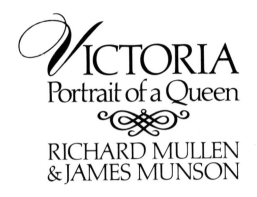

VICTORIA
Portrait of a Queen

RICHARD MULLEN
& JAMES MUNSON

BBC BOOKS

Published by BBC Books
A division of BBC Enterprises Ltd
Woodlands, 80 Wood Lane
London W12 OTT

First published 1987

First paperback edition published 1988

ISBN 0 563 20700 0

Typeset in 10/12 Ehrhardt and
printed in England by Butler & Tanner Ltd,
Frome and London

CONTENTS

To
the memory of
Jacob Munson and Eugene Wild,
Victorians

ℒIST OF ILLUSTRATIONS

REFACE

In the 150 years since the accession of Queen Victoria, numerous books about her have been published. Perhaps no other woman has ever had so many words written about her. It is certainly difficult to think of any other who wrote so many words herself.

This biography grew out of a BBC radio series designed to present a portrait of the Queen. Our emphasis throughout has been on the Queen's personality as seen either by herself or by those who came into contact with her. When she asked Theodore Martin to write a biography of Prince Albert that project grew to five volumes. Queen Victoria lived twice as long as her husband and it would take at least ten volumes to recount the story of her life and reign in detail. Even the Victorians would not have accepted a book of that length.

Sir Theodore Martin also wrote a shorter book called *Queen Victoria as I Knew Her*, which appeared shortly after her death. Max Beerbohm eventually acquired a copy and followed his usual practice of adding humorous comments throughout. Sir Theodore ends his memoir with a grand flourish: 'Victoria the Great and the Good'. To this Beerbohm added: 'The good and human, the likeable, the even lovable, and the peculiar, the never uninteresting – essentially the simple Sir Theodore and the serpentine Lytton Strachey are at one about her.' It is the aim of this biography to show how Victoria was 'good ... human ... likeable ... lovable, and ... peculiar'. Certainly she has never been 'uninteresting', for she has fascinated people ever since that June dawn of 1837 when she was called from her bed to the throne.

The authors would first wish to thank Her Majesty the Queen for gracious permission to quote material held under Crown Copyright and correspondence in the Royal Archives. They would also like to thank: the Most Noble the Marquess of Salisbury, the Rt Hon. the Earl of Clarendon, the Rt Hon. the Viscount Harcourt, Mrs Alice Russell and Sir William Gladstone for permission to quote from collections in Christ Church College, Oxford, the Bodleian Library and Clwyd Record Offices; Mr P. L. V. Mallet and Mr R. B. Backhouse, QC, for permission to use manuscripts in their possession; the Librarian and Trustees of Lambeth Palace Library; the Keeper of Western Manuscripts, Bodleian Library, Oxford; Princeton University Library; the Librarian of Congress, Washington DC; the British Library; the National Trust; the Historical Manuscripts Commission and the Record Offices of Clwyd, Kent and Staffordshire for permission to examine or quote from manuscript collections in their possession. We would especially like to thank the staff of Duke Humfrey's Library at the Bodleian in Oxford, for the kind assistance one has come to expect while using its many collections, which the thirteen-year-old Princess Victoria described in 1832 as 'immense'. We would also like to express our gratitude to the late Mr Robert Taylor for allowing us to see in his collection at Princeton University Sir Max Beerbohm's copy of Sir Theodore Martin's memoir of Queen Victoria, and to Mr Oliver Everett, the Librarian, Windsor Castle.

We would like to thank Mr Alan Haydock, who first suggested the radio series, not only for his help in the initial stages of the work, but for all he has done to preserve the richness of radio, and to Miss Gillian Hush, who undertook at short notice the actual production of the series. Finally, we are grateful to Miss Jenny Smith, Mrs Susan Kennedy and Miss Nora Mullen for their help in the writing of this book, and Mr and Mrs Reginald Evans for their hospitality to us while staying in Windsor.

Richard Mullen
James Munson
Oxford, 1986

ONE
HOPE FROM THIS CHILD

On 24 May 1819 a large, tired balding man sat down in Kensington Palace to write a triumphant letter to an English friend in Germany:

> I have now the satisfaction of acquainting you, for the information of all our friends at Amorbach with the safe delivery of the Duchess at a quarter past four this morning, of a most perfect female child. ... I never quitted her [the Duchess] for a moment the whole night and after six hours and a quarter had the satisfaction of witnessing the prosperous result of all our anxieties. We were attended by the Archbishop of Canterbury, the Bishop of London, the Duke of Wellington and Lord Bathurst, Mr Vansittart, Mr Canning, besides the Duke of Sussex and Lord Lansdowne who were there as private friends.

The writer was Edward, Duke of Kent, and it was appropriate that this 'most perfect female child' was born at Kensington Palace in London. The mellow red brick building had provided the setting for some of the most important events in the history of his family. At Kensington the last female sovereign, Queen Anne, had died just over a century before. The Duke of Kent was the great-great-grandson of George I, who had moved into Kensington when he arrived from Hanover to succeed Queen Anne in 1714.

By 1819 the Hanoverian dynasty was in a poor state. For the last decade George III had been unable, because of blindness and senility, to perform his duties as King. After a reign of half a century he was now confined to a few rooms at Windsor where occasionally the sound of his harpsichord broke the melancholy aura that hung over him and his dynasty. His eldest son, the Prince Regent, was a man who had done little to arouse respect for the monarchy. He shared his unpopularity with his six brothers, who had a reputation for immorality, rudeness, indolence and debt.

Compared with his brothers, the fourth son, the Duke of Kent, had always been a busy man. He was a strange combination of visionary and martinet. In the Army he had been an efficient officer but a hated one, notorious for his belief in flogging. Yet he was also deeply interested in social reform, a friend of leading radicals, and a supporter of numerous useful charities such as the Literary Fund for Distressed Authors and the Lying-in Charity for Delivering Poor Women at Their Own Habitations.

For many years the Duke, like several of his brothers, had lived with a woman: Madame de St Laurent was for all practical purposes his wife. The Royal Dukes showed little desire to marry what their eldest brother called a royal German *Hausfrau*, and there was little other choice if they were to make a marriage which would gain their father's approval and an increased grant from Parliament. The succession seemed guaranteed to fall upon the Prince Regent's only child, Princess Charlotte. Her popularity increased when she married, in spite of her father's wishes but to the public's great approval, Prince Leopold of Saxe-Coburg. All the nation's hopes as well as Prince Leopold's happiness were destroyed when the Princess died in childbirth in 1817 at the age of twenty-one.

Suddenly the country faced a frightening prospect. George III had had fifteen children, but now there were no legitimate grandchildren. His two eldest sons had made unhappy marriages and it seemed unlikely they would produce an heir. Thus began the 'race for brides', when several of the younger Royal Dukes shook off the comforts of non-wedded bliss and set out in search of an inoffensive princess who could produce an heir to the greatest throne in the world. The Duke of Kent was already on that trail. He had been devoted to his niece Charlotte and had helped her by smuggling notes from Leopold while her father opposed the match. Leopold had sought to repay the debt by recommending the Duke to his widowed sister, Victoire or Victoria.

Though the Coburg family was part of the ancient royal house of Saxony their duchy was small and their power insignificant. But the family suddenly displayed a useful talent: the ability to make dazzling marriages. The German Chancellor Bismarck, with his characteristic vulgarity, was to call them the 'stud farm of Europe', and this new-found talent was to take them from their little duchy into most of the royal houses of Europe. Princess Victoria's first marriage, however, had hardly been a great achievement: the Prince of Leiningen had been only a minor princeling. When the Duke of Kent appeared, carrying warm recommendations from her younger brother Leopold, Victoria was already a widow with a son, Charles, and a daughter, Feodora. She did not accept the Duke of Kent at first, but he was persistent and finally she married him in Coburg on 29 May 1818; a second ceremony was held in England a few weeks later. After that the couple returned to Germany where they could live more comfortably on his insufficient income.

The Duke's departure from England was no doubt welcomed. He was thoroughly disliked by the Regent and by most of the Royal Family, who called him 'Joseph Surface' after the renowned hypocrite in Sheridan's *School for Scandal*. Lord Holland, a prominent politician, described the Duke well:

> He was ... regular to excess in all his habits. Household and family were more strictly disciplined than a regiment or a convent, and the duties, the occupations, and the amusements of every branch of his establishment recorded, docketed, and preserved with a minuteness I hardly venture to recount.... This observance of form and details, and above [all] this restless love of business which it caused, produced other results less creditable to his memory.

Many of these traits were inherited by his daughter, but fortunately in a gentler manner. The Duke was a healthy man with a strong belief in his destiny. His friends grew weary of hearing: 'My brothers are not so strong as I am; I have lived a regular life; I shall outlive them all: the crown will come to me and my children.' As in so many other things, he was half right.

When the Duke learned that his wife was pregnant he began to plan his return to England so that the child should be born there. It cost a great deal of money to move a royal couple across Europe with a caravan of servants and baggage. He wrote to one sister that he was coming out of duty to 'dearest Victoria' if he could raise enough in loans from friends. He had asked for the royal yacht, but if the Regent refused: 'I shall bring her over in the *Packet*.' This behaviour infuriated another sister: 'Edward ... is behaving like a fool and a madman.' One younger brother, the Duke of Sussex, urged him to hurry:

> As to the legal *necessity* of the Dutchess's coming to be confined in London, opinions may differ, but as to the *feeling*, there can *be no doubt*. John Bull is a very odd animal, and he must be cajoled. You will find it very difficult to drive into his Head that *his sovereign if born in a foreign Country* is *not a foreigner*, and this *at any price* you must prevent.

(Incidentally, this letter disproves the old canard that excessive underlining was a feminine habit introduced by Queen Victoria!) The cost of the journey was eventually met by Earl Fitzwilliam and others through a large loan. The Duke, always a most considerate husband, drove the coach himself for part of the way to make the trip as comfortable as possible for his Duchess.

Only the third brother, the Duke of Clarence, who also had a new German wife, Princess Adelaide, stood between the Kents and ultimate succession to the throne. Thus the birth of a child to the Duchess was an important event, requiring the presence of many official witnesses to ensure that no colourful legend could throw doubts on its circumstances. Kensington Palace had been divided into a series of suites for the younger children of George III and the redecoration of a room for the Duchess's confinement was only completed two days before the birth. The Kents arrived with their own doctor from Germany, and it is fitting that the greatest woman of her time was brought into the world by Charlotte von Siebold, who only two years before had become the first German woman to qualify as a doctor of medicine.

The first problem for the Duke was to find a name for his child. Some urged those characteristic Hanoverian names, Charlotte or Augusta, while others thought Elizabeth an apt name for a potential Queen. The decision was not for the Duke, however, but for the Prince Regent. He refused all requests to send a name until the day of the christening. One of the godparents was Tsar Alexander I of Russia, and it was proposed that the feminine form of his name be given to the child. But the Regent hated the Tsar because of the way he had courted public opinion as well as the Regent's estranged wife on his visit to London five years before, and he would not allow the name Georgiana – after himself – to be coupled with Alexandrina. When the Royal Family gathered on 24 June 1819, the Regent finally said, 'Give her the mother's name.' So the baby was baptised Alexandrina Victoria. Though at times in childhood she was called Drina, she was normally known as

Victoria, and thus it is due to a fit of pique by the Prince Regent that the name Victoria – virtually unknown in England at that time – entered the language.

The Duchess was anxious to let her mother know all about the baby, to which news she responded with enthusiasm: 'May God's best blessings rest on the little stranger ... destined, perhaps to play a great part one day, if a brother is not born to take it out of her hands. The English like Queens.' The grandmother delighted in hearing details of the new baby from Charlotte von Siebold, who had hurried back to Coburg. Soon, too, the grandmother was writing about her daughter-in-law, the reigning Duchess: 'She was yesterday morning safely and quickly delivered of a little boy. Siebold, the accoucheuse, had only been called at three, and at six the little one gave his first cry in this world. ... The little boy is to be christened tomorrow and to have the name of Albert.'

For the Kents, the next few months were dominated by discussions about the Duke's debts. He even contemplated a lottery on his country estate as a way to raise funds. Part of the time was spent at Claremont, the lovely house in Surrey where the baby's Uncle Leopold lived. There was also a first visit to that most historic of the royal residences, Windsor, where so much of Victoria's life was to be spent. 'The Kents passed two nights at Windsor,' wrote the Duke's sister, Princess Mary:

> besides the baby she brought her daughter [Feodora] and Mlle de Spate [Spaeth, the Duchess's lady in waiting] – and they *all retired* to *rest* both evenings at 9 o'clock, the Duke and Dss of Kent, Baby, Nurse, the Pss Feodora, and Mdlle Spate *all* wished them good Night at the same time and actually *went to bed* to the very great amusement of the whole society of Windsor.

In December the Duke decided to take his family to Devon in the hope of finding some sun: 'My little girl thrives under the influence of a Devonshire climate, and is I am delighted to say, strong, and healthy; too healthy, I fear, in the opinion of some members of my family by whom she is regarded as an intruder. How largely she contributes to my happiness.' He loved to display the infant to his friends and would say 'Take care of her, for she will be Queen of England.' As with all fathers, every event of her existence was an item of news and he hastened to inform friends in Germany in the last days of 1819: 'Our little girl cut her first tooth yesterday without the least pain ... a second is almost making its appearance.' His only disappointment was the weather in Sidmouth where 'the cold [is] intense, a hard frost and everything covered with snow'.

This period of domestic happiness was all too short. The Duke was a powerful man, but on one walk he caught a chill and made the proverbial mistake of staying in wet clothes. When the chill developed into a serious illness the Duchess became alarmed and sent for her brother Leopold. He arrived with Baron von Stockmar, his secretary, who was also a physician. He told the Duchess that the Duke was dying. It was doubtful whether he had the strength even to sign his will. 'With difficulty', Stockmar recalled, 'he wrote "Edward" ... looked attentively at each separate letter, and asked if the signature was clear and legible. Then he sank back exhausted on his pillow. The next morning all was over.'

The Duke's last words to his wife had been: 'Act uprightly and trust in God.' She had little else to trust in on the morning of 23 January 1820. Here she was, a woman in her mid-thirties, twice widowed, with little knowledge of English and without money. She had her two elder children to consider. Above all the eight-month-old infant, now fatherless, was one of the closest heirs to the throne. The Duke's father, George III, followed him into the royal vaults at Windsor within a few days. Now only three ageing uncles stood between Victoria and the crown.

The Duchess was lucky in having her brother Leopold at her side. He was rich, for Parliament had set his allowance at £50,000 a year. Leopold often liked to boast to Queen Victoria, particularly when he was in need of her diplomatic support, of all he had done in those dark days of January 1820. Yet it is true that it was he who paid for the return to Kensington Palace, back to those rooms glistening with their new decorations and Empire furniture that had contributed so mightily to the mountain of debts that had encumbered the Duke of Kent.

Prince Leopold counselled his sister that the young Victoria must be brought up in England as an English princess. In the history of the British monarchy, it is difficult to think of anyone who was faced with a more daunting task without any preparation than the Duchess of Kent. It is easy enough to criticise her mistakes. Yet this German princess managed to produce the best-educated heir in centuries. Her achievement is all the greater when the hostility of much of the Royal Family is considered. To them, Victoria was 'an intruder', as her father had said. Should she succeed to the throne, the Hanoverian dynasty would be split. Women could not reign in Hanover itself as long as a male member of the family were alive, and so one of her uncles would succeed to their ancestral territory of Hanover. The only hope was for the Duke of Clarence to produce an heir to save the Hanoverian heritage from the grasping Coburgs. At the end of 1820 the Duchess of Clarence had a daughter, and George IV signified his joy by giving her the regal name of Elizabeth. 'There is great delight here', wrote one of the new King's intimates, Lady Cowper, 'at the Dss of Clarence's daughter. I suppose the King likes it to cut out Victoria and Leopold and so am I.' But Princess Elizabeth lived only a few months. Eighty years later Edward VII was making his way through the corridors of Windsor on his first visit as King when his wife asked him who was the little child commemorated in a sculpture. 'If that child had lived, you and I would not have been here,' said Queen Victoria's successor.

The Duchess of Clarence – later Queen Adelaide – is one of the kindest figures in royal history. Rather than harbour resentment against the Duchess of Kent for possessing a healthy child, she was one of the few members of the Royal Family to visit her fellow German duchess. A friend heard her speak of her infant niece:

> She also said that the ... little Girl, was a very fine Child and full of Spirits. Someone sent its Mother a Miniature Picture of the Duke, done when he was very Young, which she suspended round the Child's neck. When the little child was brought to the Dutchess of Clarence, she had her two little Hands spread over the Picture, and laughed as if delighted ... upon the Duke of Clarence entering the Child pointed to the [Garter] Star and exclaimed 'Papa, Papa'.

Victoria's grandmother was always delighted to hear about 'The Mayflower', as she called her granddaughter after the month of her birth. She often sent back similar stories about Victoria's slightly younger cousin: 'Albert is teething like his little cousin, but he is feverish with it and not at all well.' Six months later she had further news: 'The little fellow is the pendant to the pretty cousin, very handsome, but too slight for a boy, lively, very funny, all good nature, and full of mischief.' Already so many of Prince Albert's foremost characteristics were present: good looks, charm within the family circle, cleverness and weak health. The old lady in Coburg possessed the family talent for matchmaking, and from quite early on she saw a marriage between the cousins as a way to regain that glittering prospect that Prince Leopold had lost by the death of Princess Charlotte. Years later, when Queen Victoria reflected on this, it only caused her to recall her dead grandmother with more veneration: 'She could have little guessed what a blessing she was preparing not only for this country but for the world at large.'

It would be wrong to think that Victoria's only grandparent did nothing but plot marriages. Often she was full of good maternal advice. 'Do not', she warns her daughter when Victoria was almost four, 'tease your little puss with learning. She is so young still.' But the Duchess had already begun to tease her 'little puss with learning', and she had the great good fortune to have a superb assistant at hand in the person of Princess Feodora's governess, Louise Lehzen, the daughter of a German pastor. In 1824 she was appointed Victoria's governess, and three years later George IV gave her a Hanoverian title. Some of the English nobility sneered at 'the Baroness', who had the habit of chewing caraway seeds, but she proved both an excellent governess and a loyal friend.

Throughout her long life, Queen Victoria frequently reflected on her childhood. Like many people, she came increasingly to the conviction that it was not a happy time. In the last few months of her life, one granddaughter asked about her earliest memory. She required only a few moments to think back almost eighty years and replied: 'Going to Carlton House Terrace to watch Sir Thomas Lawrence painting the Duchess of Gloucester.' In her fifties, the Queen wrote some reminiscences of her childhood at Kensington:

I can remember crawling on a yellow carpet spread out for that purpose – and being told that if I cried and was naughty my 'Uncle Sussex' would hear me and punish me, for which reason I always screamed when I saw him! I had a great horror of *Bishops* on account of their wigs and *aprons*. I used to ride a donkey given me by my Uncle, the Duke of York, who was very kind to me. ... The last time I saw him ... he had Punch and Judy in the garden for me. ... I was brought up very simply – never had a room to myself till I was nearly grown up – always slept in my Mother's room till I came to the Throne. ... We lived in a very simple plain manner; breakfast was at half past eight, luncheon at half past one, dinner at seven – to which I came generally (when it was no regular large dinner party) – eating my bread and milk out of a small silver basin. Tea was only allowed as a great treat in later years. ... Up to my 5th year I had been very much indulged by every one, and set pretty well *all* at defiance ... *all* worshipped the poor fatherless child. ... At 5 years old, Miss Lehzen was placed about me, and though she was most kind, she was very firm and I had a proper respect for her. I was naturally very passionate, but always most contrite afterwards. I was taught from the first to beg my maid's pardon for any naughtiness or rudeness towards her; a feeling I have ever retained, and think everyone should *own* their fault in a kind way to any one, be he or she the lowest – if one has been rude to or injured them by word or deed, especially those below you.

Like most people, Queen Victoria liked contrasting the simplicity of her early life with the luxury her children enjoyed. She once burst out to Disraeli: 'All I know is, I was brought up very differently. I never had a room to myself; I never had a sofa, nor an easy chair: and there was not a single carpet that was not threadbare.' None of these things was a real loss. What she lacked was companionship. She was devoted to her half-sister Feodora, even though she was twelve years older, but she left Kensington to marry a German prince when Victoria was only nine. Occasionally children were invited to play with the lonely Princess. One recalled:

> I was taken by my grandmother, Lady Radnor ... when she paid a visit to the Duchess of Kent. ... A little girl was playing by herself ... the young Princess quickly and warningly told me, referring to toys scattered around 'You must not touch those, they are mine; and I may call you Jane, but you must not call me Victoria.'

The young Victoria was so possessive of her toys because they were essential to her. In the 1890s an exhibition of the dolls the Queen had made as a little girl led her to write:

> She was quite devoted to dolls and played with them till she was 14. Her favourites were small ones and small wooden ones which could be dressed as she liked ... *she* was an *only* child and except occasional visits of other children lived always *alone*, without companions. Once a week one child came.

These were not baby dolls but dolls dressed in costumes based on the works of Sir Walter Scott or on the many ballets and operas that she saw. The dolls – there are well over one hundred of them today at the Museum of London – required great artistic skill, patience, imagination and concern for detail. The ever faithful Lehzen helped to make them. She also helped her to make cushions for them, the smallest of which were about half an inch square. For these the princess and her governess could use the cloth samples that dressmakers sent to the various royal ladies in Kensington.

Even as a child, Victoria had – perhaps because of her loneliness – that capacity for self-pity which became, in time, her most trying characteristic. When she was a child it had a humorous side, as her grandmother noted on a visit from Coburg:

> Lehzen takes her gently from the bed and sits her down on the thick carpet, where she has to put on her stockings. One has to contain oneself not to burst out laughing when she says in a tragic tone of voice: 'Poor Vicky! She is an unhappy child! She doesn't know which is the right stocking and which is the left! I am an unhappy child!'

The little girl had books for companionship. One of her favourites was *Ellen or the Naughty Girl Reclaimed*, which taught proper behaviour by the use of paper dolls. The opening lines applied to a girl who, by her own accounts, was headstrong and passionate:

> This little girl, whom now you see,
> To mind mamma will not agree,
> And though her face is fair and mild,
> You view a stubborn, naughty child.

The Duchess has never been given proper credit for the education that the young Princess received. Queen Victoria has often been portrayed as a rather unintelligent woman, an idea which springs from comments by those who find the idea of an intelligent and cultured royal person almost a personal insult. Several academic historians, for example, with little ability outside their own patch, continue to dismiss a woman who was fluent in several foreign languages, a talented musician, a fine artist and a good writer. Ironically because she was a girl, she probably received a better education than many boys. Early nineteenth-century education was obsessed with the classics and almost all public schools devoted their time to beating the intricacies of Latin and Greek, and little else, into the heads of little boys. One of her ministers arrived at the Colonial Office in the 1840s with a famous reputation for Greek verse; unfortunately he had not found New Zealand on a map. This was never a problem for his Queen. It was thought to be a waste of time to teach any Greek or more than a smattering of Latin to a mere girl, and thus she had to make do with an education that fitted her for her future position. Most of her ministers could read Greek, but few of them could do much more than stumble through a few phrases with French, German or Italian diplomats. Victoria, thanks to her mother's care, had no trouble there.

The Duchess accepted 'the absolute necessity of bringing her up entirely in this Country, that every feeling should be that of her native land'. A month before Victoria's fourth birthday her mother selected a clergyman, George Davys, to supervise her education, though she regretted that he was 'most inadequately recompensed for his service, because I have barely the means allowed me, to maintain the small establishment I have'. She tried to get him preferment in the Church and he eventually became Dean of Chester. After Victoria came to the throne, he was made Bishop of Peterborough.

Davys had that laudable nineteenth-century habit of keeping a diary, and he recorded his first meeting with his pupil on Wednesday, 16 April 1823:

> She was not yet four years old. Her first lesson was the alphabet, which the Princess had learned before. ... The Duchess seems to be very anxious for the improvement of her little daughter and had promised her a reward if she said a good lesson. The Princess asked for the reward before she began the lesson.
>
> *April 21:* I wrote some short words on cards for Princess Victoria and endeavoured to interest her by making her bring them to me from a distant part of the room as I named them.
>
> *May 17:* I asked whether the little Princess had been good in the nursery. The Duchess

said she had been good that morning, but that the day before there had been a little storm. The little one very honestly added: 'Yes two storms – one at dressing and one at washing.'

Davys, much impressed, was one of the first to note what became one of Victoria's most admired characteristics, her high regard for truth: 'I have observed in the Princess a character of particular honesty, a willingness to confess when she has done wrong.' He gave the Princess basic instruction in religion as well as working with her on other subjects. Under him were other tutors in French, German, music, writing and drawing. All were men, though the Duchess insisted 'from feelings of delicacy' that a woman should instruct the little girl in dancing and 'carriage' – which evidently was a success since Victoria was renowned throughout her life for her excellence as a dancer and for the tremendous dignity with which, even as an old lady, she could walk through a room. She herself attributed this to her early dancing mistress. The Duchess or Lehzen was always present when a man was tutoring Victoria. Not only could the mother act as a chaperone, but she could improve her command of English.

One can only admire the sensible system that Davys adopted. Unlike many nineteenth-century teachers, he adhered to Plato's advice that for young people learning should be mixed with enjoyment. Each day had its own schedule. Take the schedule for Monday as an example: at 9.30 Davys started with an hour of geography and natural history; that was followed by an hour devoted to instruction in drawing by the distinguished watercolour artist Richard Westall. From the first, Victoria showed great skill in drawing. Then came three and a half hours for walking, playing and dinner. Work resumed at three with Latin, followed by more time for drawing, which then gave way to an hour's French. Between five and six o'clock her music master instructed her in singing, a talent she inherited from her mother. A final half hour was given over to more playtime. This, it must be stressed, was all for a young girl not yet ten. Other days featured other subjects, but all had the same sensible balance between work and play. On Saturday, Victoria repeated to Davys all she had learned that week.

Contrast all this with a schedule drawn up by Prince Albert for himself only a few years later. There the emphasis is on constant work, starting with French at six in the morning and ending with Latin at eight in the evening. It is perhaps no wonder that Albert lived only half as long as Victoria!

The lists that Davys kept of her reading show a wide and sensible choice of books. As early as seven she was reading *The Child's Grammar* by the delightfully named Mrs Lovechild. In 1829 the ten-year-old girl was reading a history of France and some Cicero, as well as poetry by Goldsmith and the very popular Cowper. Another book dealt with the wealth of the British colonies and was her introduction to a relevant subject.

In the spring of 1830, the Duchess gathered reports from all the tutors which she sent to two bishops. She feared that the King would assume direct control of his niece's education, but a favourable response from the bishops would strengthen her hand. Davys reported: 'The Princess is better informed in History than most

9

young Persons of the same Age. The same remark is applicable in Geography. The Princess can read Poetry extremely well. ... We are not far advanced in Latin.'

In other languages, though, she was making greater progress. She had begun French before she was six and her tutor said 'her pronunciation will be perfect', an opinion verified in later years by numerous Frenchmen. Contrary to most people's experience, she was better at speaking French than at writing it. Many people assumed that German was Victoria's first language, and some still assert that she spoke English with a slight German accent. This is not so: the Duchess was determined that English would be Victoria's mother tongue. The tutor's report noted that she had a German vocabulary of about 1500 words and had translated a children's book, *Mary and Her Cat*, into her mother's language. The German master praised her 'correct German pronunciation, which is particularly remarkable for its softness and its delicacy'.

It was with a pardonable sense of pride that the mother summed up her daughter's character:

> The general bent of Her character is strength of intellect, capable of receiving with ease information, and with a peculiar readiness in coming to a very just and beneficent decision. ... Her adherence to Truth, is of so marked a character, that I feel no apprehension of that bulwark being broke down, by any circumstance.

This was a remarkably accurate assessment. Almost every one of Victoria's ministers would have endorsed it. The 'adherence to Truth' was the facet of her character that Gladstone was repeatedly to stress.

People in the nineteenth century were just as interested as their descendants are today about that moment when an heir to a throne realises his or her future. In our age it was answered by the Prince of Wales in a television interview. For his great-great-great-grandmother the problem was more complex: her succession remained uncertain, for it was always possible that her Aunt Adelaide would have a child. So in March 1830 her mother informed the two bishops to whom she sent the tutors' reports:

> As yet, the Princess is not aware of the station that she is likely to fill; – she is aware of its duties and that a Sovereign should live for others! So that when her innocent mind receives the impression of her future fate, she receives it, with a mind formed to be sensible of what is expected from Her, – and, it is to be hoped, she will be too well grounded in her principles, to be dazzled with the station she is to look to.

On 10 March the Duchess spoke with the Bishop of London. In her memorandum of this conversation she recorded that she 'had not made up her mind to tell it [her possible succession to the throne] to the Princess in the hope she would come to the knowledge by accident'. At this point a note has been added: 'That occurred on the 11th in looking over Howlett's tables.' Lehzen later claimed that she deliberately left this chart of the royal succession for Victoria to discover, and that when she did she held up her right forefinger and said: 'I will be good!

I understand now, why you have urged me so much to learn, even Latin.' This anecdote became a standard ingredient in all the Victorian biographies. It is impossible now to decide how much of it may be true. The story originates in a letter that Lehzen sent to the Queen in 1867, in the margin of which Victoria wrote, 'I cried much on learning it and ever deplored this contingency.' The Duchess told the Bishop of London:

> It was not possible for anything to occur more naturally; what accident has done ... no art could have done half so well; and the result as to *impression* was that, I confidently anticipated. ... I cannot sufficiently express the happiness I feel. ... We have everything to hope from this child.

This favourable account may seem coloured by a mother's natural prejudice. But others, too, reported glowingly on the young Princess. One Whig lady recorded a visit to Claremont, where Victoria spent her happiest days as a child:

> The little Princess is the most delightful, intelligent and lively child. She lives a good deal with the grown up people as she sits thro' half the dinner, which is her supper. She is very observing, not at all shy, and seems to have amazing spirits. She is so interested in everything about other children, and never forgets one thing. ... I think her very pretty; her features are grown more delicate. She is still short for her age, tho' she has certainly grown lately; but from her being stout, her hair turned up, and her dress very womanly, the effect is shorter than she really is. Her education appears to me excellent, constant care and watchfulness without fuss or parade. She is allowed to run and romp as much as she pleases. ... She is very much advanced in her studies and is very quick. She seems also to have a great deal of fun about her and is very amusing; her manner is very good and she is at the same time very natural.

Victoria's accomplishments seemed to be one of the few things that were not dividing the two political parties, for the Tory Lady Wharncliffe recorded her impressions of the Princess about six months later. She had been to dinner at Kensington. It was a good dinner – 'not usual' Lady Wharncliffe says – but the main attraction was 'our little future Queen':

> Her Mother's conduct is the most sensible thing I ever saw – her own manner excellent, and the way she brings the child *gradually* forward quite perfect. When she went to bed we all stood up ... she curtsied ... and then walked off with her governess. She is very accomplished by *taste*, being very fond both of music and drawing, but fondest of all of her Dolls. ... I look to her to save us from Democracy, for it is impossible she should not be popular when she is older and more seen.

Yet behind all of these charming scenes lurked a horrible spectre in the shape of the Duchess's 'confidential servant', Sir John Conroy, who was to make the next few years a misery to Victoria. Conroy had been equerry to the Duke of Kent and remained in the Duchess's service, where he gradually became the most powerful person in her Household. Society gossip was convinced that the Duchess had become Conroy's mistress. There is no proof of this and the general tenor of her life would make it unlikely; yet she was certainly infatuated with him and became dependent upon him as her principal adviser and friend. Conroy was an ambitious man who formulated a plan known as the Kensington System. Its purpose was to maintain him as a permanent influence – it was quite possible that Victoria could succeed to the throne before she was eighteen, which meant that the Duchess would be Regent. Conroy controlled the Duchess, and he assumed that he could control the Princess too. That is where he went wrong, for Victoria increasingly resisted him. Conroy controlled all the Household except Lehzen, who always remained faithful to her Princess.

The Conroy saga is a sorry episode in Victoria's life. It caused great unhappiness between mother and daughter, and at times they were not on speaking terms. Yet it was not without value in forming Victoria's indomitable character: she learned how the insatiable drive towards power can obsess people, and to be wary of attempts to control her; she learned how to keep her own counsel; above all, she learned how to resist.

Conroy's bid for power did not go unnoticed. The Duchess of Northumberland held the title of Governess to the Princess, although Lehzen 'the sub Governess', actually performed the duties. Nevertheless the Duchess was concerned about developments at Kensington and in 1833, three years after her appointment, she wrote to Lord Liverpool, a prominent Tory, to express her fears:

Are you as anxious as I am about the influence that is gaining ground, with persons to whom we are so devotedly attached? I fully believe that excellent Mother is totally unconscious of the drift of his advice but she is fast in the Toils – not only is he admitted but he is courted.

Lord Liverpool was cautious in his reply, but he did spot the crucial point that Conroy's power sprang from the fact that the Duchess of Kent was isolated. 'Pray remember', he wrote in his draft reply, which has survived, 'with what asperity she is considered by almost every part of the Royal Family whereby every action of hers and those about her is seen with malevolence and ill will.' Victoria was even more isolated than her mother. Her half-sister and half-brother were in Germany. Her Uncle Leopold, who always had her best interests at heart, had become the first King of the Belgians in 1831; so, although he had watched over his niece's early years, he was not able now to guard her from Conroy's machinations.

What of the English Royal Family? George IV was in increasing ill health. His hostility to his sister-in-law never wavered, but he did show occasional kindness to his niece. Once he sent her a piano as a gift; she gave him one of her drawings in return. In 1826 Princess Victoria was taken to Windsor where her 'Uncle-King' lived with the last of that long line of mistresses, Lady Conyngham. It was an unforgettable experience for a girl who had just passed her seventh birthday. Among the guests was the Duke of Wellington, who noted: 'The King was very drunk, very blackguard, very foolish, very much out of temper at times, and a very great bore! . . . The little Princess is a delightful Child. She appeared to please the King.' Also there was that arch-intriguer Princess Lieven, wife of the Russian Ambassador, who wrote to her old lover Prince Metternich in Vienna:

> It was a family reunion, the first to my knowledge. The little future Queen was there. In spite of the caresses the King lavished on her, I could see that he did not like dandling on his sixty-four year old knee this little bit of the future, aged 7. . . . His Majesty got drunk one day, in a way people don't get drunk any longer; he was full of attentions towards me . . . and, as a result our good Duke [of Wellington] was in such ecstasies of hilarity that he laughed in his face. It was really the madhouse that he calls it.

Forty years later, Queen Victoria remembered this visit to Windsor:

> When we arrived at Royal Lodge the King took me by the hand, saying: 'Give me your little paw.' He was large and gouty but with a wonderful dignity and charm of manner. . . . Then he said he would give me something for me to wear, and that was his picture set in diamonds. . . . I was very proud of this, – and Lady Conyngham pinned it on my shoulder.

The next day Victoria saw the King driving in his phaeton with his sister. When he spotted his niece he roared:

> Pop her in, and I was lifted in and placed between him and Aunt Gloucester who held me round the waist. (Mamma was much frightened.) I was greatly pleased.

Victoria thus managed to see what court life was like in her uncle's time. It would be her life's mission to ensure that never again would a monarch live in idle frivolity amongst ageing mistresses.

In June 1830 George IV died and the Duke of Clarence succeeded as William IV. He was a bluff sailor who restored some popularity to the throne, but he lacked the essential attribute of dignity. He and Queen Adelaide were anxious to help their little niece and wanted to see her at court, but the Duchess resisted all their kind offers; she did not want her daughter in contact with the court. William IV's court was in fact a moral one except for the fact that his illegitimate children – the Fitzclarences – were at Windsor, where Queen Adelaide, with her customary kindness, made them welcome. Years later Victoria recalled these tensions in a letter to her own daughter:

> Always on pins and needles, with the whole family hardly on speaking terms. I (a mere child) between two fires – trying to be civil and then scolded at home. Oh! it was dreadful, and that has given me such a horror of Windsor, which I can't get over.

The Duchess refused to allow Victoria to attend the coronation of King William IV. Years later Victoria told a granddaughter how she recalled sitting at a window in tears as she watched all the carriages go by in the glorious pageant in which she had no place. Queen Adelaide was offended by this behaviour, and the blunt old King was furious. His anger only increased when Victoria and her mother began a series of travels round his kingdom. Sovereigns are rarely entirely happy (Victoria herself would be no exception) when too much attention is paid to their heir. To an old man like William IV, the chill of mortality was particularly unwelcome.

It was the Duchess who was anxious for her daughter to visit various parts of the country:

> I really think it will form a very sensible and discreet part of Victoria's education that we should *without form* move about the United Kingdom ... that she should, with her own eyes and ears, receive those valuable impressions, that such an interesting tour would give rise to.

Victoria's travels were of great benefit to her, not the least of which sprang from her mother's gift of a journal in which to record her impressions. For some time afterwards the Duchess and Lehzen inspected the entries, which at least ensured that this Journal, unlike most people's, went beyond its first week. It went on for almost seventy years and would eventually reach to over 120 volumes, though it is a great loss that Victoria's youngest child burned almost all of it after copying out selected passages that were used for the numerous published volumes of the Queen's writings. Even with this 'editing', however, her reactions to small as well as to great events can still be seen.

Two habits formed the outlook of many Victorians. To keep a journal forced a person to account for his time both to himself and to God: that is why the practice became so widespread. Secondly, children, particularly girls, were taught drawing so that they could understand and retain what they saw. Victoria, unlike most of her subjects, became adept both at writing her Journal and at drawing, skills which taught her to observe and to remember.

> Wednesday August 1st, 1832: We left K.P. at 6 minutes past 7 and went through the Lower-field gate to the right. We went on, and turned to the left by the new road to Regent's Park. The road and scenery is beautiful. 20 minutes to 9. We have just changed horses at Barnet, a very pretty little town.

Thus begins the thirteen-year-old girl's account of her travels. Obviously she was writing as the carriage bounced along, and she was already showing her devotion to precise facts: it is not just 'about 7', it is '6 minutes past 7'. This trip to Wales allowed the young heiress to take a close look at her inheritance. She was travelling when there were only a few miles of railway in the whole country, so she was able to experience the old way of travelling by coach with stops at places like Barnet for fresh horses. But she also saw the new England, the England of the Industrial Revolution that was springing up:

> We have just changed horses at Birmingham where I was two years ago and we visited the manufactories which are very curious. It rains very hard. We just passed through a town where all coal mines are and you see the fire glimmer at a distance in the engines. ... The men, women, children, country and houses are all black. But I can not by any description give an idea of its strange and extraordinary appearance ... wretched huts and carts and little ragged children.

Very few young ladies had any idea that such sights existed, but it was the

Duchess's view that her daughter should see things like this. Two years before, she had explained the purpose of Victoria's first visit to Birmingham to the Duchess of Northumberland: 'This was a valuable lesson to my child, and will make a lasting impression upon her.' It did make an impression. Queen Victoria became the first modern monarch to see the way ordinary people lived, and throughout her life she took a deep concern in improving their lot. Some of this she did by private charity, but she also tried to interest her ministers in promoting better housing. Such a concern sprang from some of the sights she saw on her early tours: in this, as in so many other things, her mother's care led to good results.

However, the main purpose of these travels was not to introduce the Princess to the problems of the people but rather to let the people see their Princess. In particular, the Duchess felt that the Princess should get to know the great aristocratic families, and mother and daughter began to pay visits to country houses. Most of their hosts were prominent Whigs, a fact which further angered William IV, who was becoming increasingly annoyed with his Whig ministers. In replying to public addresses of welcome, the Duchess's responses – drafted by Conroy – always stressed her daughter's commitment to the 'popular' cause.

Visits to two country houses give a flavour of their travels. Eaton Hall in Cheshire was the seat of the fabulously rich Marquess of Westminster. The prospect of a royal visit caused some concern. Victoria's 'Uncle Sussex', an enthusiastic country house visitor, had created havoc on one visit to Eaton Hall when he tumbled out of bed, pulling down all the bed hangings about his unwieldly person. The Duchess and her daughter were, however, perfect guests: they were impressed when they arrived, they were polite while they remained, and they knew when to depart. Victoria was amazed at the opulence:

> The breakfast-room is magnificent. There are 4 fireplaces; and the windows are of stained glass. ... A massive lustre of gold with an eagle likewise in gold hangs from the ceiling. ... The breakfast was served in handsome silver tea and coffee pots; a crown of gold with precious stones contained the bread. ... We then went into our own rooms and I wrote my journal. At 12 Mamma went into the great saloon where all the ladies were and an address from the mayor and corporation of Chester arrived and then another from the gentlemen and inhabitants of Chester.

The Marquess's daughter-in-law, Lady Elizabeth Grosvenor, praised the Duchess's behaviour:

> It really is an enterprise for a woman by herself in a responsible situation to meet all those Addresses and Testimonials, which she does so well and manages so cleverly under the semblance of a quiet journey, making the Princess known and securing friends for after times.

Tents were erected in the park so that 260 guests could sit down to a dinner and watch displays of archery. Inside the house the Duchess entertained the family by singing; she had a good voice, a fact which even George IV had been forced to admit. The Princess had inherited this gift and she too sang; she 'will have a fine voice,' wrote Lady Elizabeth. The Duchess, in spite of her limited means, bestowed charity in any neighbourhood she visited; the Chester Infirmary received £100 and the debtors (perhaps in memory of her husband) were sent £25.

It was a long day's carriage trip from Cheshire to Derbyshire to visit the greatest of the Whig grandees, the Duke of Devonshire, at Chatsworth. There the Duke had arranged some charades from *Bluebeard*, *Tom Thumb* and *Kenilworth* for his royal guests. Among those taking part was Henry Greville, a well-known society figure. Like his brother Charles, he kept a diary:

> The Princess ... appears gay and intelligent, and her manner is both childlike and royal. The dinner was very handsome: thirty-five people, with a great display of plate, and a band of music which was more noisy than harmonious. ... I sat next to the Baroness [Lehzen], who assured me that the Princess was a delightful child, not at all shy, fond of music and drawing, and has a great facility for learning modern languages. She always sleeps in her mother's room, and from the time she could speak has never been left alone with a servant. The Baroness always sits and reads to her while she dresses, and sits in her bedroom until the Duchess goes to bed.

Even before Conroy achieved his dominance at Kensington Palace, the Duchess had never allowed the Princess to sleep alone, nor did she permit her to have idle chatter with servants. At first this was to keep the child in ignorance of her closeness to the throne. However, there was another reason, which Conroy appears to have played upon. If anything happened to Princess Victoria, the throne would go to her uncle the Duke of Cumberland, George III's fifth son and the most hated man in England. It was popularly believed that he was guilty of incest with his sister Princess Sophia, and had killed his own valet – though in self-defence. Some whispered that he was planning to seize the throne from his niece; others feared he might even poison her. Whether the Duchess ever fully credited such rumours is not known, but they gave her further reason to protect her child. It also gave her cause to feel she must gather the support of the Whig aristocrats of Eaton Hall and Chatsworth.

The last few years of Victoria's childhood at Kensington were times of increasing tension. Conroy intensified his campaign to force Victoria to promise him a powerful position. Rivalry between the Duchess at Kensington and the King at Windsor also grew. The question of a husband for the young heiress began to become more important. The Duchess and her brother Leopold continued to favour their nephew Prince Albert, who was brought over to be introduced to his cousin. When King William heard that Victoria had been impressed, he did all he could to prevent another visit: the King wanted his niece to marry into the Dutch Royal Family, who were hostile to King Leopold of the Belgians. Other members of the Royal Family hoped that Victoria would marry one of her Hanoverian cousins, thus preserving the dynasty.

With all these tensions swirling round her, Victoria had great need of prudence. It was a virtue she had already closely cultivated. Perhaps that is why her confirmation, on 30 July 1835 – the first time she took the lead in a ceremony – so deeply affected her:

I went with the firm determination to become a true Christian, to try and comfort my dear Mamma in all her griefs, trials and anxieties, and to become a dutiful daughter to her. Also to be obedient to *dear* Lehzen who has done so much for me. I was dressed in a white lace dress, with a white crape bonnet with a wreath of white roses round it. . . . The King went first leading me, the Queen followed leading Mamma, and all the others followed after. . . . [I] knelt down and received the benediction from the Archbishop . . . who read also a very fine address to me, composed by him expressly for the occasion. . . . I felt the whole *very deeply*.

Archbishop Howley's address survives, in a handwritten copy bound in blue silk, at the Bodleian Library in Oxford. Like everyone else who spoke of Victoria, he stressed her 'love of Christian truth'. He then turned to her future:

The eminence on which you are placed by Divine Providence imposes on you the necessity of more particular caution: the conduct of persons in high stations is more particularly liable to observation, and whether for good or for evil the influence of their example and the weight of their authority have great and extensive effect. In return for the privileges they enjoy, they owe a debt to God and to man, and incur a more than ordinary responsibility. . . . They are consequently engaged . . . to walk humbly before God. . . . Persevere then without interruption in the course on which you have entered, and let the whole tenor of your life be conformable to this beginning.

'The whole tenor' of her life would indeed conform to the Archbishop's sermon. As her proud tutor, by then the Dean of Chester, wrote on the day after the confirmation: 'There is a beautiful promise of good in the princess.' Yet not even the sacredness of confirmation was free from dispute. More than sixty years later the elderly Queen Victoria said that the Duchess of Kent had asked Conroy to be at the service, but when William IV heard of this he told her: 'If he attends *I* stay away.' The King won that battle. However, the Duchess arranged that Conroy would receive Holy Communion with Victoria and herself a few days later.

Perhaps nothing reveals Victoria's developing personality as much as her comments on the books she was reading. Of one religious book she wrote: 'Just the sort of one I like: which is just plain and comprehensible and full of truth and good feelings. It is not one of those learned books in which you have to cavil at almost every paragraph.' This would remain her taste for life. Much of her reading was devoted to history, where she tried to understand both sides of a question. Having read Clarendon's royalist account of the Civil War, she then read the Puritan version by Mrs Hutchinson. Lehzen read to her while she was dressing and they got through ten volumes of Madame de Sévigné's letters – in the original French of course – which were considered the model for all letter-writers. The comment of the seventeen-year-old Princess could well describe the correspondence she was to conduct for many years with her eldest daughter:

I like them more and more, they are so beautiful, so easy, they show the character of the person who wrote them so perfectly, you become acquainted with her and hers, and there are such tender and beautiful feelings expressed in them, towards that daughter. . . . There is certainly nothing so beautiful of the kind, in any language as these letters.

She also read biography, particularly great literary classics like Boswell's *Life of Johnson* and Lockhart's *Life of Scott* which had just been published. Victoria was characteristic of her generation when she burst forth in her Journal: 'Oh! Walter Scott is my *beau idéal* of a Poet: I do so admire him both in Poetry and Prose.' As of yet she had not read any of his novels, though she knew some of the plots either from operas or from creating dolls based on his characters. She did not read any real novels until she came to the throne, for novels were considered frivolous and time-wasting.

As well as reading, Victoria enjoyed various hobbies to replace the dolls who had now been carefully retired. She began a collection of autographs, and Uncle Leopold would frequently send her interesting ones from the Continent. She even sought them further afield, asking an American diplomat to get her some autographs from his country; most of all she wanted James Fenimore Cooper's. In return she gave the diplomat a drawing of a scene from Cooper's novel of Renaissance Venice, *The Bravo*, which might imply that she had a little more acquaintance with the dangerous practice of novel-reading than 'Mamma' suspected.

Her greatest joy, however, was music, particularly opera. In one of her first breaks with Hanoverian tradition, she rejected Handel. Even the splendour of York Minster did not make *The Messiah* a favourite for her as it had been for her predecessors: 'It is considered very fine, but I must say that with the exception of a few choruses and one or two songs, it is very heavy and tiresome. . . . I am not at all fond of Handel's music, I like the present Italian school such as Rossini, Bellini, Donizetti.' She frequently went to the opera and preserved her impressions as well as sharpening her critical faculties by making perceptive criticisms of the singers in her Journal and by producing drawings or watercolours based on the operas. Opera gave her a taste for spectacle and drama, a valuable sense that she never lost. She made great progress in her singing lessons under the supervision of a well-known opera singer, Luigi Lablache.

Possibly she may also have found that some of the plots echoed the intrigues at Kensington Palace. In the last months before she came to the throne, Victoria resisted an outright demand by Conroy to appoint him her secretary. William IV was watching all this from afar and possibly, if his health had not been declining rapidly, he would have intervened. The King made his feelings plain at his seventy-second birthday dinner in August 1836 at Windsor. He had just discovered that the Duchess had 'stolen' an additional seventeen rooms for herself at Kensington. In front of a hundred horrified guests – including Victoria and her mother – the King said he hoped to live until 'that Young Lady' came of age in May 1837; this would prevent his sister-in-law, whom he referred to 'the person now near me, who is surrounded by evil advisors', from becoming Regent. The secret of Kensington was now all over London society. Years later, Queen Victoria pointed out one room at Windsor and said she still hated going into it as it was the room she had retired into after this outburst.

A few days before her eighteenth birthday, the King sent a letter to his niece. Lord Conyngham, the Lord Chamberlain, who delivered it, brushed aside Conroy as he tried to intercept him, saying that he had the King's command to give it directly to the Princess. The letter offered her an income of £10,000 a year which would be free from control by her mother and Conroy. Now the final battle began. Conroy spread rumours that the young girl was mentally unstable and incapable of reigning. Things got so bad that the Princess and her mother stopped speaking to each other. The government were aware of some of what was going on. The Foreign Secretary, Lord Palmerston, who had ambassadors' despatches opened whenever he could (this in the age when the sanctity of 'the diplomatic bag' was invented) discovered from an Austrian diplomat's letters that Conroy had been boasting that he would soon be ruling England.

As the cheers rang out in London for the eighteenth birthday of the young Princess on 24 May 1837, the old King's life was ebbing away at Windsor. On 12 June Palmerston considered the future in a letter to the British Ambassador in Vienna:

> The transition from 72 to 18 is great. ... The nation will not so readily believe in the will or will not of a girl of 18 as they have been accustomed to do in the determination of men of mature age. ... Few people have had the opportunities of forming a correct judgment of the Princess, but I am inclined to think she will turn out to be a remarkable person, and gifted with a great deal of strength of character.

TWO
*R*OSES WITHOUT THORNS

Thursday, 15th June, 1837. – After 9 we breakfasted.... Lehzen and I drove out and came home at 10 minutes to 11. The news of the King are so very bad that all my lessons save the Dean's are put off.... I regret rather my singing-lesson ... but duty and *proper feeling* go before *all pleasures.* – 10 minutes to 1, – I just hear that the Doctors think my poor Uncle the King cannot last more than 48 hours! Poor man! he was always kind to me, and he *meant* it well I know; I ... shall ever remember his kindness with gratitude.

Thus wrote the eighteen-year-old Princess Victoria a few days before succeeding to the throne. The story of her accession became a legend to the Victorians: countless biographies recounted how an unprepared and nervous girl was summoned from bed to throne without warning. That is all quite wrong. When Queen Victoria read one of these accounts in 1886, she was furious: 'The Queen ... referred to her Journal written at the time.... It shows the value of keeping a Journal, laborious and often overwhelming as she frequently finds it. It contradicts the *whole story* from *beginning* to *end*. She was NOT nervous.'

Nor was she entirely alone. The Duchess had summoned her son, Prince Charles of Leiningen, from Germany to persuade Victoria to appoint Conroy her permanent adviser. Prince Charles overheard Conroy say to the Duchess: 'If Princess Victoria will not listen to reason, *she must be coerced.*' The Prince warned his mother, in German, against any such plan. King Leopold had not been idle either, for he had sent over the ever-trusty Baron Stockmar to advise Victoria. Stockmar was a great help both in these dramatic days and for years to come. He had two great passions: the British constitution and the Coburg family, both of which he believed had been sent as a blessing to the world. It was his lifelong goal to have his two passions work in harmony. His belief that the monarch must be above moral reproach and party intrigue became the hallmark of Victoria's reign and her greatest legacy to the modern British monarchy.

On 19 June Princess Victoria retired to her room – or rather her mother's, for they still shared a bedroom – shortly before ten o'clock. While her hair 'was undoing', she read some more of Lockhart's *Life of Sir Walter Scott*. The next day, Tuesday, 20 June 1837, is one of the most dramatic in British history. It has been portrayed in paintings, engravings and films, yet the best account remains Victoria's own:

I was awoken at 6 o'clock by Mamma, who told me that the Archbishop of Canterbury and Lord Conyngham were here, and wished to see me. I got out of bed and went into my sitting room (only in my dressing-gown), and *alone*, and saw them. Lord Conyngham (the Lord Chamberlain), then acquainted me that my poor Uncle, the King, was no more, and had expired at 12 minutes p. 2 this morning, and consequently that I am *Queen*.

As soon as Lord Conyngham said 'Your Majesty', the little Queen put out her hand for him to kiss. Both peers knelt down to kiss their new sovereign's hand. The Archbishop had been sent by Queen Adelaide to describe the King's last hours, and Victoria heard how her uncle struggled to live through Waterloo Day and how he gasped: 'Aye the day, the day . . . quite right,' when the French flag with its Napoleonic eagle was laid at his feet. Seven years before William IV had been awakened – strangely also at six – to become King. Gossip claimed that he returned to bed saying that he had never before slept with a Queen! His niece and successor returned to her room and dressed.

While Queen Victoria dressed she pondered, and, as always when she pondered, she committed her thoughts to her Journal:

> Since it has pleased Providence to place me in this station, I shall do my utmost to fulfil my duty towards my country; I am very young and perhaps in many, though not in all things, inexperienced, but I am sure, that very few have more real good will and more real desire to do what is fit and right than I have.

That passage, with its blend of humility, confidence, patriotism, religion and a desire to do good, was characteristic of Queen Victoria. From that June dawn at Kensington until a January evening at Osborne almost sixty-four years later she would strive and she would succeed to live by that pledge in the role in which Providence had placed her. There would never be one day in all those years in which she could cast off her burden.

Breakfast was her first meal as a monarch. Throughout her reign it was an almost invariable rule that breakfast was not a time for business. But on this first day, when every moment was precious, she had 'good faithful Stockmar' to talk to her. There was time to write short notes to the two dear figures of her youth: her sister Feodora and Uncle Leopold. Then she received a letter from the Prime Minister, Lord Melbourne, announcing that he was on his way to Kensington.

Queen Victoria was not unprepared for this meeting. The customary accounts have always claimed that she had no knowledge of the political scene when she came to the throne. This is shown to be wrong by the diary of a member of the Cabinet, Lord Holland, who recorded that

> the King on his deathbed found means to convey a message to her, unknown to her Mother, advising her . . . to continue Lord Melbourne and his Colleagues and to signify that intention to them without loss of time. . . . The conveyance of such messages must have required some management, if there be any foundation in the reports of the extreme watchfulness of the Duchess of Kent and the excessive and injudicious restraint under which she kept her daughter.

The messenger may well have been Lord Liverpool, who had 'a highly important conversation' with Victoria on 15 June. The King had also sent 'a very kind message' to her on his last day by Feodora's husband, who was visiting Windsor.

That, then, was the background for this first important audience:

At 9 came Lord Melbourne, whom I saw in my room, and of COURSE *quite* ALONE as I shall *always* do all my Ministers. He kissed my hand and I then acquainted him that it had long been my intention to retain him and the rest of the present Ministry.... He then again kissed my hand. He then read to me the Declaration which I was to read to the Council.... I like him very much and feel confidence in him. He is a very straightforward, honest, clever and good man.

William Lamb, 2nd Viscount Melbourne, was in his late fifties. A devotion to the delights of the table had led to an expanding figure, but his face still retained the handsome remains of youthful beauty. About him clung a romantic aura of melancholy, for his life had not been a happy one. His wife, Lady Caroline Lamb, had carried on a torrid love affair with Lord Byron which had been gossiped about in every drawing room in London. Both Lady Caroline and their one child, who had been retarded, were now dead. Melbourne was a moderate Whig who affected a pose of cynical boredom which disguised considerable ambition and ability. This witty, wise and essentially kind man now found in his loneliness perhaps the greatest love of his life, a love that was chaste and pure. Victoria was to be a daughter whose destiny he could mould. For Victoria, the fatherless and isolated girl, this friendship was a startling awakening into a world of grace and charm. The greatest joy of her first years as Queen was the chance to talk with 'dear Lord M' and to record his anecdotes.

At 11.30 on that busy morning Victoria went to meet her Privy Council, escorted by two of her uncles. It had been 'Uncle Sussex' who had urged her parents to return to England for her birth. He, too, lived in Kensington Palace where the youthful Victoria had been in dread of disturbing him. 'Uncle Cumberland', in spite of his fierce reputation, behaved with perfect courtesy to the young Queen. He was now King Ernest of Hanover, for Victoria, as a woman could not succeed to that throne. Thus Victoria was the first British sovereign in over a century – and actually one of the few in history – to have no lands on the Continent. King Ernest performed two great services to his niece: he removed the old charge that the monarch used British wealth to support a foreign crown, and he made Victoria all the more popular because people dreaded his return should anything happen to her.

The meeting with the Privy Council allowed the principal statesmen and bishops who made up the body to assess their new monarch as she took the traditional oaths to preserve cherished rights which had been conceded by her ancestors. Among those gathered there was Charles Greville who, as Clerk of the Council, recorded the official proceedings. He was a cynical aristocrat who spent his fortune on horse-racing and yet despised himself for it. He confided his spleen to a diary in which he portrayed the great personalities of the age. Yet even he – normally so rude about royalty in the privacy of his diary – was impressed: 'It was very extraordinary, and something far beyond what was looked for. . . . she went through the whole ceremony . . . with a graceful modesty and propriety.' Another account gives an even clearer picture. Lord Rosebery described the occasion to his grandson, who became one of Victoria's last Prime Ministers:

> Her behaviour, though a great red spot on either cheek showed her mental agitation, was perfectly composed and dignified. The scene was a plain dining room. The Queen entered supported on either side by a Royal Duke. . . . She then took possession of a dining room chair at the top of the room as Sovereign and read out a written speech. . . . Ld Melbourne then wrote on a slip of paper hurriedly 'I appoint Henry, Marquis of Lansdowne, President of my Council' which she read aloud. . . . Several Councillors were affected to tears, none more so than Lord Melbourne.

Lord Lansdowne, an old friend of her father's, had been present at her birth. An even more distinguished figure who was present at both events, the Duke of Wellington, wrote to the Duchess of Nothumberland, who had only recently retired as the Queen's official governess, 'I think the race of nervous young ladies will soon be out of fashion.'

Victoria took one crucial decision on her accession day: she ordered that she would have her own bedroom. It was a declaration of independence from 'Mamma'. She also dined 'alone' that night – one of only a few such occasions in her life – because, as she told a granddaughter half a century later, she feared her mother would speak of Conroy during meals.

Conroy was lingering at the door when Melbourne left the Council, and thrust into his hand a paper recounting his services to the Kent Household. He demanded a pension and a peerage. It took months of negotiation, with the Duke of Wellington acting as final arbiter, before Conroy departed from the Duchess's service with a pension but without a peerage. He left a legacy of bitterness between the Queen and her mother. The Queen made it plain on the very first day of her reign that she would not be held on leading strings by her mother, hence the constant allusions in her Journal to 'alone' when recording her audiences and meetings.

For the Duchess of Kent 20 June was a bitter-sweet day. She had brought up her daughter as her dying husband had wished, and had seen that she was well educated. She had made only one real mistake: she had fallen under the domination of an evil man who cast a shadow between her and her daughter. Time and the intervention of 'an angel' would heal the rift. For the time being, Victoria had one real confidante: 'My *dear* Lehzen will Always remain with me as my friend.' The rift with her mother was hidden from the public. One artist who saw her at the Royal Academy in August wrote 'towards her mother she appears the same affectionate girl we saw at the Academy on the 1st May, still calling her "Mamma".'

Victoria signalled her independence by moving to Buckingham Palace within a few weeks. She was the first monarch to live there; William IV had hated it and tried to give it away. The new Queen enjoyed tremendous popularity. The wife of the American Minister (the United States were not important enough to have an Ambassador until the end of her reign) wrote:

> Everybody is run mad with loyalty to the young Queen. Even the Americans here are all infected. In all societies nothing is talked about but her beauty, her wisdom, her

gentleness, and self-possession. A thousand anecdotes are related to her goodness, and the wonderful address with which she manages every body and every thing. The poor old King is already forgotten.

Anecdotes about the young Queen, most of them concentrating on her natural kindness, added greatly to the wave of loyalty. She would not permit the flag to be raised from half-mast when she went to visit her aunt at Windsor. She also announced that she would continue to pay out of her own income the sizeable pensions that the King had given to his illegitimate children, the Fitzclarences.

Of course, not everyone was happy. The actor Charles Macready, like most who spouted republicanism during the reign, was furious not so much with the Queen but with the stupidity of people who did not agree with him: 'Does it not sicken a rational mind to see the great gifts of reason enslaved and debased to such senseless folly as that *men* should set up these golden calves to worship?' In time he came to calmer views after Queen Victoria became a notable patron of the theatre and applauded his efforts. The poet Elizabeth Barrett was closer to the national mood when from her invalid's couch she wrote to a friend: 'The young Queen is very interesting to me.... There is something hardening, I fear, in power.... But our young Queen wears still a very tender heart – and long may its natural emotion be warm within it.'

These warm emotions – what Queen Victoria herself often called 'my passionate nature' – did give her ministers pause for thought. The last three kings had caused great difficulties by their volatile personalities, which had seemed to verge – at least to those whom they opposed – on madness. Lord Holland discussed this with the Prime Minister and recorded:

> Melbourne is I think struck with her sagacity and yet more with her calm and deliberate determination, pleased *on the whole* with her feelings, but not without misgivings that her aversion to Conroy, and her estrangement from her mother ... may break out in some way harsh and unamiable.... Her family complexion and blood, her period of life and her inordinate love of *musick*, all in his judgement indicate the germ of a warm constitution.

This was a fear that remained through the whole of Victoria's reign. It may seem absurd now, but at various crises, personal and political, there was always the whispered worry: would the Queen's Hanoverian blood show itself? That is why so many descriptions of her by those in the know always comment on her complexion, as this was thought to indicate her mental state. She herself worried about her mind giving way because of overwork, which explains why she often refused to do everything she was asked by her ministers. She was always conscious that only death could end her duties.

Because her mother had kept her away from court, Victoria had little training in the actual business of monarchy. Yet she learned it all with remarkable speed. She grasped the royal method of writing official letters in the third person, and for the next six decades an endless torrent of missives with 'The Queen thinks', 'she must insist' or 'The Queen is grieved' poured forth from her many desks. In reply, her ministers always began their letters: 'With humble duty'. Only her letters to fellow monarchs, her family, and very rarely to those whom she considered friends such as the poet Alfred, Lord Tennyson, would be in the first person. Since many letters had to be in her own hand it is hardly surprising that her handwriting became worse as the reign advanced. Copies were made by Lehzen or a Lady in Waiting.

The Queen's most crucial constitutional function was to see the Prime Minister. With Melbourne, she held conversations lasting about one hour several times a week; with later Prime Ministers the audiences were not that frequent. In these audiences, she gave formal permission to introduce legislation or received the Cabinet's advice. Unlike her uncles, George IV and William IV, the Queen normally dealt with business quickly, but she always tried to follow King Leopold's advice: never take an important decision without allowing a day to consider it.

The Queen saw other ministers, in particular the Foreign Secretary, sometimes in audiences or at various social events. She also had daily reports, when Parliament was sitting, of what had occurred in each House. Some of her other duties were far more mundane. One of the most irksome was 'signing'. Every commission, military and civil, required a 'Victoria R' written in her own hand. Each year there were thousands of these and the Queen constantly devoted any odd moment, as when her hair was 'doing', to scrawling 'Victoria R'. In spite of that, she was always several years behind. Eventually, the number of commissions requiring her actual signature was reduced.

One of her earliest public duties was to dissolve William IV's Parliament. The cheering crowds did not know that the carriage ride to Westminster was somewhat hectic because the driver, an old retainer of over eighty, was so frail that he had to be lifted on to the box. The new Queen also had to receive addresses from important bodies like the two ancient Universities of Oxford and Cambridge. The diarist Henry Crabb Robinson described one such meeting with a group that always made Victoria uncomfortable, the bishops:

> She received them with all possible dignity, and then retired. She passed through a glass door and forgetting its transparency, was seen to run off like a girl, as she is.... Lately asking a maid of honour how she liked her situation, she said: 'I do think myself it is good fun playing Queen.' This is just as it should be. If she had not now the high spirits of a healthy girl of eighteen, we should have less reason to hope she would turn out a sound sensible woman at thirty.

She also had to make quick decisions about her Household. It is difficult now to imagine how important Household matters were during the reign. The Household existed, then as now, to provide a group of people to help the monarch in daily life. Some, like the Gentlemen Ushers, helped at ceremonies, while the Queen's Body Linen Laundress gave more mundane service. Parliament was quite generous in granting the new Queen an annual income of £385,000. Out of this she had to pay her Household and maintain many royal buildings, as well as provide a continuous round of entertaining. Compared with continental royalty,

Victoria did not have a vast fortune; and in her early years she also put a large sum aside to honour her father's debts.

The most important members of the Household were those ladies and gentlemen who were in constant attendance on the Queen. Although the total Household ran into hundreds, it was this inner core of about a dozen people who were the important figures. Their main function was to entertain both monarch and guests, and they were drawn from aristocratic families as they needed to display those ready social graces that were deemed peculiar to aristocracy. They might influence both the Queen's opinions and her reputation. Queen Adelaide, a highly moral figure, was much damaged by gossip that she was too close to the head of her Household, a well-known Tory. For a reigning queen, like Victoria, the task of arranging a Household was even more difficult. A king could draw on help from his wife; an unmarried queen had to make all the decisions herself. By the end of August she had, with considerable help from Melbourne, selected her Household.

The Mistress of the Robes, who governed all the ladies in the Household, was the Duchess of Sutherland and she became one of Victoria's few really close friends. There were several married Ladies in Waiting, for the most part wives of prominent Whigs, who shared the duties of attending the Queen at all times and assisting her in entertaining or in writing some of her vast correspondence. There were also unmarried girls, about the Queen's own age, called Maids of Honour who accompanied her on carriage drives, played the piano for her singing and occasionally smiled at one of the Gentlemen of the Household.

One post was absent from the Household: the Private Secretary. Ministers resented the very idea of a Private Secretary. One had been reluctantly permitted to George III when he became virtually blind, and his two sons, George IV and William IV, had been allowed to maintain the office because they too suffered from deteriorating sight partly brought on by the constant succession of letters and documents, often in the most appalling handwriting. The Queen worried that she might inherit the family tendency to blindness, but Melbourne laughed off these fears.

Melbourne, in effect, was Private Secretary as well as Prime Minister. It was not really a wise arrangement, because it meant that the Queen had no one free from the passions of party politics to advise her. Of course, she did have Stockmar, who took on some of the functions of Private Secretary, but his activities had to be kept rather secretive lest the public suspected that a German physician was playing such a crucial role so close to the throne. Lehzen, too, was ever ready to help with correspondence. She could, for example, write to the Clerk of the Robes to ask if the £400 a year salary of the Royal Hairdresser was to be met out of 'Her Majesty's Toilette'. Some Tories resented that under Melbourne's direction the Queen was surrounded almost exclusively by Whigs: there was a partisan air to the court. One Tory MP even wrote to Lehzen asking for a private meeting to discuss ways to have more of his party round the Queen. To preserve secrecy, he asked her to meet him in the British Museum in the Egyptian antiquities room – whether Lehzen's age or appearance suggested the unusual venue is not known. Wisely, however, she did not go, but gave a copy of the letter to Melbourne.

By October Victoria could write in the midst of all her new work: 'I passed such a very pleasant time here [Windsor]; the pleasantest summer I EVER passed in *my life*.' Part of the pleasure was due to a visit from her uncle, King Leopold, and his new wife, Louise. Victoria was in varying degrees of ecstasy throughout the visit. However, her most constant delight was the presence of Lord Melbourne. With him she could combine both work and pleasure: the two things she had longed for in those lonely days at Kensington. Greville quite naturally sneered that the Queen's feelings 'are sexual though she does not know it'.

Certainly it was delightful to listen to Melbourne. He undertook with fervour the task of instructing the young monarch and was constant in his attendance whether the Queen was at Buckingham Palace, Windsor or the Royal Pavilion at Brighton. Having no family, he could spend much time with Victoria, though she begrudged his visits to old friends such as Lady Holland. Melbourne would often be with the Queen for several hours during the day on business and then return in the evening for a court dinner. The Queen would receive him in her small sitting room (Lehzen was in a room nearby): 'I being seated on a sofa, and he in an armchair near or close opposite me.' Their discussions might be upon any of the varied political problems of the day: the Corn Laws, Ireland or foreign affairs.

Melbourne never applied a false layer of moral varnish in his clever talk with the young Queen. Her family's colourful past was a frequent topic between them. When she remarked that George IV's mistress, Lady Conyngham (who had pinned a jewel on the seven-year-old Victoria) was 'good-natured', Melbourne replied, 'She was the most good-natured, but the most rapacious; she got the most money from him.' Sometimes he discoursed on his own youth, claiming on one occasion that the only thing one learned at public school was punctuality and so he never had a clock in his room: 'I always ask the servant what o'clock it is; and then he tells me what he likes.' His aphorisms often contained thoughts of lasting significance – as, for instance, on Lady Holland: 'She has no religion, but she has every sort of superstition.'

Occasionally, just occasionally, the Queen disagreed with him. There was the time he ventured to suggest that the Queen's beloved dog Dash – the only gift from Conroy that she ever liked – had crooked legs. Straightaway Dash was summoned to assist at this conversation between monarch and minister. 'We put him on the table, and he was much petted and patted and admired by Lord M. who is so funny about him; we gave him tea, and Lord M. said, "I wonder if lapping is a pleasant sensation."'

Sometimes their conversations illustrate the difference in thought between the eighteenth century, of which Melbourne was a cultivated product, and the nineteenth, of which the Queen partook in all its seriousness and concern for reform. Melbourne had little time for education or, indeed, for any reform: 'You had better try to do no good and then you'll get into no scrapes.' The Queen had been much moved by reading Dickens's *Oliver Twist* as it first appeared in serial form. Now that she was Queen she dared to read novels, even though 'Mamma' still criticised such light reading. Melbourne had no objection to novels in themselves; his objection was to novels which preached social reform, as the Queen recorded in her Journal:

> Lord M was talking of some dish or other, and alluded to something in *Oliver Twist*; he'd read half of the 1st vol.... 'It's all among Workhouses, and Coffin Makers and pickpockets.... I don't like that low debasing view of mankind.' We defended Oliver very much, but in vain. 'I don't *like* those things; I wish to avoid them; I don't like them in *reality*, and therefore I don't wish to see them represented.... It's a bad taste ... which will pass away like any other.'

The Queen enjoyed three other great pleasures after she came to the throne. Even though she had to confine herself to quadrilles, she loved dancing. Opera and the theatre remained a great love. She was now able to indulge a new passion, riding. The Duke of Wellington tried to prevent her from attending a review on horseback: he felt a carriage was more seemly for a Queen. But the Duke met one of his few defeats and the young Queen reviewed her troops on horseback. One reason she liked riding was because it made her appear taller, for she was less than five feet in height. Mounted on a favourite horse, like Leopold, she liked nothing better than going for a vigorous ride for miles round Windsor. One of the young courtiers who accompanied her was Charles Murray. He had just returned from spending some months living with a tribe of American Indians and the young Queen was fascinated by his Indian ponies. He, for his part, was equally taken by her skill at riding, as he noted in his diary:

> Her Majesty's seat on horseback is easy and graceful, and the early habit of command observable in all her movements and gestures.... I never saw a more quick or observant eye. In the course of the ride, it glanced occasionally over every individual in the party.

Almost exactly a year after her accession came the great ritual of the coronation. George IV had given even that ceremony a bad name. His had been the grandest and most costly in history, and yet it was marred by the sordid spectacle of his estranged wife hammering on the door of Westminster Abbey demanding admission, which was denied. William IV had wanted to abolish the whole ceremony as an outdated mediaeval relic, but at last agreed to have a shortened version. Victoria restored splendour and dignity to the coronation: it is one of her many legacies to the modern monarchy.

Her coronation also saw the birth of the royal souvenir industry on a massive scale. Before, a few commemorative plates had been made for royal occasions. Now there were numerous books, pictures, medals, mugs and a thirty-foot engraving which folded out to reveal the whole procession: this cost 16 shillings for a plain copy or £1 11s 6d for a coloured version. As so often in the reign, the growth of industry and technology brought the monarchy to the people. However, Victoria would not have shared the sentiments of one popular broadside:

> What praise is due to her who rear'd,
> A Queen to England so endear'd,

> May her name by Britons be rever'd,
>   At Victoria's Coronation.
> Tho' Victoria does the sceptre sway,
> Her parent may she still obey,
> Each British heart will shout huzza
>   At Victoria's Coronation.

Thursday, 28 June dawned overcast but soon cleared, 'as if Nature smiled upon England's Hope', as Sally Stevenson, the American Minister's wife, put it. Almost all the great events of the reign were marked by excellent weather, so much so that 'Queen's weather' became a proverbial expression. The Queen was awakened early by the cannons firing in Hyde Park. Both her half-sister Feodora and her half-brother Charles were at Buckingham Palace to see her in her robes. At nine o'clock, a gun announced that the great coach carrying the Queen had left the Palace. Young Arthur Stanley was sitting in Westminster Abbey (years later he would be its Dean and husband of one of Victoria's dearest friends) and noted that at the sound of that gun 'an electric shock ran visibly through the whole Abbey'. The artist Charles Leslie had come to make sketches for a painting which the Queen later bought. Like the other guests, he had been there since 5 a.m.: 'Refreshments of every kind were to be had there,' he wrote, 'but I had taken some bisquits in my pocket which satisfied me.' Later a new MP, Benjamin Disraeli, saw one peer with his coronet askew gulping champagne from a pewter pot.

Meanwhile the huge procession was making its stately progress towards the Abbey. Cheers went up as the carriage containing the Duchess of Kent came in view. Twelve carriages, each drawn by six horses, carried the Ladies of the Household. Then a squadron of the Life Guards, helmets glittering in the sun, and the Mounted Band of the Household Brigade, followed by the Royal Huntsmen, Yeomen Prickers and Foresters announced the approach of the glorious though unwieldy State Coach. In it, accompanied by the Mistress of the Robes and the Master of the Horse, sat the little Queen, full of smiles for 'the millions of my loyal subjects . . . their good-humour and excessive loyalty was beyond everything, and I really cannot say *how* proud I feel to be the Queen of *such a Nation*'.

It was approaching eleven o'clock by the time the Queen began her procession up the nave of the Abbey. Galleries had been erected in every conceivable spot so that as many people as possible could crane their necks to see. Lord Melbourne carried the sword of state in front of the Queen, who wore a royal robe of crimson velvet and ermine over a dress of white, bordered with gold lace. Young Stanley saw her entrance:

> She paused, as if for breath, and clasped her hands. The orchestra broke out into the most tremendous crash of music . . . 'I was glad when they said unto me, Let us go into the house of the Lord.' Everyone literally gasped for breath from the intense interest, and the rails of the gallery visibly trembled in one's hands from the trembling of the spectators. . . . But at last she moved on to her place by the altar and (as I heard from one of my cousins who had a place close by) threw herself on her knees, buried her face in her hands and evidently prayed fervently.

Sally Stevenson, seated among the ambassadors, observed that the Queen 'was very pale, but calm, dignified and self-possessed'. Then came the greatest moment, as the Queen herself wrote:

> The Crown being placed on my head; which was, I must own a most beautiful impressive moment; *all* the Peers and Peeresses put on their Coronets at the same instant. My excellent Lord Melbourne, who stood very close to me throughout the whole ceremony was *completely* overcome at this moment, and very much affected; he gave me *such* a kind, and I may say *fatherly* look.

The shouts of 'Long Live Queen Victoria! May the Queen Live for ever!' were so great that the Duchess of Kent was too overcome to lift her coronet and her Lady in Waiting, Lady Flora Hastings, had to put it on for her. Mrs Stevenson admitted that this great acclamation 'had a most thrilling effect even upon my democratic nerves'. One humorous incident relieved the emotion of the day's events. When the peers came to do homage, an aged noble slipped and rolled down the steps of the throne; on his next attempt, the young Queen rose and gently helped the old man. The fact that he was named Lord Rolle convinced all the foreigners that this was some peculiar English custom. A more serious mishap was recorded in pencil by one of the canons in his copy of the order of service: the Bishop of Bath and Wells, turning over two pages instead of one, told the Queen the service was over; she retired to a side chapel, but had to be summoned back so that the service could resume. She was surprised to see that the altar in the side chapel was covered with food, but Melbourne told her that 'whenever the clergy ... had anything to do with anything, there's sure to be plenty to eat'.

In her long Journal entry, the Queen makes no comment about her mother's presence other than to state that 'Mamma' was there. Her emotional observations are reserved for 'my good Lord Melbourne' and Lehzen 'whose eyes I caught when on the Throne, and we exchanged smiles'. 'Loaded', as the Queen delightfully puts it, with her sceptre and orb – which the Archbishop had given her at the wrong time – the Queen left the Abbey. Her hand was sore, for the Archbishop had pushed the ring on to the wrong finger.

The writer Anna Jameson was among the vast crowds who saw her return:

> Poor child, she went through her part beautifully; and when she returned, looking pale and tremulous, crowned and holding her sceptre in a manner and attitude which said: 'I have it, and none shall wrest it from me' even Carlyle, who was standing near me, uttered with emotion a blessing on her head.

Charles Leslie, who had gathered enough impressions to start his superb painting *The Queen Receiving the Sacrament at Her Coronation*, recounted the story he had heard of the Queen's arrival back at the Palace:

> She is very fond of dogs, and has one very favourite little spaniel, who is always on the look out for her return when she has been from home.... When the state coach drove up to the steps of the palace, she heard him barking with joy in the hall, and exclaimed,

'There's Dash!' and was in a hurry to lay aside the sceptre and ball she carried in her hands, and take off the crown and robes *to go and wash little Dash.*

The last word on the coronation may be left to Lord Melbourne. After that evening's banquet, and with tears in his eyes as always, he told the newly crowned Queen 'You did it beautifully – every part of it, with so much taste; it's a thing that you can't give a person advice upon; it must be left to a person.'

Victoria was now so popular that the only place her reputation could go was down, and this it rapidly did in the next year. The cause was the celebrated Lady Flora Hastings Affair, which grew out of the Queen's bad relations with her mother and from listening to court gossip. Victoria had not cared much for Lady Flora, the Duchess's Lady in Waiting, in those now distant days at Kensington. When Lady Flora, an unmarried daughter of the Marquess of Hastings, suddenly began to put on weight, gossip could see no other cause than pregnancy. Victoria listened eagerly to all the rumours; her belief in them grew because Conroy was assumed to be Lady Flora's lover. The gossip was most unfair, as Lady Flora was highly moral and, as one rather unkind Whig put it, 'Lady Flora pregnant otherwise than by a legitimate husband would be a miracle.'

Victoria, as she came later to admit, behaved very badly in all this. All that can be said in her defence is that she was ill advised both by Melbourne and by her court physician. Eventually Lady Flora was subjected to the indignity of an examination by Sir James Clark, the Queen's doctor, who declared her a virgin. Victoria attempted rather feebly to be kind to the unhappy lady; in June she went with the Queen to see Donizetti's new opera *Lucrezia Borgia* (which must have caused some reflections about the dangers of court intrigue).

Politics had entered into the battle because the Hastings family, who were Tory, saw the rumours as a Whig plot. Lady Flora's brother published pamphlets and sent letters to the papers denouncing the royal persecution of his sister. All the publicity made the Queen quite unpopular. A young Tory MP, William Gladstone, recorded 'the really sad story' that as the Queen rode into Hyde Park someone shouted: 'Mrs Melbourne, why don't you turn off the doctor?' A few weeks later the Duchess of Montrose and another lady hissed when the Queen appeared at Ascot. Many years later the Queen discussed this incident, and her balanced reflection is the best comment on the whole affair: 'They sent to let me know privately they didn't hiss me. They hissed Lord Melbourne. He was an excellent man but too much a party man and made me a party Queen. He admitted this himself afterwards.'

In the midst of all this occurred the first great political crisis of the reign, the moment Victoria had dreaded: Melbourne resigned after a defeat in the Commons. The Queen disliked the Tory leader, Sir Robert Peel: he was a man of tremendous ability but to everyone except his close friends he appeared a cold man. When, in 1839, Victoria was forced to ask Peel to form a new government, she refused his request that some of her Whig ladies be replaced by Tory ones. The Queen's refusal meant that Peel felt unable to take office and Melbourne returned for another two years, to the Queen's great delight. This so-called Bedchamber Crisis harmed the Queen's reputation still further. She had shown great determination, but many saw it as an obstinacy worthy of her grandfather, George III. It was not only the Tories who were furious; the young Radical writer William Thackeray exploded to his mother:

> Don't talk about the spirit of a woman – the Queen has no business to be a woman. She is a machine worked by ministers, and a set of Whig chambermaids about a dull, obstinate, vain, silly creature like this little Vick are enough to pull down the institutions of the whole country. The rascally, lying, pettifogging Whigs were beaten ... came back – how? upon the shoulders of the maids of honour ... shame, humbug. I am furious at the cant which makes a saint out of the self-willed vulgar little mind which has no right for the sake of her little partialities to stop the march of parties in England.

Thackeray's fury was so vehement because he had sent a similar – 'only better written' – version to a Whig newspaper, which had refused to publish it! He was, however, expressing the widely held view that the Queen's prejudices towards her Whig ladies had preserved a weak government in office. 'Will the country submit', asked the Tory newspaper *The Standard*, 'to be governed by a female camarilla at the palace?'

The reputation of the Queen and 'the female camarilla' was further damaged when Lady Flora died a few weeks later. The embarrassing swelling in her stomach had been caused not by Conroy but by a tumour. In no other event in her long reign did the Queen again behave in such a foolish and unjust manner to anyone. She greatly regretted what had happened, and learned a valuable lesson about the harm which court gossip can cause.

One way to limit the influence of the Ladies in Waiting was for the Queen to marry, and in any case the country needed an heir to prevent the return of 'Uncle Cumberland'. The plan for Victoria to marry her cousin Albert had been opposed by William IV, who distrusted the Coburgs. King Leopold, however, was as anxious as ever to promote the match, and was always ready with advice for Albert, who for many years had accepted that his destiny was to marry Victoria. In May 1836 – about the time of Victoria's seventeenth birthday – Albert and his older brother Ernest had visited England and the cousins met for the first time. Victoria quite liked Ernest, but she thought that neither his mouth nor nose were good. Albert, from that very first meeting, seemed perfection: 'Albert ... is extremely handsome; his hair is about the same colour as mine.' Victoria missed him greatly when he left after a month's visit: 'Albert used always to have some fun and some clever witty answer ... he used to play and fondle Dash so funnily too.'

However, a year after Albert's departure Victoria became Queen, and for the next two years she was immersed in the round of her duties. Military reviews, daily rides, the coronation and those ever joyous conversations with 'Dear Lord M' allowed her little time to think of marriage. Some in court circles thought it was time for the young Queen to marry. It was noticed how infatuated she was when the Tsar's heir visited Windsor, and she enjoyed herself to the full in one of her favourite pleasures, dancing. When she first came to the throne, it was considered indecorous for her to waltz, but she had conquered that notion.

One Friday in July 1839 the Queen discussed her views on marriage with Lord Melbourne. She had 'no great wish to see Albert, as the whole subject was an odious one, and one I hated to decide about; there was no engagement between us.... I said it was disagreeable for me to see him'. The reason why it was disagreeable was because Victoria would have to make a decision and then, if she decided to marry Albert, she would have to propose to him. The younger son of a minor German Duke could not propose to the Queen of England. Victoria also worried that she was a few months older than Albert. Although Melbourne saw no difficulty in that, he did think it best to wait a year or two. Victoria then burst out that she would prefer not to marry at all. 'I don't know about *that*,' replied Melbourne.

The Queen often brooded on '*that*' in later years, and in the 1860s after Albert's death she wrote a memorandum for her husband's biographer. This, like so many of her most intimate thoughts, she was willing to publish for all her subjects to read:

> Nor can the Queen now think without indignation against herself, of her wish to keep the Prince waiting.... The only excuse the Queen can make for herself is ... that the sudden change from the secluded life at Kensington to the independence of her position as Queen regnant ... put all ideas of marriage out of her mind.... A worse school for a young girl, or one more detrimental to all natural feelings and affections, cannot well be imagined than the position of a Queen at eighteen, without experience and without a husband to guide and support her.

On Thursday, 10 October 1839, Victoria was walking on the terrace at Windsor enjoying a talk with Lord Melbourne when a page ran up with a letter from Uncle Leopold saying that his nephews, Albert and Ernest, were on their way to England. At 7.30 that evening the twenty-year-old Queen walked to the top of the staircase as her cousins' carriage drove up. 'It was with some emotion that I beheld Albert who is *beautiful*.'

The next evening there was dancing which, like all court events, began quite late. This was torture for Albert who, throughout his life never liked to stay up at night; but Victoria revelled in both dancing and late nights. By now she was clearly in love with Albert: 'so excessively handsome, such beautiful blue eyes, an exquisite nose, and such a pretty mouth with delicate moustachios ... a beautiful figure, broad in the shoulders and a fine waist.' The Queen flung herself into the dancing with even more than her usual energy. There were numerous quadrilles, gallops and waltzes in that age when dance music had reached the peak of perfection. She managed to dance quite a few with 'dearest Albert, who dances so beautifully'. When not dancing she could sit and talk with Lord Melbourne – who naturally was next to her – and observe Albert: 'It is quite a pleasure to look at Albert when he gallops and valses,' she said. 'He does it so beautifully, holds himself so well with that beautiful figure of his.'

On the Sunday the Queen told Melbourne that her views about marriage had changed, but that a decision was still difficult. On the Monday, the Queen made up her mind and told the Prime Minister, who was '*so fatherly*' in his reply:

'You will be much more comfortable; for a woman cannot stand alone for any time, in whatever position she may be.' The next day the two Coburg Princes went out hunting in the morning. When they returned Albert received a message that the Queen wished to see him. It was shortly before one o'clock when Albert entered the Queen's little room:

> I said to him, that I thought he must be aware *why* I wished them to come here, – and that it would make me *too happy* if he would consent to what I wished (to marry me). We embraced each other, and he was *so* kind, *so* affectionate. I told him I was quite unworthy of him.... I really felt it was the happiest moment in my life.... I feel the happiest of human beings.

Victoria hastened to write to Uncle Leopold: 'He seems like perfection, and I think that I have the prospect of very great happiness before me. I love him *more* than I can say.' The wise old uncle had already sensed what was developing, for at the same time he was writing, 'May Albert be able to strew roses without thorns on the pathway of life of our good Victoria.'

Prince Albert was not only remarkably handsome, but a man of great ability. Although he was a few months younger than his cousin Victoria, he appeared several years older. He had grown up in his tiny German duchy with a deep devotion to his older brother Ernest. Although Albert had never really known his mother, who had been banished because of a love affair, his childhood had been happy. He had studied both at a German university and on his travels in Italy, where he acquired his lifelong love of art. It has often been assumed that Albert's love for Victoria was not as intense as hers was for him. This is not the case. He wrote less about it, but then few people have ever equalled Victoria in writing about their devotion.

As soon as Albert was back in his room at Windsor he was writing to his betrothed (he had apparently already learned her habit of sending notes even to people in the same palace): 'How is it that I have deserved so much love, so much affection? ... Heaven has sent me an angel whose brightness shall illumine my life.' Yet a few weeks later, before he returned to Germany, he wrote of his fears to his family in Coburg in a letter which shows his ability to analyse problems:

> My future position will have certain dark sides, and the skies above me will not always be blue and unclouded. Still, life, wherever one is, has its storms, and it is a support to one to feel one has used all one's endeavours and strength in some great object, decisive for the welfare of so many.

Victoria accepted – reluctantly – that Albert would have to return to Coburg while plans for the marriage went ahead. Before it could be announced publicly, she had to inform the Privy Council. Lord Holland was present at this 'strange' ceremony: 'A modest girl of twenty, unaccompanied by any of her own sex, had to announce to a grave and observant assembly of 85 men her *determination* to take as bedfellow a young man who had lately left her palace.' One Tory overcame his annoyance at her behaviour in recent political events and wrote:

I cannot describe to you with what a mixture of self-possession and feminine delicacy she read the paper. Her voice, which is naturally beautiful, was clear and untroubled; and her eye was bright and calm ... there was a blush on her cheek which made her look both handsomer and more interesting; and certainly she *did* look as interesting and as handsome as any young lady I ever saw.

When her aunt, the Duchess of Gloucester, asked if she had been frightened, Victoria replied: 'A little, but not much, for I had to propose it to Albert himself and had gone thro' that much more awkward ceremony before I mentioned it to the Privy Council.'

For the next few months messengers hurried back and forth between Windsor and Coburg with almost daily letters to and from 'Dearest, Deeply Loved Victoria'. By 7 February 1840 Albert was back in England. He was never a good sailor and this crossing of the Channel was dreadful. He hastened to send a note to his beloved, assuring her of his safe arrival at Dover even though 'our faces were more the colour of wax candles'. Thousands stood on the quay and cheered him loudly.

However, not everyone was cheering. The Tories in Parliament had already taken their revenge on the Queen by halving the proposed allowance to Prince Albert. There was also considerable popular dislike at the idea of another German marriage. To many Englishmen, Germans were dirty, poor and they all smoked pipes (this was a favourite view of Melbourne's). As so often, popular prejudices found their way into broadsides such as 'Prince Albert in England':

> I am a German just arrived,
> With you for to be mingling,
> My passage it was paid,
> From Germany to England;
> To wed your blooming Queen.
> For better or worse I take her,
> My father is a duke,
> And I'm a sausage maker.

> *Chorus*

> Here I am in rags and jags,
> Come from the land of all dirt,
> I married England's Queen,
> My name it is young Albert.

However, most of her subjects were delighted at the thought of the wedding. Men, in particular, were stirred by the idea of the young Queen whom costuming and kind engravers made quite beautiful. Charles Dickens, no emotional royalist, told a friend that he and the artist Daniel Maclise were both 'raving with love for the Queen'. They even went down to Windsor and were allowed not only to wander in the private grounds but to peep into 'the very bedchamber'.

Monday, 10 February was one of those few public occasions in the Queen's reign when the weather did not promise well. Victoria, however, did not really mind. She was up shortly before nine o'clock, 'having slept well ... the last time I slept alone'. 'Mamma' brought in a nosegay of orange blossom and 'dearest kindest Lehzen' gave her a little ring. Then, in violation of all folk wisdom, Albert arrived and she saw him 'for the *last* time *alone*, as my *Bridegroom*'. It took some time to dress, as the Queen wore a 'white satin gown with a very deep flounce of Honiton lace, imitation of old ... my Turkish diamond necklace and earrings and Albert's beautiful sapphire brooch'.

The marriage took place in the Chapel Royal in St James's Palace, which was so small that there was hardly any room for guests. Amongst the few who watched the Queen led in by her 'Uncle Sussex' was Sally Stevenson:

> After two mortal hours of shivering, the trumpets proclaimed the approach of royalty.... The train was held by twelve fair girls, daughters of the highest nobility, all in white, with orange flowers in their hair. The deportment of the royal bride was really beautiful. It blended the sensibility of the woman with the dignity of the queen and that calm and quiet self-possession for which she has been so remarkable ever since her accession to the throne.... Her agitation was only discoverable in the marble paleness of her brow and the shaking of the orange flowers.... The only comic part of the whole affair was when the poor German prince 'endowed her with all his worldly goods'.

One of the Queen's oldest Ladies in Waiting, Lady Lyttelton, struggled to see the bride, though her view was blocked by the 'portly form' of the Duchess of Bedford. When she caught sight of the Queen's face, she noted 'her eyes swollen with tears, but great happiness in her face'. Afterwards, Victoria noted simply: 'The Ceremony was very imposing and fine and simple, and I think OUGHT to make an everlasting impression on every one who promises at the Altar to *keep* what he or she promises.'

The Queen and her husband then drove back to Buckingham Palace; they were able to have half an hour of privacy when they sat on a sofa in her dressing room and talked. Then Prince Albert led his bride downstairs to greet their guests. Weighing 300 pounds and nine feet wide, the wedding cake was decorated with turtle doves and cupids bearing the arms of England, Scotland and Ireland. It needed to be a large cake, as pieces were sent everywhere. Sally Stevenson sent several to her relatives in America, while Lady Holland dispatched a large piece to the English residents in Florence. Nor did the Queen forget to send some to those whom she had known as a child. One was sent to the daughter of a former American diplomat 'with a letter enclosed in a beautiful satinwood box, on which the letter V is emblazoned in diamonds'.

Before leaving with Albert for Windsor, the Queen enjoyed ten minutes of praise from Lord Melbourne, who was dressed in a new coat for the occasion. It was not quite three years since he had walked through a door at Kensington Palace to kiss the hand of an eighteen-year-old Queen. Now he bent again to kiss the hand of a twenty-year-old bride: 'God bless you, Ma'am.' Then, after a briefer farewell to 'Mamma', the carriage was on its way to Windsor with cheering crowds lining much of the way. Inside sat 'I and Albert alone'.

THREE

*A*LL MY ALBERT'S WORK

Windsor Castle, 11th February, 1840

My dearest Uncle, – I write to you from here, the happiest, happiest Being that ever existed. Really, I do not think it *possible* for anyone in the world to be *happier*, or as happy as I am. He is an Angel, and his kindness and affection for me is really touching. To look in those dear eyes, and that dear sunny face is enough to make me adore him. What I can do to make him happy will be my greatest delight. Ever your affectionate,
VICTORIA R.

This letter to King Leopold reveals Victoria's joy on the day after her wedding. In her Journal she recorded quite frankly her happiness on her wedding night:

I *never*, *never*, spent such an evening!! my *dearest dearest dear* Albert sat on a footstool by my side, and his excessive love and affection gave me feelings of heavenly love and happiness I never could have *hoped* to have felt before! He clasped me in his arms, and we kissed each other again and again! His beauty, his sweetness and gentleness – really how can I ever be thankful enough to have such a *Husband*!

Victoria never wavered in this view from 1840 until the Prince's death in 1861, nor in the forty years of her widowhood which were devoted to commemorating his ideals both in her own life and in marble. Yet if it was a marriage with great love and passion, it also contained its tensions, particularly about Albert's position both in her Household and in her kingdom. As the Prince wrote to a close friend three months after the wedding, 'In my home life I am very happy and contented; but the difficulty in filling my place with the proper dignity is, that I am only the husband and not the master in the house.'

Most people assumed that royalty dwelt on a different level from ordinary mortals. However, a few who knew them thought deeply about the personalities of Prince and Queen and attempted to analyse them. The most perceptive of these was Mary Ponsonby, granddaughter of a Whig Prime Minister, who began a lifetime at court by becoming a Maid of Honour in the 1850s. Her uncle, General Grey, was Secretary to Prince Albert and later to Queen Victoria. Mary Bulteel, as she then was, married Henry Ponsonby who would later become the Queen's Private Secretary. She had a questioning mind that led her to abandon most of the political and religious principles of her youth and to dabble with socialism. Thus her assessment of Prince and Queen is no ordinary courtier's tribute.

Mary Ponsonby started to write an analysis of their characters in the early 1870s:

I became accustomed to see the door leading to the Queen's rooms shut silently behind the page who came backwards and forwards for orders, and I rather longed to get on the other side and see what her tastes and occupations were, and to get to know her opinions.

In 1901, just a few days after the Queen's death, she provided Edmund Gosse with information for an anonymous article on 'The Character of Queen Victoria', which infuriated people who only wanted unconsidered praise at that time. It still remains the best assessment.

In many ways Mary Ponsonby admired Prince Albert:

> He had a calm, philosophical way, intensely German, of weighing the pros and cons of predicting what the effect of such and such a measure would be, of theorising on the abstract qualities and faults of a nation, and then deducing what would be the right mode of dealing with each case.

The problem was that this type of mind 'made him unsatisfactory to our statesmen of the empirical and hand-to-mouth class'. She admired Albert's moral character even more than his mind. He was 'unselfish, patient, kindhearted, truthful, and just', though she did not find him 'very civil' in his treatment of the Household, particularly towards women, as he was ever anxious to avoid scandal or opening his wife's vast reservoir of jealousy.

> That he was a happy man I very much doubt, for with all his love of dry formulas there was a strong vein of poetical feeling ... it showed itself in his appreciation of music and his feeling of keen pain at the miseries of other lives.... His manner was the least pleasing thing about him.... There was a complete absence of that frankness which was such a charm in the Queen's manner.... He gave one much more the idea of being an excellent tutor, and this was the cause of his being unpopular with those who judged entirely by his manner.

The Queen was never, in any sense, an intellectual like the Prince. That is by no means a fault. 'I have always thought', says Mary Ponsonby, 'the Queen possessed an instinct and a quick appreciation of people (without being able to reason about them) in a far more marked way than the Prince.' Victoria once described her own mind as 'matter of fact'. This was a great strength which enabled her to judge, usually with alarming accuracy, what the outcome of a policy would be. Hers was never a theoretical mind and when she occasionally wandered into the fields of theory, as in some of her theological views, she would often become quite confused. Most of these traits were already present at the time of her marriage, while others were either developed by her husband or matured during her widowhood. She had a 'discriminating shrewdness' which allowed her to consider carefully both politicians and their measures. The bad side of this was that she had strong views which could degenerate into 'obstinacy'.

> In her inspection of a strange minister, or a newly appointed member of her household, she had a method well understood by those who observed her narrowly. She received the unfamiliar person with a look of suspended judgement.... Her eyes and her mouth took on their investigating aspect. She could be seen to be making up her mind almost as though it were a watch which had to be wound up. If the analysis was easy, and the

result of it satisfactory, the features would relax.... But if the presented type was complex or difficult, those who knew the Queen extremely well would perceive that her mind was not made up after all. The lines of the mouth would continue to be a little drawn down; the eyes, like sentinels, would still be alert under eyebrows faintly arched. But sooner or later she would succeed in her analysis.... She was scarcely ever wrong, and she was slow to admit a mistake.

She was, of course, ever conscious of who and what she was, though never proud in any haughty way; in fact, she could be quite humble. The Queen was never one to overrate her mental abilities or to attribute any great beauty to herself. Yet she was always determined that her position be respected: 'Those who were much with her were never allowed to forget that she was the most important person in the room. Without the least emphasis, or need for emphasis, her character imposed itself on her surroundings.' Although she was in many ways a shy woman, she was unconcerned with what others thought of her. When one courtier wondered what a newly presented politician thought of the Queen, she was puzzled by the question: 'Dear me. I did not give a thought to that. It is so beside the question. What really signifies is what I think of him.'

She had a tremendous, at times even a 'tyrannical', love of order and punctuality which were all aided by her phenomenal memory. From her childhood, her Journal entries always give the exact time of any event. After she became Queen, time and its allotment became of crucial importance: 'I can't afford to be kept waiting,' she once said. 'If I am to get through my work, I mustn't have my moments frittered away.' As the reign went on, an inflexible schedule governed the whole movement of the court.

Victoria had a wonderful sense of presence and the ability in spite of shyness and later her size, to glide into a room with awe-inspiring dignity. Her innate dramatic sense was sharpened by frequent visits to the opera and theatre. She prided herself on being well informed about her guests, and at receptions would do a 'circle', talking to them. Sir Henry Wood, the great conductor, met the Queen in 1898 and was amazed at 'the rare beauty of her voice, the gentle sweetness of which has ever remained with me'. The famous actor Squire Bancroft, who performed before her, said the Queen has 'perhaps the most beautiful and winning voice I ever listened to'. Victoria's other assets were her sense of humour and her smile which, as Mary Ponsonby observed, was seen whenever she was enjoying some court joke or performing one of her many acts of kindness.

No smile was the least like it, and no shadow of it is preserved ... under the evil spell of the photographic camera.... It came very suddenly, in the form of a mild radiance over the whole face, a softening and a raising of the lines of the lips, a flash of kindly light beaming from the eyes.... Her smile, in fact, was the key ... to the secrets of the Queen's character.

These, then, were some of the traits of character and personality already apparent in a young woman who was a Queen, a wife and about to become a mother, even though she was not yet twenty-one. People like Charles Greville had grumbled that a few days' honeymoon at Windsor, with dinner parties every evening, was 'not the way to provide us with a Prince of Wales'. However it was soon whispered in society that the Queen was expecting her first child.

Victoria's attitude towards pregnancy and children was quite complex. To put it briefly she adored marriage, disliked pregnancy, did not care much for babies but quite liked older children. She was to have a total of nine children between 1840 and 1857. The last two births were aided by the use of chloroform, to the fury of religious fundamentalists who believed that the Queen was violating the biblical assertion that man is born 'in sorrow'; her action helped to get chloroform accepted. She explained her attitude towards child-bearing to her first-born when that daughter was herself expecting a child:

> If I had had a year of happy enjoyment with dear Papa, to myself – how thankful I should have been! But ... I was in for it at once – and furious I was.... I had constantly for the first 2 years of my marriage – aches – and sufferings and miseries and plagues ... and enjoyments etc. to give up – constant precautions to take, you will feel the yoke of a married woman! Without that – certainly it is unbounded happiness – if one has a husband one worships! It is a foretaste of heaven.... I had 9 times for 8 months to bear with ... real misery (besides many duties) and I own it tried me sorely; one feels so pinned down – one's wings clipped – in fact, at the best (and few were or are better than I was) only half oneself. This I call the 'shadow side'.... And therefore – I think our sex a most unenviable one.

The role of 'our sex' was a difficult one for the Queen. In many ways she felt that her sovereignty placed her in an unnatural position since, in her view, politics was not a proper concern for women. Men should hold power, and yet she did not entirely trust them. Sometimes these views about her public role leapt into her private life and her attitude towards men. 'Those very selfish men', she told her eldest daughter, would not 'bear for a minute what we poor slaves have to endure.' Men are guilty of 'despising our poor degraded sex – for what else is it as we poor creatures are born for man's pleasure and amusement, and destined to go through endless sufferings and trials?' Even Prince Albert, that veritable paragon of perfection, was not without this fault.

Because she was the Queen she could not withdraw during her pregnancies into that seclusion which her 'interesting condition' prescribed for Victorian ladies. She had to carry on her duties, often in public, and had to see ministers within days of a birth. It was worse because several of those same ministers would have to gather outside her bedroom at the time of birth to attest that it truly was her child. Within a few weeks she would be discussing politics or diplomacy with them. It is amazing, given this background, that her attitude towards pregnancy was not more extreme.

The nation awaited the birth of her first child with concern. The Queen's popularity had increased greatly since the Flora Hastings affair. Should anything happen to Victoria, the dreaded King Ernest would come lumbering back from Hanover. Added to this was speculation as to how child-bearing would affect her 'Hanoverian nerves', a worry which increased after 10 June when, in the midst of her pregnancy, she and Prince Albert had set out for a drive to visit the Duchess of Kent. Prince Albert described what happened:

> We had hardly proceeded a hundred yards from the palace, when I noticed ... a little mean-looking man holding something towards us ... a shot was fired, which almost stunned us both, it was so loud, and fired barely six paces from us.... Suddenly he again pointed his pistol and fired a second time. This time Victoria also saw the shot, and stooped quickly, drawn down by me. The ball must have passed just above her head.... I called to the postillion to go on, and we arrived safely at Aunt Kent's. From thence we took a short drive through the Park, partly to give Victoria a little air, partly also to show the public that we had not ... lost all confidence in them.

The Queen had not recognised the first shot for what it was, and remarked to Albert, 'How imprudent that persons should be allowed to shoot at birds in the park!' But she knew what the second shot meant, and she later told Lehzen that her immediate thought was: 'If it please Providence I shall escape.' This was the first of seven attempts on the Queen made during her reign. No other British monarch has experienced so many attacks. Each understandably upset the Queen and, in time, made her nervous about driving in London.

'Throughout the whole Kingdom', the American Minister reported back to Washington, there was 'the deepest indignation and horror'. Fortunately this awful experience did not affect the Queen's health or make her more nervous about the expected birth. Charles Locock was the doctor appointed to look after the Queen during her first pregnancy, and his account of her behaviour at his first examination found its way into a letter to the Duke of Wellington from a well-informed friend:

> Locock says he felt shy and embarrassed; but the Queen soon put him at his ease.... She had not the slightest reserve and was always ready to express Herself ... in the very plainest terms possible. She asked Locock whether she should suffer much pain. He replied that some pain was to be expected ... 'Oh yes' said the Queen, 'I can bear pain as well as other People.'

What did surprise Locock was that the Queen did not have 'stays or anything that keeps Her shape within bounds and that she is more like a barrel than anything else'.

On the night of 21 November doctors were summoned to attend the Queen. Various Privy Councillors hurried to be in the room next to the Queen to act as official witnesses. The Duchess of Kent was there and started a letter to her nephew Ernest, Albert's brother. At noon she wrote, 'our good angel Albert remains at the side of his beloved'. A few hours later she added: 'A daughter was born at 2 o'clock, mother and child are as well as they can be, God be praised.' Albert found time to write: 'Victoria is well and happy. It is hardly to be believed that only a few hours ago she lay in dreadful pain.... Albert, father of a daughter, you will laugh at me!'

Dr Locock informed the Queen, 'Oh Madam it is a Princess.'

'Never mind,' replied Victoria, 'the next one will be a Prince.'

The nurse immediately carried the baby through the door, which had been left partially opened, and laid her, wrapped in flannel, upon a table so that the Privy Councillors could see her. Stockmar was amused when the Queen told him, 'It is rather a bore it is a girl.' A bore was certainly one thing this child never was. Princess Victoria, as she was christened, inherited her father's intellectual abilities and her mother's 'passionate nature'.

The birth of Vicky, as she was always known, was an important event for her parents in more than the normal way. The Queen had been determined to exclude the Prince from any of her constitutional duties, for, as she had warned him before their marriage, 'The English are very jealous of any foreigner interfering in the government of this country.' Disregarding Melbourne's advice that she should discuss all business with her husband, she decided that Albert would occupy a role similar to that of a Queen Consort: he would share her social duties, but the affairs of state were not for him. Melbourne had suggested that Albert could act as Private Secretary for the Queen and conduct some of her enormous correspondence.

Officially, the Queen still did not have a Private Secretary, but Lehzen had come to undertake some of the work. This was particularly the case within the Household. The Ladies knew that if they could get Lehzen on their side, a victory in any little battle was more likely. Albert soon saw that he would have to oust Lehzen if he was ever to be 'the master in the house', particularly because they frequently disagreed on his own role. For example, Lehzen thought it ill advised for Albert to be in the royal carriage when the Queen went to Parliament. It was the arrival of Vicky that led to Albert's assuming a political role. The day after the little Princess was born, Melbourne wrote to the Foreign Secretary, 'Will you send the Foreign boxes to the Queen as usual? The Prince has her key and will open them and inform her of the contents.' Albert was able to tell his brother two days later: 'I also look after V.'s political affairs.' Albert began to assume a daily role in political life by reading all the documents that came to the Queen and drafting many of her responses. Thus with Vicky's birth the reign of Victoria ended and that of Albert and Victoria began.

Even before this, Albert had gradually begun to take on more public responsibilities. Only a few months after the marriage he had made his first public speech to the Anti-Slavery Society – identifying himself with those progressive movements that were the driving force of Victorian England. Yet his real political importance was the way he could look at a complicated problem and prepare a memorandum on the possible solutions. This strengthened the Queen's hand when she spoke with the Prime Minister.

One of Albert's earliest goals was to make the Household more economical and better organised; it was governed by ancient customs which time had rendered sacred and inefficient. It was said that to have a fire lit in a royal grate, permission was needed from two officials: one gave the order to lay the fire, while the other gave the command to light it. Inevitably Albert's reforms made enemies. Several royal servants, for example, had a profitable sideline in selling things like partially used candles. The rule was that candles were never lit twice, so partially burned candles were sold by the royal servants to Miller of Piccadilly, who resold them as 'Palace Ends' in packets which were snapped up because of their superior quality. Under the new regime old candles could continue to grace a royal table.

Albert's other great enemy was court intrigue. He insisted that he should be the final arbiter in the running of the royal palaces, and the greatest obstacle to this was Lehzen. In particular, Albert was determined that he and not Lehzen would be in charge of the royal nursery. This led to considerable arguments between Albert and Victoria, but eventually she accepted that Lehzen must depart. After a tense interview in which Stockmar arranged her pension, Lehzen was on her way back to Germany. The Queen did as much as she could to smooth Lehzen's departure; they continued to correspond, and Victoria sent her old friend engravings and photographs of each royal child as the nursery grew. A quarter of a century later, Lehzen would stand on a railway platform in Germany just to watch the Queen's train speed by.

The day after the Baroness left, Lady Lyttelton, the governess to the royal children, encountered the Queen, who said:

> It was very painful for me, Lady Lyttelton, waking this morning, and recollecting she was really quite away. I had been dreaming she had come back to say good-bye to me, and it felt very uncomfortable at first. I had heard it mentioned before – that odd feeling on waking – but I had no experience of it. It is very unpleasant.

When Lady Lyttelton, one of the wisest women at court, wrote of this to her family she added a very perceptive comment:

> There is a transparency in her truth that is very striking – not a shade of exaggeration in describing feelings or facts; like very few other people I ever knew. Many may be as true, but I think it goes often along with some little reserve. She talks all out; and just as is, no more and no less.

From his first days in England, Albert had been very friendly with the Duchess of Kent. She was, of course, his aunt as well as his mother-in-law and the only person at court with whom he could speak of Coburg. One of the happiest fruits of Victoria's marriage was a reconciliation between the Queen and her mother. From this time on 'Mamma' resumed an important place in Victoria's life and the Duchess developed into an ideal grandmother. She had her own residences near the Queen's, and the two of them were in almost daily contact. The Duchess, however, was never really allowed to play any important role either in the education of the children or in the Queen's confinements. Only one person was allowed to do that – Prince Albert. The Queen described this in a memorandum which she wrote for the biography of the Prince:

> No one but himself ever lifted her from her bed to her sofa, and he always helped to wheel her ... into the next room. For this purpose he would come instantly when sent for from any part of the house. As years went on and he became overwhelmed with work (for his attentions were the same in all the Queen's confinements), this was often done at much inconvenience to himself; but he ever came with a sweet smile on his face. In short his care of her was like that of a mother, nor could there be a kinder, wiser, or more judicious nurse.

On the morning of 9 November 1841 – less than a year after Vicky's birth – the Duke of Wellington hurried to Buckingham Palace. When he saw a midwife he asked, 'Is it a boy?'

The reply came: 'It's a Prince, Your Grace.'

The Queen wrote to King Leopold, 'I wonder very much, whom our little boy will be like. You will understand *how* fervent are my prayers, and I am sure everybody's must be, to see him resemble his Father in *every*, *every* respect, both in body and mind!' It would cause considerable misery to both parents and to the little boy that he never resembled his father. On 14 December 1841 the Queen wrote again, reflecting on that mixture of private happiness and public worries that made up her life. In the midst of her second pregnancy the Whig government of Lord Melbourne had been defeated:

> We must all have trials and vexations; but if one's *home is happy*, then the rest is comparatively nothing. . . . I had this autumn one of the severest trials I could have, in parting with my government, and particularly from our kind and valued friend . . . but my happiness at home, the love of my husband, his kindness, his advice, his support, and his company make up for all, and make me forget it.

Fortunately the Queen could not foresee that exactly twenty years to the day this happiness would end in the same castle. But for now all was joy, at least at home. The Queen exalted in her Journal for Christmas 1841: 'To think that we have two children now, and one who enjoys the sight already, is like a dream.' The Prince described the occasion to his father:

> This is the dear Christmas Eve, on which I have so often listened with impatience for your step, which was to usher us into the Gift-room. Today I have two children of my own to make gifts to, who, they know not why, are full of happy wonder at the German Christmas-tree and its radiant candles.

Prince Albert did not actually introduce the Christmas tree into England. Victoria's grandmother, Queen Charlotte, and her aunt, Queen Adelaide, had both observed this German custom: Albert and Victoria popularised it. The illustrated magazines which were starting up in the 1840s carried engravings of the royal trees, of which there were always several, and the Victorian middle classes quickly copied this happy practice.

The birth of a son entailed many decisions. The Queen had decided that his name would be Albert Edward, honouring both her husband and her father. It was her wish that every male descendant would bear the name Albert, which would show that a new dynasty had begun in 1840. The baptism allowed yet another innovation. Royal christenings had formerly been performed privately, but for Prince Albert Edward, St George's Chapel, Windsor provided a more public setting. The Dean of Windsor was not exactly tactful when he congratulated the Queen for 'saving us from the incredible curse of a female succession'. The organist at Windsor had composed a special anthem. But Prince Albert, with his great knowledge of music, knew how little people liked those long endured but quickly forgotten compositions: 'No anthem. If the service ends by an anthem, we shall go out criticising the music. We will have something we all know – something in which we can all join – something devotional. The Hallelujah Chorus; we shall all join in that, with our hearts.' This is a perfect example of Albert's gift for uniting the practical with the artistic.

The birth of the Prince reminded the Queen of an old problem: the question of Prince Albert's rank and precedence. Before their wedding she had attempted to settle the matter but the Tories (mainly out of spite for her behaviour during the Bedchamber Crisis) and the 'old Royal Family' opposed her wish to give her husband precedence over the rest of the Royal Family. The issue continued to worry the Queen in private, but it led to a farcical incident two years later when King Ernest of Hanover appeared for the christening of the Queen's second daughter, Princess Alice. Prince Albert was rather relieved that the King was late, so that the baptism and banquet were over by the time he arrived 'in a hackney coach'. Uncle Ernest, however, decided to stay on in his native land for a few weeks to attend the wedding of a niece. Prince Albert described to his brother how the inevitable fight for precedence took place:

> He insisted on having the place at the altar, where we stood. He wanted to drive me away and, against all custom, he wanted to accompany Victoria and lead her. I was to go behind him. I was forced to give him a strong push and drive him down a few steps.... We had a second scene, when he would not allow me to sign the register with Victoria. He laid his fist on the book. We manoeuvred round the table and Victoria had the book handed across.... After a third trial to force Victoria to do what he commanded, but in vain, he left.... Uncle Leopold was highly amused.

It would be some years before the Queen found a solution to the problem of Albert's precedence.

Victoria and Albert were both concerned that the royal children be protected from those illnesses that threatened Victorian nurseries; few Victorian mothers could match their record of raising nine children without one death. Albert himself kept the key to the nursery (mainly because of horrible letters threatening the royal children) and he made the final decisions about the children's health and education. The Queen was anxious to have the infant Prince vaccinated, an occasion that provides a charming vignette of how both the Queen and Prince Albert behaved with people outside the orbit of the court. The royal doctor searched for a baby of the right age from which the 'vacci' could be taken for the Prince of Wales. Eventually he found the child of Charlotte Bailey, wife of an ironmonger in Holborn. Mrs Bailey, her baby and a nurse came to Windsor. The proud mother described what followed:

> Sure enough there was her little Majesty standing at the end of a small room and Prince Albert (that Adonis) at her side.... I had sense enough to make my obeisance to the Majesty of England (Majesty forsooth! I towered over the little lady).... The operation was then performed and my baby behaved admirably and the Queen and the Prince admired him.... The Prince said 'see how sweetly he smiles'.... She expressed a hope

that my baby would not take cold.... Then Prince Albert came across the room and making the most graceful of bows and with the sweetest of smiles and softest of voices said 'I thank you, Madam for allowing our child to be vaccinated from yours.'

Mrs Bailey then backed and bowed her way out of the royal presence; later, as she was taking a glass of sherry and a biscuit, the doctor said that the Queen had expressed a wish to be revaccinated (she had been vaccinated as a baby). Some more specimen was taken and Mrs Bailey could hear Prince Albert laughing, but the Queen saying 'take care of my skin it's very thin' as they were vaccinated. The Queen sent the nurse £5, and the baby a scarf pin of rubies and turquoises with the Prince of Wales feathers. She would have been delighted to learn that Mrs Bailey's baby was re-named Edward Albert.

In the election of 1841 the Queen identified herself with the Whigs, 'our party', by making a tour of Whig country houses such as Woburn and Melbourne's own house, Brocket, which she had long wished to visit. The ageing Prime Minister led the Queen round his house and grounds, all of which she inspected with great care and admired with suitable enthusiasm. A memento of her visit to Woburn remains in the superb series of drawings by the Queen, engraved by Prince Albert, which they gave to the Duke of Bedford. Ironically, she was embarrassed to ask many questions about the artistic masterpieces that adorned Woburn then as now. Despite this display of royal support, the Whigs lost the election. It was a sad day for the Queen when it became obvious that Melbourne would have to leave her. It was just over four years since he had greeted her at Kensington Palace. By her obstinancy about her Ladies she had kept him in power for two more years, but a defeat in the election left no alternative to resignation.

After bidding a sad farewell to Lord Melbourne the Queen had to receive her incoming Prime Minister, Sir Robert Peel. Among her new ministers was the young Gladstone, who throughout his long political career made extensive memoranda of all his actions to serve as both a record and a self-justification, much as the Queen's Journal did for her. One of Gladstone's memoranda describes the Privy Council ceremony when the new government was sworn in:

3 September, 1841. The Queen sat at the head of the table, composed but dejected – one could not but feel for her.... We knelt down to take the Oaths of Allegiance and Supremacy and stood up to take (I think) the Councillor's oath – then kissed the Queen's hand, then went round the table shaking hands with each member, beginning with Prince Albert who sat on the Queen's right.... Then the Chancellor first and next the Duke of Buckingham were sworn to their respective offices. C. Greville forgot the Duke's Privy Seal and sent him off without it: the Queen corrected him and gave it. Then were sworn the secretaries of State ... Greville again forgot the seals ... but the Queen again interposed.... Then were read and approved several Orders in Council.... These were read aloud by the Queen in a very clear though subdued voice: and repeated 'Approved' after each.... Then the Queen ... retired bowing.... Peel looked shy all through.

It is amusing to see that Greville, always so critical of everyone else, did not know how to conduct the ceremony but that the Queen, presiding at her first change of government, knew exactly what to do. But Greville did at least record a conversation with Melbourne in which he sent sensible advice to his successor:

> Have you any means of speaking to *these chaps*? I said 'Yes'.... 'Well' he said, 'I think there are one or two things Peel ought to be told.... Don't let him suffer any appointment he is going to make to be talked about, and don't let her hear it through anybody but himself; and whenever he does anything, or has anything to propose, let him explain to her clearly his reasons. The Queen is not conceited; she is aware there are many things she cannot understand, and she likes to have them explained to her elementarily, not at length and in detail, but short and clearly.'

Prince Albert had already begun to make arrangements to ensure that there would be no repetition of the 1839 Bedchamber Crisis. Even before the election his secretary opened negotiations with Peel, and a compromise was agreed: important Household offices would go to those who supported the government, but not every Maid of Honour must be banished if her family's party was defeated. The Queen accepted that she must appoint some Tory ladies and end the partisan appearance of her court.

In spite of her initial hostility to Peel, Victoria soon came to have a great respect for him. Peel urged the Prince to take an active role both in politics and in promoting the arts. This delighted the Queen, who called her new friend Albert's 'second father'. Albert and Peel shared a common outlook on government. Both were 'liberal-Conservatives' who believed that the rising power of the middle classes demanded that the old order make sensible and well-considered reforms, based not on some intellectual theory but rather on the pragmatic needs of the British people. Both the Queen and the Prince supported Peel throughout his five years of office, years in which he increasingly alienated his more reactionary followers. When Peel died in 1850, Prince Albert paid him a remarkable tribute at a banquet in York. His definition of Peel's political attitudes could also stand as an apt summary both of his own and of the Queen's:

> He was liberal from feelings, but conservative upon principle. Whilst his impulse drove him to foster progress, his sagacious mind and great experience showed him how easily the whole machinery of a state and of society is deranged, and how important, but how difficult also, it is to direct its further development in accordance with its fundamental principles, like organic growth in nature.

One small but highly symbolic change occurred at this time. In her first years as Queen, Victoria had acted in many ways like her Hanoverian ancestors, showing her support for 'our party'. Now Prince Albert, following Stockmar's preaching that the monarchy should avoid a partisan approach, stopped royal involvement in elections. It had always been accepted in the town of Windsor that the monarch could control the election of the local MPs just as the Duke of Marlborough did at Woodstock. Albert, with Peel's enthusiastic support decided that the Queen would no longer do this. There was no idea in all this that the monarchy should withdraw from proper involvement in political questions; it was only that the

Queen respected the integrity of the elected house just as she demanded that they respect her power.

Prince Albert's influence increased greatly throughout the 1840s. He was now present at every audience the Queen gave to her Prime Minister. In the royal residences of Windsor and Buckingham Palace, husband and wife had adjoining desks so that Albert could draft most of the Queen's letters or prepare careful memoranda. It is often stated that the Queen had little power because she had to agree anything sent by Parliament. This facile generalisation neglects the custom which had developed by which the Prime Minister secured the Queen's approval *before* legislation went to Parliament. The royal approval for a bill only reiterated what the Queen had already agreed weeks before.

This did not mean that the Queen always liked what a Prime Minister proposed; yet she accepted that he had the right to implement a policy which he had been elected to enact, provided it was not unconstitutional. The Prime Ministers who were successful with the Queen were those who studied her personality, as Melbourne had done and as Disraeli would do, and who knew how to manage it. Peel confided his method of dealing with the Queen to his young follower, Gladstone. If Gladstone had absorbed this advice, his own premierships would have been much easier. Peel was talking about a plan the Prince and Queen had for visiting King Leopold. Some practical difficulties of the visit worried the government. The royal pair 'will be as reasonable as possible', said Peel, 'but it does not do to thwart them – I know how to manage them – the way is to receive the proposal without objection and show a willingness to meet their desire – then as difficulties appear they will grow cool.' It is interesting to note that the visit to King Leopold went ahead in 1843 as the Queen and Prince planned. Charlotte Brontë was in Brussels studying French at this time, and she caught a glimpse of her sovereign:

> I saw her for an instant flashing through the Rue Royale in a carriage and six, surrounded by soldiers. She was laughing and talking very gaily. She looked a little stout, vivacious lady, very plainly dressed, not much dignity or pretension about her. The Belgians ... said she enlivened the sombre Court of King Leopold, which is usually as gloomy as a conventicle.

King Leopold was anxious for good relations between Britain and France as security for his new throne. His wife was a daughter of the French King, Louis-Philippe, who was disliked by most conservative monarchs for replacing his cousin in one of those periodic revolutions that the French enjoy. Queen Victoria had no patience with reactionary monarchs, such as the Tsar of Russia, and she promoted friendship with France. She became the first English sovereign to set foot in France for centuries when she visited Louis-Philippe at his château in Normandy in 1843 and 1845.

The French King also visited her at Windsor in 1844, which caused much correspondence between the Queen of the Belgians and Victoria. Queen Louise was concerned that her father might eat too much in England, and she asked Victoria to see that the King had only a bowl of chicken broth in the mornings.

As to a bed, she suggested that her father's mattress should have a board underneath it. (Visiting monarchs could cause problems about beds. Tsar Nicholas I of Russia had stayed at what he called the 'prison' of Windsor earlier in 1844; although a large bed surmounted with a crowned 'N' was prepared, His Imperial Majesty flung his usual sack of straw on the floor and slept like a Russian soldier. It would be ten years before a proper use for that bed could be found, when it was slept in by the Emperor Napoleon III.) The Queen became very fond of Louis-Philippe, and she always remained kind to his family throughout the rest of her reign.

The visits to France allowed the Queen to use the royal yacht, which she much enjoyed. On the trip in September 1843 one of her Maids of Honour noted a group of sailors staring at the Queen and grumbling. When the captain of the yacht, Lord Adolphus Fitzclarence (one of William IV's sons) came forward, the Queen asked whether there was a mutiny:

> Lord Adolphus laughed, but remarked he really did not know what *would* happen unless Her Majesty would be graciously pleased to move her seat. 'Move my seat' said the Queen, 'why should I? What possible harm can I be doing here?' 'Well, ma'am' said Lord Adolphus, 'the fact is, your Majesty is unwittingly closing up the door of the place where the grog tubs are kept, and so the men cannot have their grog!' 'Oh very well' said the Queen, 'I will move on one condition ... that you bring me a glass of grog.'... After tasting it the Queen said 'I am afraid I can only make the same remark I did once before, that I think it would be very good if it were stronger!'

In 1845 the Queen was able to make an emotional visit to Germany. She and the Prince stood on a balcony at Bonn, where he had been a student, and watched as a statue of Beethoven was dedicated. Though the Queen was a little annoyed that the concert that evening did not contain much of Beethoven's music, the next evening's entertainment did delight her. Meyerbeer was the conductor, with Franz Liszt and Jenny Lind among the performers. The evening was all the more delightful because Uncle Leopold and his wife were also present. On this visit Dr Charlotte von Siebold was presented to the Queen and Prince, both of whom she had brought into the world twenty-six years before. However, the highlight of the trip was the visit to that most sacred of shrines, Rosenau, a charming, neo-Gothic castle whose yellow stucco walls were a colourful sight in the countryside near Coburg:

> How happy, how joyful we were on awakening, to feel ourselves here, at the dear Rosenau, my Albert's birthplace.... He was so happy to be here with me. It is like a beautiful dream.... Before breakfast we went upstairs to where my dearest Albert and Ernest used to live.... The view is beautiful, and the paper is still full of holes from their fencing.

This trip to Germany saw the early stirrings of a public criticism that was to increase: the Queen often looked unhappy. Lady Lyttelton decided to speak to her about the rumours of the Queen's frown which had reached English newspapers. Victoria listened meekly to this rebuke from her children's governess and said that she might have looked cross from 'fatigue and shyness'. She asked Lady Lyttelton and the Prince, 'What *am* I to do another time?' The Prince advised her to behave like a ballet dancer and show all her teeth in a fixed smile. 'He accompanied the advice with an immense pirouette and prodigious grin of his own, such as few people could perform just after dinner without being sick, ending on one foot and t'other in the air.'

However, not all her travels had the purpose of seeing foreign rulers. The Queen's first visit to Scotland in 1842 marked the beginning of her love for her northern kingdom. Her yacht was escorted north by a fleet of ten ships, each carrying various court luminaries from the royal physician to Albert's favourite dog, Eos. The old royal yacht was slow: 'How annoying and provoking this is!' They were breakfasting on deck on 1 September when the hills over Edinburgh came into sight through the fog. They were a day late and Peel, who was waiting to greet them, was furious with the Edinburgh civic authorities for not being on hand. 'Half the effect of the entry', he claimed, was 'spoiled by their stupidity and negligence.' It did not spoil the arrival for the Queen, who was delighted with the city: 'Quite beautiful, totally unlike anything else I have seen; and what is even more, Albert, who has seen so much, says it is unlike anything *he* ever saw.'

Prince Albert was never one to miss a good opportunity to persuade the government to spend money on the Royal Family and he spoke to Peel about the need for a new steam yacht. The Prime Minister wrote to the First Lord of the Admiralty: 'Utilitarianism must prevail over the Romantic and Picturesque even in the case of Royal Voyages. Towing after all is an ignoble process.'

The books of Sir Walter Scott, the Queen's favourite poet, had put Scotland in the forefront of the Romantic imagination. For the Queen the next few weeks were perfect: the 'very good' porridge at breakfast, bagpipes, handsome highlanders in kilts dancing reels by torchlight, and above all the stunning scenery. Victoria also loved the clean air. She was always very sensitive to climate and hated hot, stuffy rooms; even as an old lady she would do her work outdoors in a tent far into the autumn rather than be closed up inside. Generations of courtiers shivered and grumbled at the Queen's hatred of warm rooms. She and Albert both disliked the polluted air that hung over London: this increasingly became the excuse for avoiding the capital whenever possible. She also loved the people of the Highlands, their simple manners and their lack of pretence. Victoria never felt so much at ease as when in Scotland. From this September visit in 1842 the rest of her life almost always saw her pass many weeks there each year.

The Queen was not able to visit Ireland until 1849. She had hoped to go a few years before, but the horrors of the potato famine, which began in 1845, delayed the visit. In the earlier part of her reign she had been full of sympathy for Ireland. Daniel O'Connell, the Irish leader, had a great sentimental devotion to 'the little Queen', whom he always exempted from the sins of her government. Ireland was, however, one place where Albert's influence was not helpful: 'the Irish baffle all human ingenuity to help them by their behaviour,' he wrote to Peel. Nevertheless Victoria enjoyed her first visit there as well as the three others she made. She was particularly struck with the women: 'such beautiful dark eyes and hair, and such fine teeth; almost every third woman was pretty'. Victoria was greeted with noisy affection wherever she went, from Cork to Dublin and Belfast. As the Queen, Prince and royal children entered Dublin one old woman shouted out: 'Oh! Queen, dear, make one of them Prince Patrick, and all Ireland will die for you.' As a compliment Victoria did give the Prince of Wales a new title: Earl of Dublin.

Lord Dufferin described the Queen's departure in a letter to the Prime Minister's wife:

> I never witnessed so touching a sight as when the Queen from her quarter-deck took leave of the Irish people. It was a sweet, calm, silent evening, and the sun just setting behind the Wicklow mountains bathed all things in golden floods of light. Upon the beach were crowded in thousands the screaming bother-headed people, full of love and devotion for her, her children, and her house, surging to and fro like some horrid sea and asking her to come back to them, and bidding her God-speed.... It was a beautiful, historical picture, and one which one thought of for a long time after the Queen and ships and people had vanished away. I suspect that she too must have thought about it that night as she sat upon the deck and sailed away into the darkness – and perhaps she wondered as she looked back upon the land, which ever has been and still is, the dwelling of so much wrong and misery, whether it should be written in history hereafter, that in *her* reign, and under *her* auspices, Ireland first became prosperous and her people contented.

Ireland was to know more prosperity and contentment during parts of Victoria's reign than ever before, but always there were the smouldering embers of past wrongs readily ignited by an agitator's rhetoric. The Queen, moved by the loyalty shown her, wrote to her mother: 'The enthusiasm and Loyalty of the Irish is most striking – and *we never* can forget, or feel otherwise than most warmly and kindly towards them.' Victoria's greatest failing as Queen was her refusal to display those feelings. She was to visit Ireland twice more during Albert's lifetime, but then followed a long period when Ireland did not see its 'little Queen' until the last days of her reign. By then, in spite of her good intentions, it was too late.

It was the same search for good air and privacy that had endeared Scotland to Victoria that led her to settle in the Isle of Wight. In her first few years as Queen she had carried on using that exotic creation, the Royal Pavilion at Brighton, but the Prince particularly disliked the place. Then one day in 1845 they were attempting to walk from the Pavilion to the chain pier when a crowd of two hundred people ran after them to get a close look. Some even ran alongside the Queen and peered under her large bonnet. The *Sunday Times* dismissed these beings as 'chiefly tradesmen's boys ... with baskets on their arms'.

Sir Robert Peel was soon able to come to their assistance. He had heard of an estate for sale on the Isle of Wight, which was now accessible enough from London thanks to the spread of the railways. Prince Albert drove a hard bargain for the estate, which was bought with the Queen's private funds, supplemented by the sale of the Brighton Pavilion. Albert was soon able to use his skill and energy in planning a new house in which he could display his ability at uniting art with science. It went up at record speed because much of it was prefabricated. Albert also organised the laying out of the lovely grounds by standing on a high platform and using a system of flags as signals to show where to plant the trees. 'We are proceeding rapidly here with all our building and gardening and get to like the place better every day,' he wrote to Peel. Only fifteen months after the Queen had laid the foundation stone, Lady Lyttelton saw the Royal Family move into their new 'Marine Residence':

> After dinner we rose to drink the Queen's and prince's health as a *house-warming*, and after it the prince said very naturally and simply, but seriously 'We have a hymn' in Germany ... and he quoted two lines in German ... meaning a prayer to 'bless our going out and coming in.' It was dry and quaint being Luther's; but we all perceived that he was feeling it.

The Queen described the setting to Lord Melbourne, for she continued to write to the lonely old man after he had left office:

> It is impossible to imagine a prettier spot – valleys and woods which would be beautiful anywhere; but all this near the sea (the woods grow into the sea) is quite perfection.... The sea was so blue and calm that the prince said it was like Naples. And then we can walk about anywhere by ourselves without being followed and mobbed.

The 'paradise' of Osborne would always remain a favourite home of the Queen, as with each year the grounds that Albert had planned grew in splendour. It was here that she could escape the heat, the noise, the formality and the politics that she associated with London. She could not escape her work, but at Osborne she could breathe in peace.

Osborne allowed Albert ample space to develop his many practical ideas. Great attention was paid to modern sanitation, for older royal residences were notorious for their bad drains. The Queen shared her husband's concern about the need to install lavatories, and years later she warned her eldest daughter that 'these very necessary conveniences ... are totally wanting in Germany [which] ... really make one's life very uncomfortable and very unwholesome'. Osborne also provided privacy for the growing family. The children had a 'Swiss Cottage' where they could learn practical things like cooking and gardening, and there was even a fort where the boys could play at soldiering. Yet underlying all this practicality and pleasure was a strain of melancholy. Lady Lyttelton paints an admirable scene of one night at Osborne in July 1850:

> Last evening *such* a sunset! I was sitting gazing at it ... when from an open window below this floor began suddenly to sound the Prince's organ, played by his masterly hand. Such a modulation, minor and solemn, and ever changing, and never ceasing ... up to the fullest swell, and still the same 'fine vein of melancholy'! And it came in so exactly as an accompaniment to the sunset. How strange he is! He must have been playing just while the Queen was finishing her toilette. And then he went in to cut jokes and eat loads at dinner, and nobody knows what is *in him* – except, indeed, by the look of his eyes sometimes.

Music was one of the greatest pleasures that Victoria and Albert enjoyed, and she loved to sing his songs. Nothing brought either of them closer to anyone than

Princess Victoria, aged 15, with her mother, the Duchess of Kent. A lithograph from a drawing by Sir George Hayter, 1834. Princess Victoria had this drawing in her room at Kensington Palace

I

Right *The Duke of Kent, Queen Victoria's father, in 1818, the year of his marriage. From a painting by Sir William Beechey*

Centre *A drawing by Princess Victoria of her governess, Louise Lehzen. Amongst her many other duties, Baroness Lehzen often agreed to be drawn by the young princess who was a promising artist*

Far right *Sir John Conroy in 1836, at the time when he was trying to coerce Princess Victoria into promising him permanent power. The painting is by Alfred Tidey, who later did miniature portraits for Queen Victoria*

Left *The Duchess of Kent in 1857, when she was 71. From a painting by Franz Winterhalter, one of Queen Victoria's favourite artists: an 'old friend' whose 'work will in time rank with Van Dyke'*

Right *Queen Victoria, a few months after she came to the throne, riding between Lord Melbourne on her right and Lord Palmerston on her left. A sketch by the best known caricaturist of the day, John Doyle, who signed his works 'H B'*

II

SUSANNAH AND THE ELDERS

III

Queen Victoria receiving the Sacrament from the Archbishop of Canterbury at her Coronation. She purchased this painting from the artist, Charles Leslie. Lord Melbourne stands behind her

THE WONDER OF WINDSOR.
*The Artist Poet, Fiddler here we see
And all is Tweedle dum and Tweedle dee.*
PUB.ᵈ BY J.W.LAIRD 1 LEADENHALL Sᵗ.ᵗ 1841

Above *'The Wonder of Windsor', an 1841 lithograph making fun of the Coburg family: Albert is seated; behind him is his cousin King Ferdinand of Portugal; Uncle Leopold, with violin, and Prince Ernest, Albert's brother, are performing; Victoria is followed by her mother*

Right *Victoria and Albert waltzing, about 1840. 'It is quite a pleasure to look at Albert when he ... valses, he does it so beautifully, holds himself so well with that beautiful figure of his,' wrote Victoria*

IV

MESS.RS PHILPOT,

BY

CHARLES COOTE.

LONDON, PUBLISHED BY CHAPPELL, MUSIC SELLER TO HER MAJESTY, 50, NEW BOND STREET

V

VI

Above *Seven of the royal children photographed by Roger Fenton in their costumes portraying the seasons, a tableau arranged to celebrate the Queen's fourteenth wedding anniversary on 14 February 1854. Arthur (whose lack of stockings upset the Queen) lies between his sisters, Alice and Vicky. Helena presides, dressed as Britannia. Alfred, holding the cup, portrays autumn. Next to him is Louise and then Bertie, dressed as winter*

Left *The Queen and Prince Albert photographed in June 1854 by Roger Fenton at Buckingham Palace. Fenton, one of the earliest professional photographers, was much encouraged by the royal couple and received Prince Albert's support for his trip to the Crimea where he became one of the first war photographers*

Queen Victoria receiving the Emperor Napoleon III, followed by the Empress Eugénie with Prince Albert and the elder royal children at Windsor, 16 April 1855. A painting by G. H. Thomas

The Royal Family at Osborne House in May 1857. Queen Victoria holds her youngest child, Beatrice. The other children, from left to right are: Alfred (next to Prince Albert), Helena, Alice, Arthur, Victoria, Louise, Leopold and the Prince of Wales

a shared love of music. Mendelssohn described to his mother a wonderful afternoon at Buckingham Palace, which he called 'the one really pleasant and thoroughly comfortable English house, where one feels *á son aise*'.

> Prince Albert had asked me to ... try his organ ... as we were talking away, the Queen came in ... in simple morning dress. She said she was obliged to leave for Claremont in an hour, and then suddenly interrupting herself, exclaimed, 'But goodness, what a confusion.'

The wind had swept in through an open window and scattered music all over the floor, so the Queen knelt down and started to pick it up, joined by Prince and composer. Albert then persuaded the Queen to sing one of Mendelssohn's songs.

> 'If it is still here' she added, 'for all my music is packed up for Claremont.' Prince Albert went to look for it, but came back, saying it was already packed. 'But one might perhaps unpack it,' said I 'We must send for Lady ——,' she said.... So the bell was rung, and the servants were sent after it, but without success; at last, the Queen went herself.... Then the Queen came back and said, 'Lady —— is gone, and has taken all my things with her. It really is most annoying, ... The Duchess of Kent came in too, and while they were all talking I rummaged about amongst the music, and soon discovered my first set of songs. So, of course, I begged her rather to sing one of those ... it was really charming, and the last long G I have never heard better, or purer, or more natural from any amateur ... she said 'Oh, if only I had not been so frightened; generally, I have such a long breath' ... then I took leave; and down below I saw the beautiful carriages waiting, with their scarlet outriders, and in a quarter of an hour the flag was lowered, and the Court Circular announced, 'Her Majesty left the Palace at twenty minutes past three.'

When, five years later, Mendelssohn died, tragically young, the Queen and Prince sent a message to his widow mourning 'the greatest musical genius of the age'.

Music was a respite from the constant succession of boxes containing official letters, despatches and documents. In the 1840s Peel was coming round to the belief that Britain's economic interest demanded free trade, but many Tory MPs refused to follow him. Peel received constant support from the Queen and Prince Albert, and the Prime Minister managed to spare the Queen a government crisis until the month after the birth of her fifth child, Princess Helena. With support from the Whigs, Peel enacted his free trade policy, repealed the protectionist Corn Laws, and then resigned in 1846. The Queen told him that it was 'very painful' to lose him. She commissioned Winterhalter, her favourite artist, to paint a portrait of her and the Prince as a special gift for Peel, who requested that they be portrayed in 'that simple attire' he recalled from his many audiences.

In the new Whig government led by Lord John Russell, the activities of the Foreign Secretary, Lord Palmerston, would cause continual annoyance to the Queen. His bombastic methods made Britain unpopular on the continent where rumblings of radicalism were spreading through many capitals. On 3 March 1848 a 'Mr William Smith' stumbled ashore at Newhaven and a few hours later wrote a note to Queen Victoria. 'Mr William Smith' was actually King Louis-Philippe, driven from his throne by a sudden revolution. Britain soon seemed clogged with refugees escaping from revolutions in Austria, Prussia and France. Victoria, as ever, offered kindness and hospitality to those princes and cousins who had been forced to flee. Yet both she and Albert felt that their policy of constitutional government and steady reform was justified by the awful events of 1848.

Many were worried that England would feel the whirlwind of revolution. A large Chartist demonstration, called by those demanding radical reform, was scheduled to march on Parliament on 10 April. The Queen, who was recovering from the birth of her sixth child, Louise, in March, was not afraid. 'Great events make me quiet and calm', she wrote to King Leopold, but 'little trifles fidget me and irritate my nerves.' Nevertheless the government insisted that the Royal Family repair to the safety of Osborne. The Chartist demonstration fizzled out when it encountered the well-laid plans of the Duke of Wellington.

Just a week later, the Queen asked Lord Ashley to come to Osborne. This extremely religious Tory MP was the best-known social reformer of the age. The Queen told him, 'We have sent for you to have your opinion on what we could do ... to show our interest in the working classes.' Ashley urged the Prince to 'put yourself at the head of all social movements in art and science, and especially of those movements as they bear upon the poor, and thus show the interest felt by Royalty in the happiness of the Kingdom.' Ashley asked him to speak to the Society for Improving the Condition of the Labouring Classes. Before his speech, Albert inspected some model housing that the Society had built. Better housing was one of his great interests, uniting as it did his practical and artistic sides. Prince Albert said:

> Depend upon it, the interests of classes too often contrasted are identical, and it is only ignorance which prevents their uniting for each other's advantages. To dispel that ignorance, to show how man can help man, notwithstanding the complicated state of civilized society, ought to be the aim of every philanthropic person: but it is more peculiarly the duty of those who, under the blessing of Divine Providence, enjoy station, wealth, and education.

It is perhaps ironic that at the same time that Prince Albert was doing so much practical good, a fellow German, Karl Marx, was at work spreading misery in his gospel of class war. Eventually most of the continental monarchies returned to normal after the revolution of 1848. On the first day of 1849 the Queen told her Prime Minister Lord John Russell that she was 'glad to see that dreadful *48* closed'.

The Queen and Prince Albert put their ideas on social reform into practice. On their estates, great care was taken to provide proper employment and good cottages, which greatly impressed a rather radical American, Frederick Olmsted, who came to England to study agriculture and town planning:

> We passed Osborne ... nothing is to be seen from without the grounds, but the top of a lofty campanile.... It is the custom of the royal family, when here, to live in as retired and unstately a way as they can.... The prince himself turns farmer, and engages with much ardor in improving the agricultural capabilities of the soil.... Her Majesty

personally interests herself in the embellishment of the grounds ... and is in the habit of driving herself a pair of ponies, unattended, through the estate, studying the comfort of her little cottage tenantry, and in every way trying to seem to herself the good-wife of a respectable country gentleman.

All the aims of this first decade of the royal couple's married life were symbolised by the Great Exhibition of 1851. Prince Albert had taken the lead in planning this display of the achievements of industry and technology, symbolised by the vast Crystal Palace built especially for the Exhibition. Cynics said it would be a disaster: either the Crystal Palace would collapse or hordes of foreign desperadoes would subject London to rape and revolution. Poor old King Ernest of Hanover, drawing to the end of a life in which he had opposed every change, wrote to his friends urging them to avoid Albert's latest scheme.

On the first day of May 1851 the Queen, with Prince Albert and the Duchess of Kent, opened the Great Exhibition. Only two of the seven royal children were there: ten-year-old Vicky and her younger brother, Bertie, resplendent in his kilt. The Queen walked up on the dais and stood bowing for over five minutes in response to tremendous cheers. A young man, William Harcourt (later to become one of her Home Secretaries), was among the vast throng and for his sister's edification noted that the Queen was 'in a pink satin gown with a simple circlet of diamonds'. She declared the Exhibition open as the Hallelujah Chorus rang forth, and then made the first of several visits to inspect the numerous exhibits. As she made her way round she agreed to stop at one stall which featured engraved glass. The craftsman was so overcome that he had difficulty in explaining the meaning of his work. To assist him, the Queen pointed to one glass which depicted a boy jumping from a boat while a large eye looked down from the clouds. The man stammered: 'The boy, Madam, is the Prince of Wales, and the eye is the eye of God looking out with pleasure for the moment when His Royal Highness will land on his kingdom and become the reigning sovereign.' The courtiers surrounding the Queen were aghast, but she retained her composure until she had passed this stall, when she burst out into hearty laughter.

For the Queen there could be only one thought, which she described to her Uncle Leopold:

I wish you *could* have witnessed the *1st May* 1851, the *greatest* day in our history, the *most beautiful* and *imposing* and *touching* spectacle ever seen, and the triumph of my beloved Albert.... Many cried, and all felt touched and impressed with devotional feelings. It was the *happiest, proudest* day in my life.... Albert's dearest name is immortalised with this *great* conception, *his* own, and my *own* dear country *showed* she was *worthy* of it.... I feel *so* happy, so proud.

Ever your devoted Niece,
VICTORIA R

FOUR

THE GREATEST AND WIDEST GOOD

One obligation which the Queen shared with her humblest subject was that of taking part in the census of 1851. On the night of Sunday, 30 March 'Her Majesty Alexandrina Victoria' and Prince Albert, both aged thirty-one, and their seven children were at Buckingham Palace. The census also showed a population of 27 million, an increase of over one third since her birth. Much of this tremendous growth had been in the great cities of the north, and Prince Albert was anxious that the Queen should be seen by her subjects in these expanding cities. One of their great achievements was taking the monarchy to the people. It was said that George III never went north of Worcester, but his granddaughter used the railways in order to be seen throughout her realm.

In October 1851 the Royal Family, including the four eldest children, visited Lancashire. In Liverpool the Queen's proverbial luck with the weather deserted her; she had to wrap Albert's cloak about her to keep off the rain. She was anxious to see the docks and Seamen's Refuge, both of which had been dedicated by the Prince five years before. She was quite delighted with St George's Hall, 'one of the finest of modern buildings ... worthy of ancient Athens'. Yet far more importantly for her, it won the approval of the Prince: 'Albert ... never really admires what is small in purpose and design, what is frittered away in detail, and not chaste and simple.'

They spent the night at a nearby country house where a large party including the Duke of Wellington greeted them. The next morning they set out with an escort of yeomanry; as they entered Manchester a regiment of lancers added greater colour. The Queen observed her people as much as they stared at her: 'The mechanics and work-people, dressed in their best, were ranged along the streets, with white rosettes in their button-holes; ... a very intelligent, but painfully unhealthy-looking population they all were, men as well as women.' The Queen's physician saw this as well: 'I was struck with the small stature of the manufacturing people, particularly the women, who were generally pale, but with a remarkably intelligent expression.'

In Peel Park the Queen enjoyed a

totally unprecedented sight – 82,000 school-children, Episcopalians, Presbyterians, Catholics (these children having a small crucifix suspended round their necks), Baptists, and Jews, whose faces told their descent.... All the children sang 'God Save the Queen' extremely well together.

She shared the cheers with the eighty-two-year-old Duke of Wellington. The Duke was virtually deaf, and someone in his carriage had to wake him, saying,

'Duke, Duke, that's for you.' 'Thereupon he opened his eyes and obediently made his well-known salutation, two fingers to the brim of his hat.'

It was to be one of the last occasions on which the Queen saw the hero of Waterloo. In September 1852 the Royal Family was back in Scotland. Before they left for an expedition, a newspaper report reached them of the sudden death of the Duke, but Albert dismissed it, as 'the *Sun* is not a very creditable authority'. The Queen had just begun to make a sketch of a mountain when a servant brought a letter: 'Alas! it contained the confirmation of the fatal news: that *England's* or rather *Britain's* pride, her glory, her hero, the greatest man she ever had produced, was no more! . . . One cannot think of this country without "the Duke".' His death left many important posts vacant, but Prince Albert rejected Stockmar's advice that he should assume these offices. The Prince preferred influence to public notice:

> The position of being merely the wife's husband is, in the eyes of the public, naturally an unfavourable one, inasmuch as it presupposes *inferiority*, and makes it necessary to demonstrate, which can only be done by deeds, that no such inferiority exists. Now *silent* influence is precisely that which operates the greatest and widest good, and therefore much time must elapse before the value of that influence is recognised. . . . I must content myself with the fact that constitutional monarchy marches unassailably on its beneficent course, and that the country prospers and makes progress.

Yet the Queen increasingly felt that Albert should take the lead in political questions. She explained her reasons to King Leopold:

> I love peace and quiet – in fact I hate politics and turmoil. . . . Albert grows daily fonder and fonder of politics and business, and is so wonderfully *fit* for both – such perspicacity and such *courage*. . . . We women are not *made* for governing – and if we are good women, we must *dislike* these masculine occupations; but there are times which force one to take *interest* in them.

Then she added: 'I must now conclude, to dress for the opening of Parliament.' This accounts for some of her vehemence, for she never disliked politics as much as when she was surrounded by politicians.

Early in 1851, Lord John Russell resigned as Prime Minister after an unexpected defeat in the Commons. As soon as the Queen heard the news she hurried up to Stockmar's room in Buckingham Palace. Prince Albert was already there. She snatched a moment to write to King Leopold:

> We have got a Ministerial crisis. . . . This is very bad, because there is no chance of any other good Government, poor Peel being no longer alive, and not one man of talent except Lord Stanley in the [Tory] Party. . . . Altogether, it is very vexatious, and will give us trouble.

Lord Stanley was not popular with the royal couple, but their real dislike was for his lieutenant, Benjamin Disraeli, who had risen to prominence by his attacks on Peel. This distrust even appeared in a book by Disraeli's fellow novelist,

Anthony Trollope, which mentions 'the whispered dislike of an illustrious personage' for Sidonia, the name of a character in one of Disraeli's novels. Returning from a royal audience, Lord Stanley described what had taken place to his son, who noted it down in his diary; this gives one of the best pictures of how the Queen behaved in a political crisis. She frankly told Stanley, 'I do not approve of Mr Disraeli. I do not approve of his conduct to Sir Robert Peel.'

'Madam,' replied Stanley, 'Mr Disraeli has had to make his position, and men who make their positions will say and do things which are not necessary to be said or done by those for whom positions are provided.'

It is characteristic of the Queen that as soon as she heard this explanation she replied, 'That is true. And all I can now hope is that, having attained this great position, he will be temperate. I accept Mr Disraeli on your guarantee.' This, however, did not apparently satisfy the Prince, who was inclined to 'enter into argument', but the Queen indicated that she wished to change the subject. Young Stanley summarised his father's impressions:

> On his admission to the Palace, he could see plainly that she had been in tears. His impression was that since their communication began, she had become much more cordial and unreserved.... With the Prince the reverse was the case: he remained present during every conversation that passed, suggesting difficulties faster than they could be disposed of, and endeavouring to alarm the Queen.... He began to talk ... of the unpopularity of the Minister affecting the Sovereign personally, quoting the instances of Polignac and Guizot [the ministers who were charged with causing the 1830 and 1848 revolutions in France]. My father bore this insinuation with temper; and the Queen, feeling it to be offensive, used some words intended to do away its effect.

This is a good example of why Prince Albert was often disliked by the aristocracy. It was certainly indiscreet to throw foreign examples in the face of such an insular Englishman as Lord Stanley. The Queen, on the other hand, in spite of her initial tears, was trying to do all she could to be both polite and fair.

In the event Stanley could not form a new government. The Queen's attempt at arranging a coalition also failed, and Russell agreed to carry on with a much weakened government in which the most powerful figure, Lord Palmerston, was a cause of increasing annoyance to the Queen. If the audience with Lord Stanley showed Victoria's ability to change her attitudes, the clash with Palmerston showed her determination to withstand a minister whom she felt was dangerous. Palmerston should have listened to his wife's advice about the Queen:

> I am sure the Queen is very angry with you! I am afraid you contradict her notions too boldly. You fancy she will hear reason, when in fact all you say only proves to her that you are determined to act on the line she disapproves, and which she still thinks wrong. I am sure it would be better if you *said* less to her – even if you *act* as you think best.... You always think you can convince people by arguments, and she has not reflection or sense to feel the force of them.... I should treat what she says more lightly and courteously, and not enter into argument with her, but lead her on gently, by letting her believe you have both the same opinions in fact and the same wishes, but take sometimes different ways of carrying them out.

The Queen also had personal reasons for disliking Palmerston. In Society he was called Cupid because of rumours about his many affairs; the Queen disliked him not for his reputation but because of his shocking behaviour in 1839. Charles Greville recorded the story:

> Palmerston ... took a fancy to Mrs Brand ... and at Windsor Castle, where she was in waiting ... marched into her room one night. His tender temerity met with an invincible resistance ... it came to the Queen's ears ... the Queen has never forgotten and will never forgive it.

Behind all the Queen's reactions to Palmerston's policies was a feeling, held even more strongly by Albert, that her Foreign Secretary had virtually attempted to rape her Lady in Waiting in a royal residence.

The final reason for disliking Palmerston was his refusal to keep the Queen informed. Throughout her long reign, she insisted on a special role in foreign affairs. With her wide knowledge of foreign courts she was well informed and able to offer valuable advice. In particular she always wished to act as a brake on hasty actions that could lead to war. The Queen was often denied her right to see Palmerston's frequently vehement despatches until they were on the way to a foreign government. In December 1851 he went too far. The French President, Louis Napoleon Bonaparte, staged a military coup. Without consulting anyone, Palmerston immediately congratulated the French Ambassador. He not only outraged the Queen and Prime Minister, but for once he had not carefully calculated public opinion. Victoria demanded that Russell get an explanation of his action; when Russell did so he did not find it acceptable. Both he and the Queen had had enough, and the Prime Minister dismissed Palmerston from the Cabinet.

The Queen's behaviour reflects credit upon her. She had determined that Palmerston was not fit to be Foreign Secretary. She believed one of her most important functions was to preserve peace and harmony among the nations. She saw Palmerston as a threat to that peace and harmony. She determined that Palmerston must go. And he went.

It would take a book in itself to describe the political manoeuvres of the 1850s, whose main theme was Palmerston's struggle for power, carried out against the backdrop of the events that eventually culminated in the Crimean War, Britain's only European war in Victoria's long reign. It was the first war in which a mobilised public opinion would hunt for scapegoats and traitors. This wild hunt was to bring misery next to the throne itself when it sought out Prince Albert as its prime victim.

Prince Albert had never been highly popular. Even at the time of his triumph with the Great Exhibition, Lady Lyttelton, who admired him intensely, spoke of 'the contempt for the Prince among all fine folk'. He was not liked by large sections of the fashionable classes for a variety of reasons. Petty stories circulated about him: he did not dress like an Englishman, said one; he did not shoot like an Englishman, said another; and even his manner of getting out of a carriage was ridiculed. Many found the Queen's idolisation of her husband difficult to take and, in the normal human manner, visited their annoyance on the blameless idol rather than the relentless worshipper.

In late 1853 rumours began to circulate that drew on this undercurrent of dislike. The main international question was Turkey, a decaying power that controlled most of south-east Europe. Russia's desire for influence there frightened France. Queen Victoria and the Prince urged a peaceful settlement to the dispute. They were content with the coalition government that the Peelite Lord Aberdeen had formed with the Whigs in 1852, in which Palmerston was once again a minister. Aberdeen had a deep hatred of war, yet somehow events seemed to be dragging Europe and Britain towards it. In the midst of all this tension, Palmerston resigned from the government. To many there could only be one real reason: Prince Albert had once again undermined Palmerston, the one minister who stood up to Russia. Articles began to fill newspapers about 'the Austro-Belgian-Coburg-Orleans clique, the avowed enemies of England'.

This was just a new version of an old fear: that Victoria would be a puppet controlled by her clever Uncle Leopold for the benefit of the Coburg family. The attacks grew so strong that people actually gathered outside the Tower of London because of a rumour that Prince Albert was being imprisoned for treason. One version of the rumour even had the Queen herself on her way to her own Tower! These unjust attacks greatly distressed both Queen and Prince. Albert determined to show that he was not afraid of his critics and rode without escort through the City.

In spite of efforts by the royal couple and their pacifist Prime Minister, Britain went to war with Russia. The Queen – ever conscious that she was 'a soldier's daughter' – described one scene at Buckingham Palace:

> The last battalion of the Guard ... embarked to-day. They passed through the courtyard here at seven o'clock this morning. We stood on the balcony to see them – the morning fine, the sun rising over the towers of old Westminister Abbey – and an immense crowd collected to see these fine men and cheering them immensely.... They formed line, presented arms, and then cheered us *very heartily*, and went off cheering. It was a *touching and beautiful* sight; many sorrowing friends were there, and one saw the shake of many a hand. My best wishes and prayers will be with them all.

The war set off a surge of patriotic fervour. *Punch* summed up the national mood:

> Fight – with determined fury fight!
> We know that we are in the right,
> For Freedom's holy sake we rise
> And have the best of battle-cries –
> > Victoria!
> Fight for the Queen in the Queen's own name,
> 'Tis an omen of conquest, an earnest of fame,
> On with it, brave men, through smoke and flame –
> > Victoria! Victoria!

Yet in the midst of rumour and war, the Queen was supported by the serenity of family life. On 10 February 1854, her wedding anniversary, she recorded in her Journal: 'Fourteen happy and blessed years have passed, and I confidently trust many more will, and find us in old age, as we are now, happily and devotedly united! Trials we must have; but what are they, if we are together.'

They now had four sons and four daughters. Arthur, in many ways the Queen's favourite, had been born in 1850, and the youngest son, Leopold, followed three years later, the only one of her sons to suffer from the haemophilia which Victoria and her daughters carried to the royal houses of Europe, including Russia. The Queen enjoyed being surrounded by her children once they were past the baby stage, but she insisted on proper behaviour. Henrietta Ward, an artist who painted several of the children, had excellent opportunities to observe the royal parents. She noticed that Albert had 'the tenderness of a woman' in dealing with a child and she saw him gently rocking and singing the younger children to sleep. It was Victoria who was much more the 'martinet'. When the children grew tired of hearing their mother talking about painting with Mrs Ward, they began to get restless and pull at her dress.

> The Queen had a method of reducing them to order.... She would stamp her foot, once, very decidedly, and that meant she had read the 'Riot Act' ... the children vanished quietly to another part of the room. The Queen laughing heartily, said 'I expect you often have to do that with your children.'

Leopold was the only child not to take part in a special performance to celebrate the fourteenth wedding anniversary. Among the guests was the wife of the Prussian Ambassador, Baroness Bunsen:

> We all sat in darkness till the curtain was drawn aside, and the Princess Alice, who had been dressed to represent Spring, recited some verses taken from Thomson's 'Seasons'... she did it very well, speaking ... with excellent modulation and a tone of voice like that of the Queen. Then the curtain was (again) drawn up and the whole scene changed, and the Princess Royal represented Summer, with Prince Arthur lying upon some sheaves.... Then there was another change, and Prince Alfred, with a crown of vine-leaves, and a panther's skin, represented Autumn ... another change to Winter landscape, and the Prince of Wales represented Winter, with a white beard and a cloak with icicles ... and the Princess Louise, warmly clothed, who seemed watching the fire.... Then another change was made, and all the seasons were grouped together, and far behind, on high, appeared Princess Helena ... pronouncing a blessing on the Queen and Prince in the name of all the seasons.

The Queen was delighted and ordered the curtain lifted up again so she could see her children. A Maid of Honour witnessed the sequel:

> The Prince called to them to ... jump down ... but one of them piteously remarked, 'We can't get through the atmosphere' (the gauze behind which they act); ... the Queen was so shocked at Prince Arthur's scanty attire (though his nurse assured her he had 'flesh-coloured decencies' on) that she sent him away to be dressed, but when he came back all the difference I saw was a pair of socks that hardly came above his ankles.

The royal couple asked Roger Fenton, one of the earliest professional photographers, to photograph the children in their costumes. This interest had grown out of the visit which Victoria and Albert had paid to the first exhibition of the Photographic Society. Both learned how to take photographs and had their children instructed. Victoria was an avid collector of photographs of family, friends, celebrities, servants and even of an Eskimo family who visited Windsor. Eventually she possessed over one hundred albums of photographs. A few years later one of her servants said that the Queen 'could be bought and sold for a photograph'. Yet the war was not far away from these innocent amusements, and soon Fenton was on his way to the Crimea, laden with letters of introduction from Prince Albert, to become one of the first war photographers.

Britain was in the unusual role of being allied with France – a France ruled by Napoleon III, for the President Louis-Napoleon Bonaparte, who had come to power in 1848, had now become Emperor. In September 1854 Prince Albert went to Boulogne to discuss strategy with this new ally. The thought of his five-day absence made the Queen quite distressed. Only a few hours after parting, Albert wrote:

> Whilst you sit at breakfast with the children, and are teased by wasps... I sit in the cabin at my table (yours is there empty) and wish you on paper a friendly good-morning.... It was close upon twelve when I got to bed in the cabin, which had a very blank and desolate look.

Albert paid Napoleon III the greatest compliment he could think of by saying that the Emperor did not really think or act like a Frenchman, but like a German. The Queen was fascinated with his report; its assessment of the Emperor was to be repeated in many of her letters for the next quarter of a century.

The Queen invited the Emperor to visit England with his new wife, Eugénie. There was tremendous public enthusiasm to see England's ally, but the old anti-French feelings lingered as one popular broadside proclaimed:

> The Emperor and Empress are coming so keen
> To England, to visit our sweet little Queen....
> The Emperor of France and his lady so gay,
> Are coming to England – get out of the way....
> There'll be baked frogs, and fried frogs, and frogs in a stew,
> And all the young ladies shall sing *parlez-vous*!

On 16 April 1855, the Queen awaited her visitors at Windsor:

> The evening was fine and bright. At length the crowd of anxious spectators lining the road seemed to move, then came a groom, then we heard a gun, and we moved towards the staircase. Another groom came. Then we saw the *avant-garde* of the escort; then the cheers of the crowd burst forth. The outriders appeared, the doors opened, I stepped out, the children ... close behind me; the band struck up ... the trumpets sounded, and the open carriage, with the Emperor and Empress, Albert sitting opposite to them, drove up and they got out. I cannot say what indescribable emotions filled me – how much all seemed like a wonderful dream. These great meetings of sovereigns, surrounded by very

exciting accompaniments, are always very agitating. I advanced and embraced the Emperor, who received two salutes on the cheek from me, having first kissed my hand. I next embraced the very gentle, graceful and evidently very nervous Empress. We presented ... our children (Vicky with very alarmed eyes making very low curtsies); the Emperor embraced Bertie; and then we went upstairs.

The next few days were a whirl of pageantry and excitement: a military review, visits to the Crystal Palace and to the Opera. They were to be among the most colourful and happy days of the Queen's reign. When the Garter was conferred on the Emperor, the Queen complained to Bishop Wilberforce, the Chancellor of the Order, 'I was afraid of making some mistake. You would not let me have in writing what I was to say to him. Then we put the riband on wrong! But I think it all went off well, on the whole.' At last a use was found for the bed with the crowned 'N' at Windsor that was originally intended for, but rejected by, Nicholas I who had preferred to sleep on a straw sack; it was ironic that Napoleon III used it while on a state visit to discuss the war against the Russian Tsar.

At the grand ball Henry Greville, on duty as a Gentleman Usher, was furious to see the Waterloo Gallery at Windsor Castle renamed the Picture Gallery for the evening lest it hurt Imperial pride: 'for in these times we even go so far as to apologise for *history*'. The Queen, who was born four years after Waterloo, and the Emperor who had embraced his uncle before he set out for that battle, had become friends as well as allies. 'How strange,' she reflected:

> How strange to think that I, the granddaughter of George III, should dance with the Emperor Napoleon, nephew of England's great enemy, now my nearest and most intimate ally, in the *Waterloo Room*, and this ally only six years ago living in this country, an exile, poor and unthought of.

Two days after a tearful departure, the Queen gave her impression of her new 'sister' to Princess Augusta of Prussia, a close friend since her own visit to Windsor nine years before. This is an unique letter in which the future Empress of India comments on the Empress of the French to the future Empress of Germany:

> The Empress is a very charming, lovable creature, also extremely tactful, yet natural, in her manner ... very pretty, with a charming profile and figure, and with a sweetness and friendliness that win all hearts. She was deeply touched by my affection and care for her.

Part of the 'care' was a talk about a subject that disturbed the Emperor. According to a well-informed German diplomat, Napoleon 'begged her Majesty, as the mother of eight children, to persuade the Empress to consult a physician. Sir Charles Locock ... was accordingly summoned; and so successful was the treatment ... that nine months afterwards the Prince Imperial was born.' Victoria paid Eugénie the supreme compliment of not even being jealous: 'Altogether I am delighted to see how much Albert likes and admires her, as it is so seldom I see him do so with any woman.' The Queen did not wait long before paying a return visit to her Imperial friends.

The two eldest children accompanied their parents to France on 18 August, a trip that marked the debut of the new royal yacht, the *Victoria and Albert*, which took nine hours to cross from Osborne to Boulogne. Napoleon III was waiting almost on the very spot where his uncle had raged in vain at his inability to cross the Channel. This was to be the grandest state visit of Victoria's reign. Her Journal entries reveal a deeply sentimental nature particularly stirred by the sadness of history, and show her considerable ability as a writer who could capture a great and colourful scene with simplicity. Her writing was like her drawing, by which it was much influenced; she could pick out the salient lines of anything that stirred her emotions.

At Boulogne, the royal party – like all tourists – began a long rail journey to Paris. The August sun was starting to set when she saw 'a glimpse of Montmartre, my first sight of Paris ... and at last we passed the fortifications and Paris opened upon us'. They drove down the new Boulevard de Strasbourg and made their way to the Palace of St Cloud outside the city, where the Empress who – as Prince Albert put it – was 'in expectation of an heir and suffering', awaited them. The week that followed was a kaleidoscope of brilliant events. Everything was done for the Queen's comfort: one of her rooms glittered with furniture that had belonged to Marie Antoinette, but the legs were shortened to make the pieces more comfortable. Another room was a replica of one of her own at Windsor, and the Queen jokingly said that all it lacked was her dog. The next day a French messenger arrived from Osborne with the dog.

One purpose of the visit was to see the Exposition, which was a French version of the Great Exhibition. The Royal Family's frequent visits to both the Exposition and other places allowed the Queen to see a fair amount of the city. The Emperor was an enthusiastic guide, illuminating historic spots with some personal anecdote. As their carriage trotted across the Seine on the way to the Sainte Chapelle, he pointed to the grim Conciergerie: '*Voilà où j'étais en prison!*' This was after one of his two attempts to overthrow Louis-Philippe. 'Strange contrast,' reflected the Queen, 'to be driving with us as Emperor through the streets of the city in triumph.' The Emperor even took the thirteen-year-old Prince of Wales on a drive through the city and amidst the haze of the Imperial cigar smoke was born his undying love of Paris and its pleasures.

The Queen also managed an incognito drive about the city:

> We got into a *remise*; I and Miss Bulteel, having put on common bonnets, I with a black veil down, and a black mantilla. We sat together, while Albert, and Vicky, (who had also a bonnet and mantilla which we sent for in a hurry,) sat backwards ... by help of my veil I was able to look out and we took a charming long drive by the Rue de Rivoli ... Place Vendôme ... all along the Boulevards des Capucines, des Italiens, Montmartre, Poissonnière ... the Place de la Bastille ... and along the Quais, everything there looking so light, and white, and bright ... people sitting and drinking before the houses, all so foreign and southern-looking to my eyes, and so gay.

We are fortunate that Mary Bulteel, the Maid of Honour, also described the outing in a letter to her mother:

67

First we were presented with some ordinary-looking bonnets that came from the Magazin du Louvre.... The Queen took tremendous interest and delight in quite ordinary circumstances, such as the people having their food out of doors outside the cafés, or at a cutler's shop because the knives and scissors were arranged in a circle in a window.

'But this should also be done in England.'

I tried to explain that it was done, only that she didn't see it. As we were driving back ... some woman shouted out '*Celle-là ressemble bien à la Reine d'Angleterre.*' The Queen bridled, as she always has a *penchant* for being recognised when she was incognito. When she said 'They do not seem to know who I *am*' it was a sure sign that she was beginning to be bored.

Perhaps it was on this venture that the Queen stopped to buy a toy for young Jenny, 'the daughter of a humble Balmoral neighbour' to whom she had promised to bring a present. The Reverend Charles Bullock, who recounts this tale in *The Queen's Resolve: 'I Will Be Good'*, one of the most popular of the Golden Jubilee books, comments: 'These are the links that bind the people to their Queen.' The Queen also did some shopping at the Exposition. Like many of her subjects she was surprised at how much she had bought when the purchases began to arrive in England. 'She was', noted one courtier, 'horrified at the price of many, and Col. Phipps more so; and they all agree in telling Lady Ely she was too soft, and did not scold the sellers into a reasonable price.'

The most symbolic and solemn moment of the visit was at the Invalides. The Queen had given her permission fifteen years before for the body of Napoleon to be brought back from St Helena, and now she went to see his tomb.

There I stood, at the arm of Napoleon III, his nephew, before the coffin of England's bitterest foe; I, the grand-daughter of that King who hated him most, and who most vigorously opposed him, and this very nephew, who bears his name, being my nearest and dearest ally! The organ ... was playing 'God save the Queen' at the time, and this solemn scene took place by torchlight, and during a thunder-storm. Strange and wonderful indeed ... the seal of Heaven placed upon that bond of unity, which is now happily established between two great and powerful nations. May Heaven bless and prosper it!

The round of festivities included a great ball at Versailles, where Victoria also had time to visit the Trianon with its haunting memories of Marie Antoinette. At the Louvre a 'rolling chair' was provided to allow the Queen to see as many of its treasures as possible. There was also a visit to the Opera with the Emperor and Empress. One of her Ladies remembered this event half a century later:

Her conquest of France happened at the gala performance at the Opera.... The Empress was looking magnificent, a dream of silken splendour; the Queen, as ever, somewhat disdainful of her clothes, had made no effort to shine. But when the party arrived at the box ... her innate genius for movement inspired her. The Empress of the French, fussing about her women, loitered at the door of the box; the Queen of England walked straight to the front.... She stood there alone for a moment, surveying the vast concourse of society, and then she slowly bowed on every side, with a smile that the most consummate actress might envy. This was a great moment.... 'La reine Mab' became from that day forth the idol of Parisian society.

The manner in which the Queen sat down won even more praise:

Did you not observe ... how the Empress looked round to see if there was a chair for her before she sat down. But your Queen, a born Queen, sat down without looking. She knew a chair *must* be there, as surely as she is Queen of England.

Victoria became the first of her family to endure the gauntlet of French comments about her toilette. Marshal Canrobert, just back from the front in the Crimea, was amazed at the Queen's detailed knowledge of the military situation, but he thought her hat and handbag quite absurd and noticed that 'when she put her foot on the steps she lifted her skirt, which was very short (in the English fashion I was told).... The Queen seemed very small; but of a most amiable appearance; above all, in spite of the shocking toilette, I was struck by her dignified air.' The Empress, perhaps a greater expert at dress than the Marshal, took a more objective view:

The Queen stepped down wearing a large white hat with streamers floating behind, and marabou feathers on the top. Her flounced dress was entirely white, and a bright green sunshade and mantle completed her costume. She wore small slippers tied with black ribbands over the instep and ankles.... A large bag or reticule embroidered with a large gilt poodle hung from her arm. This was all so different from our Paris fashion.

The day before their departure, 26 August, was Albert's thirty-sixth birthday. The Emperor led him to the window to hear a drum roll performed by three hundred drummers and specially composed for the occasion, and presented him with the painting he had most admired at the Exposition. It is no wonder that the Queen was particularly emotional at their parting the next day. Vicky and Bertie cried when they bade the Empress farewell and begged to be allowed to stay on. When Eugénie said that their parents needed them, the Prince of Wales insisted, 'Oh no! they don't really need us, they have so many more in England.' The Emperor accompanied them to their yacht and said he would build one like it, but not as big as the one belonging to the 'Queen of the Seas'.

We looked over the side of the ship, and watched them getting into the barge. The Emperor called out '*Adieu, Madame, au revoir*' to which I replied '*Je l'espère bien*'. We heard the splash of the oars, and saw the barge lit by the moon.... Then we sent up endless rockets. We watched the Imperial yacht which passed us, while our men cheered, while we waved our handkerchiefs, and then all was still, all over.

Behind all the splendour of the Paris visit lay the serious topic of the Crimean War. The Emperor, like his Marshal, had been impressed by the Queen's knowledge of the war. He said to a friend: 'The Queen is a charming woman and an astute statesman, and both to an extreme degree.' Along with that knowledge went an indomitable courage and a refusal to panic. The Queen and the Prince were furious, however, with the press for its behaviour during the war. *The Times* had reached a peak of influence that no paper has ever equalled. Its famous correspondent, W. H. Russell, sent back colourful accounts of both the soldiers' bravery and their suffering as a result of incompetent generals. *The Times* also resumed its attacks upon Prince Albert.

Nor did the Queen like the bombastic patriotism favoured by Palmerston. She scorned one of his after-dinner speeches with its 'boastings of victories not yet achieved [as] very bad taste and unworthy of this great country which has hitherto been distinguished in not partaking of that swaggering which our French allies are famous for'. She was furious when Palmerston, who became Prime Minister after Aberdeen had been forced to resign, continued his close friendship with the editor of *The Times*. Prince Albert drafted a note in the Queen's name, instructing Palmerston to show it to the Cabinet:

> Balmoral, Oct 6 1855, The Queen has been as much disgusted with the late atrocious articles in the *Times* ... as she understands the Cabinet to have been.... Lord Panmure [Secretary at War] speaks even of the desire ... to establish an 'Anti-Times League' – the Queen believes this would but aggravate the evil like any repressive laws, but she would put it to Ld Palmerston, whether it is right that the Editor, the Proprietor, and the Writers of such execrable publications ought to be the honoured and constant guest of the Ministers of the Crown? Their introduction into our higher society ... and the attention which is publicly shown to them there, is, the most direct encouragement they could receive adding both to their importance and power for mischief.

The Queen's main concern throughout the war was to alleviate the suffering of the Army. Never before had a sovereign become so involved in the welfare of the ordinary soldier. The Royal Family shared this interest. The Patriotic Fund, under Prince Albert's direction, arranged an exhibition of drawings by the elder children. The Princess Royal, already an accomplished artist, told her drawing master, 'Mamma says I may draw something, but, it must not be anything political.' Eventually the drawings were sold to raise money to help the families of the soldiers. *The Knight* by the Prince of Wales fetched 55 guineas, while the Princess Royal's *The Battlefield* brought 250 guineas. While the Queen was delighted with this charitable effort, she demanded government action as well:

> The Queen is very anxious to bring before Lord Panmure the subject which she mentioned to him the other night, viz. that of Hospitals for our sick and wounded soldiers. This is absolutely necessary, and *now* is the moment to have them built, for no doubt there would be no difficulty in obtaining the money.... The Queen is particularly anxious on this subject, which is, she may truly say, constantly in her thoughts as is everything connected with her beloved troops, who have fought so bravely and borne so heroically all their sufferings and privations. The Queen hopes before long to visit all the Hospitals at Portsmouth, and to see what state they are in.

This royal concern played a vital role in the establishment of the important military hospital at Netley.

The Queen also wanted public honours to be given, for the first time, to ordinary soldiers. After some royal prompting, the War Office had medals made for the Queen to distribute. Among those watching the first ceremony was the young Lucy Lyttelton, granddaughter of the former royal governess:

Punctually at 11 a.m. through the Horse Guards swept a whole troop of Life Guards.... Then up came the Royal carriage, drew up at a sort of low platform ... with two gilt chairs and a flag-staff; out stepped the little Queen, while loudly echoed the reports of cannon, and the National Anthem.... Then it began. The long file of wounded passed before the Queen, and as each received the medal from her own gracious hands, he passed on.... There were noble grenadiers who fought at Inkermann, and the glorious few remaining from the Balaclava Light Cavalry charge.... There was but little cheering, people felt it in a different manner to what would be expressed by that.... Her beloved Majesty drove away to the same crash as before, guns firing, bands playing 'God Save the Queen.'

The Queen was deeply moved as 'the rough hand of the brave and honest private soldier came for the first time in contact with that of their Sovereign'. 'I own,' she wrote to King Leopold, 'as if they were *my own children*.' Many of them refused to give up the medals to be engraved, lest they lose the one put in their hands by the Queen.

The Queen gave an even higher honour to those who had been cited for outstanding heroism in the Crimea: the Victoria Cross. The Crosses were made of metal from a captured Russian cannon, and at their first distribution she rode her horse slowly along the line of the first sixty-two men to receive the greatest of all awards for valour. She wore 'a scarlet jacket with a Field-Marshal's sash and the ribbon of the Garter over a dark blue habit, and a wide-awake hat with an officer's feather'. Sophisticates like Henry Greville may have found the Queen's taste for 'soldiering' mildly amusing, but she was always conscious that she was a 'soldier's daughter'.

After their return from Paris, the Royal Family went to their new holiday home in the Highlands of Scotland, Balmoral, but those September days of 1855 were clouded by rumours about the siege of Sebastopol. Lord Granville, Lord President of the Council, who was staying at Balmoral, records that one night after dinner:

I was trying to keep myself awake by arguing with Her Majesty that it was better to receive common-place messages by the telegraph which I could read, than to receive important ones in cypher which her Majesty could not understand, when the page came in with a message for each.

The Queen carried on the tale in her Journal – a selection she later published:

I began reading mine, which was from Lord Clarendon, with details from Marshal Pélissier of the further destruction of the Russian ships; and Lord Granville said 'I have still better news;' on which he read, 'From General Simpson – *Sevastopol is in the hands of the Allies.*' God be praised for it! ... In a few minutes, Albert and all the gentlemen, in every species of attire, sallied forth, followed by the servants, and gradually by all ... the village – keepers, gillies, workmen – up to the top of the cairn. We waited.... The bonfire blazed forth brilliantly, and we could see the numerous figures surrounding it – some dancing, all shouting.... Just as I was undressing, all the people came down under the windows, the pipes playing, the people singing, firing off guns, and cheering first for me, then for Albert ... and the 'downfall of *Sevastopol*.'

71

Once peace came, the greatest hero of the war was invited to Balmoral. The Queen had been deeply interested in Florence Nightingale's work among the wounded, and had written to her, sending various gifts. The Queen was impressed by their meeting: 'She has a rare presence, very simple, gentle and ladylike and modest to the last degree. At the same time she has a man's intelligence.... One can see how much she has gone through.' The royal couple had several long talks with the famous nurse: Albert enjoyed discussing theology with her, while the Queen drove the pony-cart so they could have a confidential talk about the need to improve medical care.

The Queen considered it appropriate that the news of Sebastopol came to Balmoral, because it had proved 'lucky ... for from the first moment of our arrival we have had good news'. Ever since her first visit to Scotland, in 1842, she had tried to spend part of each summer and autumn there. From the first she and the Prince were attracted by the 'wild, and yet not desolate' scenery, which reminded them of Germany: they both felt better in the mountain air. For several years they rented the old Balmoral House, but the Tory Foreign Secretary, Lord Malmesbury, who stayed at the old house in 1852, was not impressed by it:

> Balmoral is an old country house in bad repair, and totally unfit for royal personages.... The rooms are so small that I was obliged to write my despatches on my bed. We played at billiards every evening, the Queen and the Duchess [of Kent] being constantly obliged to get up from their chairs to be out of the way of the cues.

However, the large building programme which Prince Albert had set up at Osborne meant that they could ill afford another large country residence. The solution to their problem arrived during Malmesbury's stay, in the form of a telegram announcing that the Queen had been left a fortune. At first she dismissed this as a joke, but enquiries showed that an eccentric, childless miser in Buckinghamshire had bequeathed her a legacy of at least £200,000. She only agreed to accept it after increasing the amount of money willed to his executors. She then insisted on beautifying her benefactor's parish church with new stained glass and a reredos behind the altar bearing an inscription, which can still be read today, expressing her gratitude 'in the eighteenth year of her reign' to John Camden Nield.

With this unexpected fortune Prince Albert was able to carry out his plan at Balmoral. The old house was pulled down and under Albert's supervision a castle was built: its foundation stone was laid in September 1853. As at Osborne, Albert's building rose quickly, and two years later the Queen could write: 'An old shoe was thrown after us into the house, for good luck, when we entered the hall. The house is charming; the rooms delightful; the furniture, papers, everything perfection.'

In 1855, about a week after the news of the capture of Sebastopol, a young visitor came to Balmoral. Prince Frederick William was the nephew of the childless King of Prussia, and the eventual heir to that throne. For a long time English opinion had looked with contempt on Prussia as a land of martinets and despots. Prince Albert, on the other hand, believed that Prussia could unite Germany under a liberal monarchy. Fritz, as he was nicknamed, was handsome, dignified, decent and an apt pupil for Albert's endless tutorials on German unification. He had stayed with the Royal Family at the time of the Great Exhibition four years before, when he was twenty, and had been quite captivated by the clever Vicky who had guided him round the exhibits. She was the perfect guide to her father's triumph, because in so many things she was a virtual reincarnation of Prince Albert. She was to write a few years later: 'Papa is an oracle and what he decides must be right.' Like him she had a highly cultivated mind, with a passion for theories about everything from Renaissance art to modern sanitation.

One of the great difficulties that faced Queen Victoria for the next quarter of a century was arranging the marriages of her children. Although there was no law compelling them to marry royalty, this custom had not been violated, at least openly, since the seventeenth century. The law, however, did forbid marriage with a Roman Catholic, thereby ruling out the royal houses of Austria, France, Spain, Italy, most of southern Germany and even King Leopold's children. Thus when a candidate as eligible as Fritz – the heir to the most important Protestant throne on the continent – appeared, he had to be taken very seriously even though Vicky was only fourteen. Yet Victoria wanted all her children's marriages to be founded on genuine attraction as well as reasons of state.

She hastened to report the news to that master marriage-broker, her Uncle Leopold of Belgium:

> On Thursday after breakfast, Fritz Wilhelm said he was anxious to speak of a subject which *he* knew his parents had never broached to us – which *was to belong to our* Family.... I need *not* tell you with *what* joy *we* accepted him ... but the child herself is to know nothing till *after* her confirmation.... I have little – indeed no – doubt she will gladly *accept*....
>
> Now, with Albert's affectionate love, and with the prayer that *you* will give *your* blessing to this alliance, as you have done to ours, ever your devoted Niece and Child,
> VICTORIA R.

The phrase 'to belong to our Family' is significant, for one thing that attracted Fritz to Vicky was the sight of a large, happy family, something he had never known. The foundation of it lay in the Queen's own character. It was no mere diplomatic politeness that led Queen Victoria to say to the King of Prussia: 'Through my own experience, I am becoming more and more convinced that the only true happiness in this world is to be found in the domestic circle.' However, that did not mean that there were no tensions beneath the happy exterior, and as the children grew older the tensions increased. The Queen found it difficult to come to terms with them as emerging adults. She was characteristically frank about her feelings when she wrote in the following year to Fritz's mother, her old friend Princess Augusta:

> I find no especial pleasure or compensation in the company of the elder children.... Usually they go out with me in the afternoon (Vicky mostly, and the others also sometimes), or occasionally in the mornings when I drive or walk or ride, accompanied by my lady-in-waiting. And only very exceptionally do I find the rather intimate

intercourse with them either agreeable or easy.... Firstly, I only feel properly *à mon aise* and quite happy when Albert is with me; secondly, I am used to carrying on my many affairs quite alone; and then I have grown up all alone, accustomed to the society of adult (and never with younger) people – lastly, I still cannot get used to the fact that Vicky is almost grown up.... To which I must add that I have such a number of children that I shall be provided with them for many years to come.

In fact, as the Queen wrote this letter she was already expecting her ninth and final child, Beatrice, who was born in the spring of 1857. She arranged for Vicky's future doctor to be present 'to see how these things are managed here'. Like many mothers, she was always to treat the last child as her baby – indeed Beatrice was always known as 'Baby' – and to use her as companion and confidante in the years to come. Yet she maintained certain proprieties even with Beatrice, who said at the end of the Queen's life that none of the daughters ever 'see her in bed'.

As her children grew up, the Queen brooded on a problem that had plagued her since her engagement in 1839. What was the proper title for Prince Albert? To the politicians who came for an audience or who received a well-drafted state paper, Albert was, in effect, the King. This fact was suspected and from time to time denounced in the press. However his rank remained nothing but that of a younger son of a minor German ruler who had married the Queen of England. This was always a problem when the royal couple ventured abroad, particularly to Germany with its passion for the minutiae of rank. Napoleon III had won Victoria's friendship by treating Albert as a sovereign: addressing him as '*Mon Frère*' and yielding precedence even in the great question of who should face the horses in a carriage. Yet should she die before her husband, his rank would depend on the courtesy of his eldest son.

In May 1856, the Queen drew up a memorandum arguing that it was time for the Constitution to recognise not only her husband's position but '*all future Consorts of Queens*'.

> Naturally my own feeling would be to give the Prince the same title and rank as I have, but a Titular King is a complete novelty in this country, and might be productive of more inconveniences than advantages to the individual who bears it. Therefore, upon mature reflection, and after considering the question for nearly *sixteen years*, I have come to the conclusion that the title which is now by universal consent given him of 'Prince Consort' ... should be the one assigned to the husband of the Queen regnant *once and for all*.

The Queen would have preferred Parliament to grant the title, but she was warned that there might be opposition. So she granted the title herself in June 1857.

Meanwhile, Vicky had matured much in the few months since her engagement. The American Minister, James Buchanan (who later was elected President), described her as the most charming girl he had ever met: 'All life and spirit, full of frolic and fun, with an excellent head, and a *heart as big as a mountain*.' She needed both her spirit and her excellent head for her confirmation in March 1856. Queen Victoria always placed great stress on confirmation. As many of the family as possible were always assembled. In Vicky's case that meant her parents, brothers, sisters, her grandmother the Duchess of Kent, and Uncle Leopold. Many members of the Household and prominent politicians were also gathered in the private chapel at Windsor to hear her answer questions from the Archbishop of Canterbury.

Once the confirmation was over, it was time to plan for the wedding. Some Prussians, not unnaturally, assumed that the heir to their throne would marry in their country. They had not, of course, reckoned with Queen Victoria. She made her view quite plain in a letter to her Foreign Secretary that is one of her most characteristic productions:

> The Queen *never* could consent to it, both for public and private reasons, and the assumption of its being *too much* for a Prince Royal of Prussia to *come* over to marry *the Princess Royal of Great Britain* IN England is too *absurd* to say the least. . . . Whatever may be the usual practice of Prussian Princes, it is not *every* day that one marries the eldest daughter of the Queen of England. The question therefore must be considered as settled and closed.

The Queen approached her eldest daughter's marriage in January 1858 with conflicting emotions. She was convinced, quite rightly, that it was impossible to find a better son-in-law. Yet marriage meant losing her child to a man and to another country. Before leaving Windsor for Buckingham Palace, the Queen had a look at the rooms prepared for the honeymoon: 'Poor, poor child. . . . She slept for the last time in the same room with Alice. . . . Now all this is cut off.'

The court flung itself into a whirlwind of gaieties: special performances of *Macbeth* and *La Sonnambula* (odd choices for a royal marriage), and a ball for a thousand in the new ballroom at the Palace. After luncheon on the day before the marriage, Vicky and her parents examined the tables heaped with gifts. Vicky then gave her mother a brooch containing a lock of her hair and said, 'I hope to be worthy to be your child.' Later the parents accompanied Vicky to her room, 'kissed her and gave her our blessing, and she was much overcome. I pressed her in my arms, and she clung to her truly adored papa with much tenderness.'

The wedding itself was a veritable copy of the Queen's own eighteen years before. One thing was different: before leaving for the Chapel Royal, the Royal Family gathered for photographs. 'I trembled so', wrote the Queen, 'my likeness has come out indistinct.' In the photograph, she is wearing a diadem of diamonds made for George IV, while the Prince Consort looks more like a man in his late fifties than in his late thirties. 'My dress was of mauve moiré antique and silver, trimmed with Honiton lace.' This was her own wedding lace, which she wore to the christening of each of her children.

> The flourish of trumpets and cheering of thousands made my heart sink within me. Vicky was in the carriage with me, sitting opposite. . . . Then the procession was formed, just as at my marriage, only how small the *old* Royal Family has become! Mama last before me – then Lord Palmerston with the Sword of State – then Bertie and Alfred. I with the two little boys on either side (which they say had a most touching effect) and the three little girls behind. . . . Then came the bride's procession, and our darling Flower looked very touching and lovely . . . walking between her beloved father and dearest

Uncle Leopold.... My heart was so full. Then the bride and bridegroom left hand in hand ... the 'Wedding March' by Mendelssohn being played.

The use of Mendelssohn's music set a fashion that has continued in countless thousands of marriages, and the appearance of the bridal party on the balcony of Buckingham Palace also became a precedent. The wedding moved not only the emotional Queen but the American diplomat George Dallas, who was among the three hundred guests squeezed into the Chapel Royal: 'The embraces and felicitations among the newly created kindred ... the joyous aspect of the couple ... the rich and regulated music ... combined to invest the first wedding in the family of Victoria and Albert with a charm I had not expected.'

The honeymoon, like the Queen's, was but a few days in Windsor Castle. On the very evening of the wedding the Queen started a correspondence with her daughter which was to become one of the mainstays of her emotional life. For the next forty years messengers would scurry back and forth from London to Berlin, from Balmoral to Potsdam, carrying the intimate thoughts and opinions of the two Victorias. 'My own darling Child,' ran the first letter:

> Your dear little note reached me just as we were sitting down to dinner.... This has been a very trying day for you, my dearest child.... It is a very solemn act, the most important and solemn in every one's life, but much more so in a woman's than in a man's. I have ever looked on the blessed day which united me to your beloved and perfect Papa – as the cause not only of my own happiness (a happiness few if any enjoy) but as the one which brought happiness and blessings on this country!

On the day the young couple left for Germany, the Queen and Vicky came down the stairs weeping; all the children, led by the Prince of Wales, were also in tears. The servants, too, broke down. Everything had been done to ensure comfort for the newly married pair. Vicky was even given the ultimate Coburg blessing: a young Stockmar – the Baron's son – to act as her secretary and mentor. As the band played, the Queen saw her eldest daughter and son-in-law drive out of the courtyard into the snow and into history.

Vicky was bombarded by questions even before she reached Berlin: 'Has the railway carriage got a small room [toilet] to it? ... I see by the papers you wore a green dress at the Cologne concert. Was that the one with black lace? ... I am anxious to know how all my toilettes succeeded.' Advice flew across the Channel: 'I think it hardly safe to go from $9\frac{1}{4}$ till 5 without anything? ... take a bisquit or dry crust. You take, I suppose a cup of tea at night? ... No familiarity – no loud laughing.' The Queen's reflections on marriage and the role of women were also included:

> There is great happiness and great blessedness in devoting oneself to another who is worthy ... still men are very selfish and the woman's devotion is always one of submission which makes our poor sex so very unenviable. This you will feel hereafter – I know; though it cannot be otherwise as God has willed it so.

The Queen was delighted with Vicky's happiness, yet certain comparisons were not allowed: 'You know, my dearest, that I never admit any other wife can be as happy as I am – so I can admit no comparison for I maintain Papa is unlike anyone who lives or ever lived and will live.'

The Queen's constant round of duties continued throughout the late 1850s. There were frequent excursions to Aldershot for military reviews. There was a trip to Leeds to open the town hall, and another to Birmingham. There 700,000 people turned out to see the Queen open Aston Hall, which Lord Shaftesbury had particularly urged her to do to show her approval of the idea of a place where working people could have 'innocent' amusement.

The tremendous improvement in transportation made it much easier for the Queen and the Prince both to fulfil their duties and to escape to Osborne or Balmoral. However, it also made it easier for foreign royalty to visit, which could prove annoying, though sometimes humour broke the tedium of ceremony. One such visitor was King Victor Emmanuel of Sardinia, a vulgar little man who had outraged Empress Eugénie on his visit to Paris by asking: 'Is it true that French ballerinas don't wear underclothes? If so, this will be paradise on earth for me.' His visit to England was not quite as bad, though his behaviour provided many stories to amuse the Household:

> When he arrived ... he did not understand he was to kiss his sister sovereign, so the poor Queen stood putting her cheek up to him for ever so long ... however, he ... made up for his backwardness when she gave him the royal salute after investing him with the Garter, for after kissing her face he began upon her hand, and bestowed upon it three kisses that resounded through the room ... when he had to put out his leg for the Garter ... he stuck out first one and then the other, and at last said to the Queen ... 'Which one?' She nearly let fall the Garter for laughing, the Prince was in fits.

Behind all this farce lay a developing crisis in Italy where Victor Emmanuel, aided by France, was coming into conflict with Austria over his plans to unify Italy under his leadership. Napoleon III supported Victor Emmanuel, who wanted to weaken the Austrian hold on northern Italy. Victoria and Albert feared that the French policy would lead to war. The royal friendship with France began to fade away in spite of a visit by Napoleon and Eugénie to Osborne and a yachting expedition by the Queen and Prince to Cherbourg. The French increase in armaments caused great anxiety in England. Cherbourg had been heavily fortified. Apparently the royal party were not above a little spying, for a Royal Engineers officer accompanied the Queen. But they had not reckoned on the experienced conspiratorial eye of Napoleon III who said, 'That is an Engineer's uniform, I think', and 'smiled blandly'.

In 1859 France went to war with Austria, and it seemed possible that the other powers could be drawn into the battles in Italy. Palmerston, once again Prime Minister, wanted strong action. The Queen and the Prince Consort were anxious for peace, and were able to mobilise opinion in the Cabinet against the more warlike Prime Minister and the Foreign Secretary, Lord John Russell. As one member of the Cabinet put it, the Queen 'has a good deal of indirect power, and the spirit to use it'. She was much amused at her joke of calling the two elderly politicians, Palmerston and Russell, with their enthusiasm for Italian unification, 'our two Italian Masters'. As she said in a letter to Vicky, 'our two Italian Masters almost drive us crazy. Really I never saw two such obdurate ... I won't use any expression because I can't trust what it would be.'

There were also storms and unrest within the family when Fritz asked Albert to inform the Queen that Vicky was pregnant. Not only did the Queen say she was 'upset ... dreadfully' by the 'horrid news', but she went on: 'I feel certain almost it will all end in nothing.' When Vicky expressed her delight at the thought of having a child, her mother sent back a fierce blast: 'What you say of the pride of giving life to an immortal soul is very fine, dear, but I own I cannot enter into that; I think much more of our being like a cow or a dog at such moments; when our poor nature becomes so very animal.'

Yet two weeks later she admitted: 'I delight in ... being a grandmama ... at 39 and to look and feel young is great fun.' Such contradictions were an essential part of the Queen's highly emotional nature. One of the great delights of studying her life is that she recorded in her manifold writings those conflicting feelings that are an essential part of human experience. When her first grandchild was born, her joy was unbounded. To the wife of her Ambassador in Berlin, she wrote 'Thank God ... for our dear little grandson, whom we are very proud of, though he has conferred this somewhat ancient dignity on us at the age of thirty-nine. I think *my* dear Prince is one of the youngest grandfathers in existence.'

FIVE

$\mathcal{A}$ DEATH IN LIFE

Oh! if those selfish men – who are the cause of all one's misery, only knew what their poor slaves go through! What suffering – what humiliation to the delicate feelings of a poor woman ... especially with those nasty doctors.

It was July 1860 and the Queen was at 'dear Osborne' writing to Vicky, who was expecting her second child. The Queen's own youngest child, Beatrice, was amusing all the family by her cheerful obstinacy. When the Queen saw her reach for something, she tried to stop her: 'Baby mustn't have that, it's not good for Baby.'

'But she likes it, my dear,' replied the infant Princess.

Victoria and Albert were also pleased at the courtship of their second daughter, the seventeen-year-old Alice, by Prince Louis of Hesse: their engagement would be announced at the end of the year. Another daughter had been found a safe German Protestant prince, who were in short supply. The Queen had been frustrated because one of Fritz's cousins was ineligible: 'Dear good Leopold Hohenzollern ... Oh! if only he were not a R.C.!! It is sad when one sees what one would wish to have, one can't get it.' Although the Queen and Prince Albert were criticised for encouraging their daughters' early marriages, they knew that when an eligible prince turned up he had to be grabbed quickly.

Their two eldest sons were now emerging into public light. The second son, Prince Alfred, known in the family as Affie, was starting a career in the Navy as a midshipman, even if *The Times* worried that he was in danger of being treated as 'Midshipman Easy' and welcomed by 'royal salutes and royal fiddle-faddles of every description'. The Queen held a grudge against Albert for allowing the sixteen-year-old Affie to go to sea when he was so young. 'Papa is most cruel upon the subject ... it is much better to have no children than to have them only to give them up.' However, at least Prince Alfred was making progress. The eldest son, Bertie, would be nineteen in November and was causing increasing worry to his father and mother. His lack of academic ability and his immaturity meant that Victoria's prayer that he would be a copy of his father was not being answered. Even so, he was given his first taste of responsibility when he was sent to Canada to express the mother country's thanks for help in the Crimean War. The Queen also accepted an invitation for him to make a private visit to the United States, and he sailed across the Atlantic in July 1860.

Yet worries about Bertie's slow development did not interfere with the round of official work or pleasure. There were frequent visits to the opera and theatre: in one week in February, Victoria and Albert were at the theatre four times. In

79

the early part of the reign they had gone to many French plays, but for the last few years London no longer had a company regularly performing plays in French. In spite of her increasing hostility to French adventurism in foreign affairs, she urged Vicky to go to the French theatre in Berlin:

> Dear Papa – who you know is any thing but favourable to the French – used to delight in going to the French play. ... It is such good practice for the language. So, I hope dear, you will go. One's dislike to a nation need not prevent one's admiring and being amused by what is good, clever and amusing in it.

Some of their theatrical visits included lighter subjects. Victoria took Uncle Leopold's son to the Haymarket to see a ballet of 'negro life' in which the men all had blackened faces while the white-faced ballerinas were dressed as Swiss peasants. Not surprisingly, she was seen to laugh a great deal at this curious spectacle.

In August the Royal Family made their annual visit to Balmoral. Albert arranged a long expedition for himself and the Queen, accompanied by Lady Churchill, General Grey and four servants. The Queen and Prince travelled incognito as 'Lord and Lady Churchill'. On the first day they went forty miles (the Queen was on horseback for half of that) before they reached a little inn. Victoria was delighted with her 'very small, but clean' room and the dinner of 'soup, "hodge-podge," mutton-broth with vegetables, which I did not much relish, fowl with white sauce, good roast lamb, very good potatoes ... ending with a good tart of cranberries'. However, they brought their own wine. On the next day's travels some people noticed the crown on the dog-cart and began to suspect this might be a party from Balmoral. One woman stared at the Queen and said, 'The lady must be terrible rich', as she had so many gold rings on her fingers. 'When they heard who it was,' wrote Victoria, 'they were ready to drop with astonishment and fright. I fear I have but poorly recounted this very amusing and never to be forgotten expedition, which will always be remembered with delight.'

In November the Prince of Wales returned from his North American tour in triumph. Albert wrote to Stockmar to say that, just as his eldest son was opening the new bridge across the St Lawrence River, Prince Alfred was laying the foundation stone of a new breakwater in Cape Town: 'What a cheering picture is here of the progress and expansion of the British race, and of the useful co-operation of the Royal family in the civilisation which England has developed and advanced.' Even so, Prince Albert was not pleased with Bertie's lack of purpose:

> He has a strange nature. He has no interest for things, but all the more for persons. This trait in his character, which is often found in the Royal family, has made the family so popular. But it also arouses the dangerous inclination for what they here call 'small talk'.

The North American tour had interrupted the young Prince's year at Oxford, which he had begun in Michaelmas Term 1859. Albert had overcome the Queen's dislike of 'that old monkish place, which I have a horror of'. His father insisted that while there Bertie should be closely supervised, as this note from the nineteen-year-old Prince to Dr (later Sir) Henry Acland, one of his tutors, testifies:

I send you these few lines to ask you whether you will allow me to take a short walk, as I feel very much the want of a little fresh air, it is very fine now and if I put on a thick coat I should think it would do me no harm, and then I may have a chance of getting a little appetite.

The Prince would require a healthy appetite for the Christmas festivities at Windsor. Four men were employed to turn a baron of beef weighing 360 pounds and there were geese, fifty turkeys and a boar's head. In addition the Lord Lieutenant of Ireland sent his traditional gift of a huge woodcock pie made up of one hundred birds – not exactly a dainty dish to set before the Queen. *The Times* had a 'correspondent' at court, for one of the Lords in Waiting sent the editor descriptions of events like the royal Christmas of 1860:

> The Queen's private sitting-rooms ... were lighted up with Christmas trees hung from the ceiling. ... These trees, of immense size, besides others on the tables, were covered with bonbons and coloured wax lights. ... These rooms contained all the presents for the royal family. ... Each member gave a present to one another. ... I have never seen a much more agreeable sight. It was royalty putting aside its state and becoming in words, acts, and deeds one of ourselves – no forms and not a vestige of ceremony.... Lords, grooms, Queen, and princes laughed and talked, forgot to bow, and freely turned their backs on one another. Little princesses, who on ordinary occasions dare hardly to look at a gentleman-in-waiting, in the happiest manner showed each person they could lay hands on the treasures they had received.... Prince Arthur (the flower of the flock) speedily got into a Volunteer uniform ... including a little rifle ... took a pot-shot at his papa, and then presented arms.... I never saw more real happiness than the scene of the mother and all her children.

That Christmas the Queen overcame her detestation of tobacco sufficiently to give Bertie permission to smoke, but not in the house or in public. The Queen always tried to keep her sons from smoking and she tried to prevent the vile smell of tobacco from polluting her residences. In the past this was seen as an example of her fussiness. Today, particularly with the knowledge that tobacco fatally affected the health of several of her successors, her attitude, as on so many other things, illustrates her great commonsense.

On New Year's Day 1861, when Lord Palmerston sent the Queen his greetings with a wish for 'increasing happiness to Your Majesty', he quoted Pope:

> May day improve on day, and year on year,
> Without a pain, a trouble, or a fear.

It was not to be. The following day a letter arrived from Vicky describing the death of Fritz's uncle. The Queen replied: 'I have never even yet witnessed a death bed.'

On 5 February she drove with the Prince Consort to open Parliament. One diarist, A. J. Munby, saw her enthusiastic welcome from the crowd. A workman waved his cap and shouted: 'England's crown for ever!' Inside the House of Lords another diarist, the American diplomat Benjamin Moran, watched the 'grand sight':

The scene is one of the finest in the world. ... What with the beauty and splendid dress of the women, the gorgeous adornment of the House ... the rich uniforms of the Ambassadors ... the presence of the Sovereign, the authority everywhere visible, and the prevalent tone, there can be no display like it. ... The Queen read grandly as usual, and everybody was pleased.

All this time Prince Albert was hiding a secret from his wife: the Duchess of Kent was dying. Twenty years before, in the first year of their marriage, when one of her aunts died, Albert had decided that 'all sad impressions must be kept from Victoria'. The Queen knew that her mother was ill, but she did not know how serious it was until she was summoned to her bedside on 16 March. Three times the Queen crept in from the outer room to kneel and kiss her mother's hand. The Duchess's Lady in Waiting, Lady Augusta Bruce, thought the Queen was 'whispering "Mamma" so lovingly and earnestly as if the sound must rouse Her'. Lady Augusta noticed 'how tender' Albert was to the woman who had become a virtual mother to him. Victoria was given a dose of sal volatile to steady her as the family knelt round the Duchess. After she died Prince Albert gently placed his distraught wife in the arms of their daughter Alice. 'What the loss is to me – no one can tell,' she managed to write to Vicky: 'For forty-one years never parted for more than three months.'

The Queen's grief was frightening to many observers. Lady Augusta said she bordered on hysterics. Her misery increased when she went through her mother's possessions and found how the Duchess had 'treasured up every little flower, every bit of hair, touching relics of my poor Father'. From her letters the Queen discovered 'how very, very much she and my beloved Father *loved* each other. ... Then her love for *me*.' Victoria told King Leopold that she could not help but reflect on Conroy and Lehzen: 'I am so wretched to think *how, for a time, two people most* wickedly estranged us.' Yet her common sense reasserted itself enough to add: 'But thank God! that is all passed *long, long* ago'. The Duchess had lived to see her daughter raise the throne to new splendour and her descendants begin to spread their way into other royal houses. Well could Tennyson write the epitaph the Queen requested for her mother's mausoleum:

> Long as the heart beats life within her breast,
> Thy child will bless thee, guardian, mother mild,
> And far away thy memory will be blest,
> By children of the children of thy child.

In London there were 'horrid, vile rumours', according to Prince Albert, that the Queen had gone out of her mind. Rumours of insanity were nothing new: she had always been a highly emotional woman. We know her today mainly through her letters and Journal, and in these she is frank, outspoken and rigorous in her language. Her pen raced across paper without pause for correction. It is easy to jump from seeing an emotional, passionate woman who expressed her thoughts so honestly to imagining one beset by mental instability. This was not the case. Her grief for her mother was extraordinary because she was in no sense prepared for the death and she had severe guilt feelings about all the battles over Conroy and Lady Flora Hastings. Yet within a few months Albert could reassure his brother that 'Victoria is well.' Her grief had been great, but it was 'not a morbid grief but true love between the late mother and the daughter left behind'.

In the summer, the Queen and Prince were preoccupied with the Prince of Wales. Vicky was assigned the duty of inspecting eligible princesses and forwarding their photographs to London. It became obvious that the most beautiful as well as the best choice was Princess Alexandra of Denmark. However, there was a diplomatic problem: Prussia coveted the duchies of Schleswig and Holstein, which belonged to the Danish crown but had sizeable German populations. Albert was one of the few people in England who took any interest in this rather abstruse topic and he naturally favoured the German side.

Before the Danish match was arranged, however, rumours began to percolate through London society that the Prince of Wales had had an affair while stationed with the Grenadier Guards that summer in Ireland. Some fellow officers thought it would be an amusing lark to introduce an actress into his bed, and when Prince Albert heard about it he was extremely upset. At first he tried to keep Bertie's 'fall' from the Queen, but she badgered it out of him. Victoria and Albert have been portrayed by later generations as being obsessively prudish. While it is true that Prince Albert held traditional Christian views with a rigidity that was ridiculed in 'sophisticated' circles, both he and Victoria knew how easily a throne could be undermined by immorality. In his own family Albert had seen his mother banished because of a love affair, while his father and brother were notorious for their immorality. Victoria's own 'wicked uncles' had done much to undermine the foundations of the British throne. That those foundations were now stronger than they had ever been was the result of twenty years' hard work by Albert and Victoria. Further, they were worried that the rumours could reach Denmark and ruin the idea of a marriage with Princess Alexandra. Both parents were convinced that more than ever Bertie needed to be 'steadied' by a quick marriage.

All these upsets made both Victoria and Albert feel much older, and even the blessed peace of Balmoral did not restore Albert's shattered nerves. On 16 October they set out on another expedition among the mountains. While the Queen sat sketching, 'Albert wrote on a bit of paper that we had lunched here, put it into the Selters-water bottle, and buried it there.' When the Queen finished the account of this expedition in her Journal she wrote, probably with reference to their age, 'Alas! I fear our *last* great one!'

Political problems always seemed closer when they returned to Windsor, especially this autumn when a complicated international question suddenly appeared which threatened to draw Britain into the war between the Northern and Southern States in America. A Federal warship stopped the British mail steamer *Trent* and removed two Confederate diplomats who were on their way to Europe. Palmerston felt that the strongest possible protest must be sent to Washington, demanding an apology and the release of the diplomats. The despatch prepared by the government was sent first to Windsor for the Queen's approval.

On the night of 30 November, as troops were on their way to Canada, Prince

Albert revised the ultimatum. While still demanding the release of the diplomats and an apology for the violation of international law, he softened the wording to make it more acceptable. At seven o'clock in the morning, when he handed the revised draft to the Queen, he 'looked very wretched'. He was already ill. The Cabinet accepted the new draft and sent it to Washington, where it was readily accepted as a way to avoid war. Prince Albert's last act had been to prevent war between the English-speaking peoples.

By 6 December it was generally known in London that the Prince was quite ill. The Queen, although upset, was not unduly alarmed. Even when she heard it was typhoid, she took comfort in the thought that she had survived it herself as a child. Albert, however, knew that two of his royal cousins in Portugal had recently died of the disease and he felt he had not the strength to withstand it. He had once told his wife: 'I do not cling to life but you do. ... I feel that I should make no struggle if I were ill – that I should give it up at once.' On 12 December the Queen wrote in one of her daily reports on Albert's illness to Uncle Leopold: 'I can again report favourably of our most precious invalid ... there is nothing to cause alarm.' The next day, Friday the 13th, the doctors told the Queen that his illness was very serious and that death was a possibility.

Albert, who had been very restless throughout the illness, was moved into the Blue Room because it was large and cheerful. But he also knew that it was the room in which George IV and William IV had died, and to him this was just another omen. On 14 December the Queen bent over him and whispered, '*Es ist kleines Frauchen* – 'It's your little wife.' He was able to kiss her. That evening he grew worse. Outside the room, the Queen was talking 'confusedly' to Gerald Wellesley, Dean of Windsor. Princess Alice, who had been her father's companion and nurse throughout this awful fortnight, rushed from his room to summon her mother.

Once inside, the Queen took the Prince's left hand which was, she later wrote, 'already cold, though the breathing was quite gentle'. She knelt down by his side. Opposite her, on the other side of the bed, knelt Alice and at the foot knelt the Prince of Wales and fifteen-year-old Helena. As the castle clock struck 10.45 Prince Albert drew two or three long breaths and died, in silence, without pain and without effort. 'Oh yes,' the Queen cried out in one long, piercing cry, 'this is death. I know it. I have seen it before.' She fell upon the body and kissed it, calling out those endearing names which he could no longer hear. Victoria then 'suffered herself to be led quietly away. Her sobs, as she went to her solitary chamber were most affecting to us all' wrote Dean Wellesley. The Queen now called her children to her and then the doctors and the Household. When Major Howard Elphinstone approached her she gave him her hand and said, 'You will not desert me? You will all help me?' Before going to her room she went upstairs to the nursery and kissed Beatrice. Her grief was profound, as she wrote to Vicky: 'I may drag on an utterly extinguished life but it will be death in life.'

Victoria was only forty-two when she was left, unprepared, a widow with eight unmarried children, the youngest of whom was four years old. Her eldest son was immature and at times was seen by her as a cause of her beloved husband's illness.

She had come to depend on Albert for virtually everything, whether it be organising incognito jaunts to Highland inns or dealing with great issues of peace or war. The family, the Household, the royal correspondence – all were regulated by him. He never had her outspoken attitude towards love, but his was that sure and steady love which her nature craved. A dozen years before she had chided him because he had not carried her picture on one of those rare trips he made without her. 'Thy dear image', wrote Albert, 'I bear within me, and what miniature can come up to that? No need to place one on my table to *remind* me of *you*.' Her nature was different: it required constant reminders of the Prince when he was alive and even more when he was dead. Her obsession with commemorating his memory should not obscure the fact that their life together was one of the great love stories of history.

Some people feared that the 'Hanoverian madness' would overwhelm her. When her half-sister Princess Feodora, herself recently widowed, heard the news she paced up and down her room repeating, 'One of two things must happen to my sister: I know her. She must either die of this or go out of her mind.' In fact, Feodora did not know her sister's strength. Albert, who knew her better, had always understood her great passion for life. She grudgingly accepted this when talking with Disraeli in the following year: 'he *would* die: he seemed not to care to live'. Then she added, using a curious piece of slang, 'He died from want of what they call pluck.' Pluck was one thing she had in abundance. The Dean of Windsor described her only the day after Albert's death: 'It is one's only consolation under this great calamity that she has not been stupified by it – But everything with her has gone on in the *natural* course of excessive grief. Tears have relieved her plenteously.'

As the Queen retired to Osborne on her doctor's advice, she at least had the mournful satisfaction that now at last the nation appreciated Albert and his achievement. Many people only heard of his death when they went to church the next day and in many places there was sobbing when his name was omitted from the prayer for the Royal Family. In London's Regent Street the shops were draped in black and people wore mourning: the diarist Arthur Munby had to pay three times the normal price to get the last remaining print of the Prince Consort. Munby wrote in his diary: 'the whole nation seems to be sublimed by a noble sorrow ... into a purity and oneness that I never remember to have seen before ... even the private life of ordinary men is subdued.'

From Osborne the widowed Victoria wrote to her Uncle Leopold:

I am also anxious to repeat *one* thing, and *that one* is *my firm* resolve, my *irrevocable decision*, viz. that *his* wishes – *his* plans – about everything, *his* views about *every* thing are to be *my law!* And *no human power* will make me swerve from *what he* decided...

When she said on 15 December, 'They need not be afraid, I will do my duty', she quite meant it. It was some time before she could resume her Journal, now once again the only repository of her closest thoughts, but less than a week after Albert's death she was dealing with correspondence with the Prime Minister. (Palmerston himself had been very ill, and his health nearly collapsed when he heard of the Prince's death.) By 6 January a Privy Council could be held, though the Queen adhered to the idea of a widow's seclusion: she sat in an adjoining room while her approval was read out. Naturally her emotions and behaviour fluctuated. On 10 January she wrote to the Foreign Secretary: 'The things of this world are of no interest to the Queen . . . for *her* thoughts are *fixed above*.' Yet four days later he received a stinging rebuke when he read a Cabinet message to the American Minister before she had seen it: 'Lord Russell will perhaps take care that the *rule* should not be departed from, viz. that no drafts should be sent without the Queen's having first seen them.'

Victoria's first task was to secure men who could help with some of the work Albert had done. Yet she did not want another Conroy to dominate a widow. She told King Leopold: 'I am *also determined* that *no one* person, may *he* be ever so good . . . is to lead or guide or dictate to *me*.' However, she needed secretaries, without whose help her work could not be properly carried on. Her elder daughters and her Ladies could help, but she needed a man who would be a permanent official, able to speak confidentially to ministers with her authority. On 10 January one of her letters to the Prime Minister was in the hand of General Grey, who had been Private Secretary to the Prince Consort. The Queen apologised for this and Grey himself was 'a little nervous at my asking him to write . . . in my name, I signing the letter'. This was apparently the first time she made any important use of a Private Secretary, although he was not actually given the title till 1867. It was several years before the 'stupid ministers' accepted the new official, and in 1869 Grey still had to defend himself to the Foreign Secretary, Lord Clarendon: he was not a power behind the throne but simply obeyed 'Her Majesty's orders, and never even suggest an opinion unless Her Majesty——[word illegible] it.'

A Private Secretary could not, however, help in the many family problems that Victoria faced as the children approached adulthood. Soon she had to deal with the Greek proposal that Prince Alfred might wish to become their King. His mother decided that he would not. (They seemed so keen on the idea of an Englishman that there was even talk of offering the crown to Lord Stanley or to Gladstone. Years later, the Queen may well have wished that Gladstone had become a fellow monarch rather than her Prime Minister!) But as always the main worry was Bertie. Her attitude towards him rose and fell like a barometer, depending partly on what he did or on her mood. Here again she was intensely human; the only difference is that she recorded every reading of her emotional barometer. In January, she ascribed Prince Albert's fatal illness to news of Bertie's 'fall': 'I never can see B—— without a shudder.' In June, he was a 'poor innocent boy' led astray by 'wicked wretches'. Marriage would be his salvation and he would become a 'steady husband'. She was 'exceedingly satisfied and pleased with him' on his return from the Holy Land, a journey ordained by Prince Albert. Yet on 12 November, the first anniversary of Albert's hearing of the 'fall', the barometric reading plummeted, although she assured Vicky: 'he was forgiven thank God! or I never could have looked at him again – and I forgave him fully – but I wish him not to forget it.' Behind her changing attitudes lay the conviction that her heir was not the replica of his father that she had hoped for, but her own 'caricature'.

Negotiations over the Prince's marriage continued throughout the year. In the autumn of 1862 the Queen had an opportunity to meet Princess Alexandra on a private visit to King Leopold. Like everyone else she was charmed with the young girl and she almost, but not quite, disregarded her Danish nationality; the engagement was soon announced. There was also a visit of inspection by 'dear Alix' to Osborne, which she passed with flying colours particularly after asking so many questions about Prince Albert. But Victoria was furious when she learned that Bertie was writing to his fiancée in English rather than German. She accepted that this outrage arose from 'mere laziness', but she went on in her most unreasonable manner:

> The German element is the one I wish to be cherished and kept up in our beloved home – now more than ever ... as Alix's parents are inclined to encourage the English and merge the German into Danish and English and this would be a dreadful sorrow to me; the very thing dear Papa and I disliked so much in the connexion is the Danish element.

For the next decade she would be prone to frequent outbursts about this 'German element', which she wanted her family to cherish. By the 1870s, however, she had come to accept that the dreamy, idealistic Germany of Albert's imagination no longer existed.

The 'Danish match' was not the only royal romance at this time. Prince Albert had approved Princess Alice's marriage to Prince Louis of Hesse and therefore it must go ahead. On 1 July 1862 the couple were married privately at Osborne underneath the vast Winterhalter painting of the Royal Family in 1846 to indicate that the couple had received the Prince Consort's blessing. Henry Greville noted that it was 'a very lugubrious affair' with the Queen in black 'hidden by her sons'. Victoria herself admitted that it was 'more like a funeral than a wedding'. Throughout the service Prince Alfred sobbed dreadfully and the Archbishop cried as well.

The Queen was preoccupied with a desire to erect monuments to her husband wherever possible. Some, as at Balmoral, would be a simple cairn of stones to mark the spot of a happy picnic. Others would be statues, and yet others great architectural achievements like the Albert Memorial or the Royal Albert Hall. At Frogmore, within Windsor Park, she had a mausoleum built to contain Albert's remains. The Italian sculptor Baron Marochetti was instructed to carve two recumbent effigies, for her plan was that in time she would be buried beside Albert. The mausoleum is a beautiful building, full of light and colour and designed to reflect the ideas of Albert's favourite artist, Raphael. The Queen herself kept the key and made frequent visits, sometimes taking especially favoured guests. Every year on 14 December a special service was held there.

Although the Queen had resolved to carry on her constitutional duties, she was determined – as she had the Prince of Wales write to Palmerston only two days after his father's death – that 'her worldly career was closed for ever'. By that she meant she would no longer play any role in society. She would act just as if she were an ordinary widow forced to carry on the family business. Visits to the theatre or the opera were over for ever: a sad loss to one who loved them both. As much as possible all court functions such as levées, where people were 'presented', were now conducted by the Prince of Wales or one of his sisters. London came to symbolise to Victoria not only the place where her life was in danger from assassination but the abode of politicians who tried to force her to make public appearances or, increasingly, of the fashionable aristocracy who had little patience with her grief.

She never came out of formal mourning for her husband. Before his death all the royal residences had their own stationery, often with lovely vignettes of the scenery at Balmoral or Osborne. From December 1861 all Victoria's letters, private and official, were written on paper with large black borders which increasingly made her already difficult handwriting a greater trial to read. Except for one day, she never again appeared – even in the privacy of her family – dressed in anything but her solemn black dresses (she always had two made at a time) and her widow's cap. Certain days became sacred: Albert's birthday, the date of their first meeting, and of course 14 December, and every year memories and reflections of these events were written in her Journal. She took comfort in using the Prince's copy of the Book of Common Prayer which the Duchess of Kent had given him as a wedding gift. In her copy of Tennyson's *In Memoriam* she altered pronouns to make the lines apply to her grief, and the Poet Laureate was deeply moved when he saw her well-worn copy. The Queen also insisted that her husband's rooms remain as they were at his death, and photographs were taken to ensure that no changes crept in. This custom reached unusual lengths: many years later, Randall Davidson actually saw steaming water carried into the Prince's dressing room as if he were getting ready to shave. For Victoria it was necessary to carry on such a routine as a framework on which to perpetuate his memory.

The Queen did not invent the Victorian cult of mourning. It was well established by 1861, but as the decades went on she came to personify the idea of the Victorian widow. She always had a ready identification with other widows. Only a month after Albert's death she sent a message of comfort to the wives of 204 men killed in a coal-mining accident. Some of her best letters were those to widows of politicians, courtiers or people whom she knew. Few have ever been so skilled at that most difficult piece of writing, a letter of condolence.

By 1863, within the quiet of the family circle at Balmoral or Osborne, Victoria was beginning to take renewed pleasure in life. Try as she would to avoid it, cheerfulness gained little victories. She derived much enjoyment from Baby – Princess Beatrice. When Gladsone was staying at Balmoral as Minister in Attendance in the autumn, she enjoyed a wide-ranging talk with him. The next day a message came through Lady Augusta Bruce that the Queen feared 'she was too cheerful', which, as Gladstone wrote to his wife, 'she feels a kind of sin'. People who saw her were impressed with the revival of her spirits. Norman Macleod, her favourite Scottish preacher, was frequently at Balmoral (occasionally he had to give little talks to any of the princes who misbehaved), where he thought her 'much more like her old self'. She found great comfort both in Macleod's 'undogmatic'

Christianity and in his reading of Scottish poetry. She liked to sit working her spinning wheel while he read one of her favourite poems by Robert Burns. She enjoyed doing handwork such as making quilts for her grandchildren. When Professor Max Müller, the Oxford philologist who had been one of Bertie's tutors, came to Osborne to give the Queen and her children a lecture on India and its languages, he was delighted to see that, though she had arrived with her knitting, she found the lecture so interesting that her needles remained idle.

In March 1863 the rigorous court mourning was lifted to some degree for the glorious spectacle of the Prince of Wales's wedding in St George's Chapel, Windsor. People saw the occasion as an opportunity to celebrate, although Victoria had some Hanoverian twinges of jealousy at the attention paid to her heir. The public excitement of Princess Alexandra's entry into London was long remembered as one of the most joyous events in Victorian England. Not for the last time did the nation take a Princess of Wales to its heart.

The ceremony contained far more pageantry than any previous royal wedding in modern history. When there were only four places left in the choir of St George's, Windsor, the Queen decided to give two to Disraeli, who had led the Conservatives in the Commons. He had won her regard by an extravagant oration praising Prince Albert, a man who had always viewed him with suspicion. Disraeli enjoyed his social triumph: 'There is no language which can describe the rage, envy and indignation of the great world. The Duchess of Marlborough went into hysterics of mortification at the sight of my wife.' Bishop Samuel Wilberforce was among the officiating clergy and described the wedding as 'the most moving sight I ever saw'. He felt that the Queen's presence 'added such a wonderful chord of deep feeling to all the lighter notes of joyfulness and show'. Technically the Queen was not 'present': she gazed down with a mixture of pride and sorrow from Queen Katherine's Closet, which overlooked the altar. Bishop Wilberforce continued:

> Everyone behaved quite at their best. The Princess of Wales, calm: feeling: clever: self-possessed. The Prince with more depth in manner than ever before.... The little Prince William of Prussia between his two little uncles [whom] ... he bit on the bare Highland legs whenever they touched him to keep him quiet.... I was charmed with the prince of Prussia [Fritz].... 'Bishop' he said 'with me it has been one long honeymoon.'

This was the first public appearance of the Queen's eldest grandson: as Kaiser Wilhelm II he would continue the bothersome behaviour of his childhood.

Disraeli was delighted at being inside the Chapel. Because he was short-sighted, he used his opera glass to take a good look at the Queen. Unfortunately at the very moment he focused on her she looked straight down at him; 'I did not venture to use my glass again,' he admitted. Dr Macleod had better luck in his observation: he noticed that at the moment the Prince Consort's music was being sung the Queen's face bore a look of pure ecstasy.

After the wedding, the Queen took on the role of interfering mother-in-law. She did not think it wise that the young couple should allow their guests to be seated when everyone was having coffee after dinner. She insisted on the royal – and German – practice that people should remain standing in the presence of royalty. Nor did she think it wise that the Prince and Princess should be entertained too much by the aristocracy. Like her Uncle-King thirty years before, she did not like the heir to the throne attracting undue prominence.

The wedding did not interfere with the Queen's campaign to memorialise Albert. In April, Parliament voted £50,000 towards the Albert Memorial in Hyde Park. No MP voted against the measure, but Henry Greville began to find 'public and private opinion' turning against any more monuments. The following year, however, Parliament did agree – though there was considerable opposition – to buy land in Kensington to carry out one of Albert's favourite ideas. This had been for a large complex of institutions to encourage the arts and science. Cynics laughed at 'Albertopolis', but his idea led to the building of the Albert Hall, the Natural History Museum and the Victoria and Albert Museum.

With the publication of Albert's speeches in 1862 Queen Victoria began a long process of enshrining her husband in print as well as in stone. The collection was edited by Arthur Helps, a writer who was also an official of the Privy Council; in many ways the Queen was co-editor. The book's long introduction allowed her to speak directly to her people of how she 'could hardly endure' to remain silent during Albert's lifetime about all that he did for the benefit of his adopted land. Now it became a sacred mission to reveal as much as possible. The *Speeches* became a bestseller and encouraged the Queen to continue on the path of writing. She set about collecting material for a life of Albert. General Grey was assigned the task of writing the book, with the Queen combining the roles of research assistant and editor. She wrote to all who had known the young Albert so that their memories could be included, and allowed Grey to quote from her own Journal: *The Early Years of the Prince Consort* was published in 1867 and carried his life up to 1840.

On General Grey's death in 1870 the Queen was lucky to find Theodore Martin, a wealthy man of letters who was prepared to take on the work. He rejected any fee because he felt the honour of serving her and commemorating the Prince were reward enough. Needless to say, Martin won her close friendship. When the Queen liked someone, she would violate any custom of court etiquette she pleased. Martin had married an actress and the rule had long been that actresses were not received socially by the sovereign. While working on the book at Osborne, Martin had a severe skating accident and had to be confined to bed. The Queen immediately had a telegram sent to his wife to summon her to Osborne. She then arranged to walk into his bedroom with some larger pillows to make him comfortable at a time when she knew his wife was visiting: thus ended one court custom.

The Martin biography grew to five volumes, much of it consisting of extracts from the Queen's Journal. She also published *Leaves from the Journal of Our Life in the Highlands from 1848 to 1861*, which became another bestseller. Some of the royal children began to be uncomfortable about seeing their family life publicly portrayed, and some sophisticates sneered at the Queen's simple enjoyment of life. Nevertheless the book revealed her personality and made her a popular figure with whom average people could identify. Numerous editions were printed at varying prices, so that everyone could read of the joys of the Queen's married life. She earned a considerable amount of money, which she used for her many private charities. Nor was the book popular only in England. An English clergyman visiting America wrote:

> Every body in New York had read the Queen's book; in every society I found people talking about it; and I never heard it mentioned without expressions of interest and approval.... They said it made royalty appear to them in a new and more human light. ... They spoke of her as the head of the Anglo-Saxon race, almost as if they had as much part in her as ourselves. I believe that her Majesty's work has had a greater number of readers, and that a greater number of copies of it have been sold, in the United States than in the United Kingdom.

Leaves was followed by *More Leaves* some years later. In addition the Queen arranged a privately printed edition of her 1855 Journal about the visits from and to the Emperor and Empress – apparently as a tribute to her dear friend Eugénie, when she too came to the revered state of widowhood. Disraeli's well-known remark, 'We authors, Ma'am', was not undeserved.

Undoubtedly part of the reason for publishing was to show the whole world how happy she had been, so that all would appreciate how miserable she had become. Some people disliked this public display of private emotions. When Florence Nightingale was sent a copy of the *Speeches* she noted in her forthright manner: 'She always reminds me of the Greek chorus with her hands clasped above her head wailing out her irrepressible despair.' But as the books continued, a political message began to emerge. The Martin biography in particular showed in detail, as no other book ever has, just how important the role of a constitutional monarch was, although it annoyed some Liberals, especially Lord Palmerston's supporters. Anthony Trollope, for example, was spurred into writing a short book on Palmerston after reading Martin to defend his late hero against 'the Queen and Prince Albert and Baron Stockmar'. The Queen did not want the Martin biography to be just a conventional tribute. The proof copy of Martin's introduction has survived in the Bodleian Library and it shows how closely she corrected the book to make sure that a scholarly biography – the most fitting monument – had been written.

Queen Victoria thus became the first monarch to reveal to the world at large so many aspects of her life, personality and even views on contentious theological questions. Many Anglican clergymen were alarmed at the opinions of a 'Kirk-going Queen'. With her capacity for expressing ordinary human emotions, she could reach over the barriers erected by politicians and directly touch an appreciative audience. Even today, television has not revealed as much about royalty's private feelings and tastes as Victoria did in her excursions into authorship.

There was, however, an unpleasant side to her role as widow. She was quite capable of using it to manipulate family, ministers, courtiers and diplomats. Her argument was that she would fulfil her constitutional 'duty' – the term she always used – as an essential part of parliamentary government. The ceremonial and social sides were 'extras' to be bestowed sparingly when and on whom she wished. Her refusal to take part in social functions, such as court presentations, annoyed the diary-writing class. For the vast majority of her subjects, who had no hope of attending court, this was not an issue – although resentment was growing at her refusal to appear in public. Her ministers were annoyed, especially by her refusal to open Parliament in person. Any public ceremony, she insisted, upset her nerves. She had always been shy but now, without Albert at her side, she felt particularly vulnerable in public.

She avoided Buckingham Palace as much as possible, insisting that Windsor was close enough to London. When she went to Balmoral, one member of the Cabinet usually stayed at the Castle as 'minister in attendance' to transact government business with the Queen as well as to enjoy a welcome rest among glorious scenery. In September 1864 the Chancellor of the Exchequer, Gladstone, not yet regarded with disfavour, went for his tour of duty. As the wives of ministers were not invited to Balmoral on the grounds that accommodation was limited, Mr Gladstone kept his wife informed in daily letters of the happy time he was having. He found a smaller Household than at Windsor and an atmosphere 'less formal and dull'. Even in spite of splitting his trousers as he was about to go down for dinner, he thoroughly enjoyed his stay. He reported that the Queen's 'state of health and spirits' were much improved. He revealed a great secret of state to his wife: 'she weighs I am told 11 stone eight pounds. . . . Rather much for her height'. When the Queen was in a relaxed mood she could talk on a great variety of topics; as always, her knowledge of detail was marked: she corrected Gladstone when he confused one of his Lyttelton nephews with another. Gladstone noted down one dinner conversation:

> I can hardly tell you all the things she talked about. Prince Humbert – Garibaldi – Lady Lyttelton – the Hagley boys – Lucy [Lyttelton] – smoking – dress – fashion – Prince Alfred – his establishment and future plans – P of Wales's visit to Denmark – revenue – Lancashire – foreign policy – the newspaper press – the habits of the present generation – young men – young married ladies – clubs – Clarendon's journey – the Prince Consort on dress and fashion – P of Wales on do. – R. Meade – Sir R Peel – F Peel – misreading foreign names and words – repute of English people abroad – happy absence of Foreign Office disputes and quarrels.

This alone shows that the Queen was anything but isolated in her widowhood; yet only people like Gladstone or her Household knew that, and by 1864 rumblings of discontent began to be heard. In March a handbill was fixed to the walls of Buckingham Palace: 'These extensive premises to be let or sold, the late occupant having retired from business.' The newspapers suppressed the story, but it obviously got round. London tradesmen, denied the patronage of the court, complained that the Queen was insane and hid herself so that no one would know. Perhaps because of this story, *The Times* published a small item on 1 April: 'Her Majesty's loyal subjects will be very pleased to hear that their Sovereign is about to break her protracted seclusion.'

It may have been an April Fool's joke but it did not appear so to Victoria, who took the unprecedented step of writing a letter to the editor which he published as a news item entitled 'The Court', placing it above the Court Circular. It denounced the 'erroneous idea' of her return to society:

> Whenever any real object is to be attained by her appearing on public occasions, any national interest to be promoted, or anything to be encouraged which is for the good of her people, her Majesty will not shrink, as she has not shrunk, from any personal sacrifice.

She referred, as always, to her 'seriously impaired' strength and she warned that, if she were to resume 'these mere State ceremonies', she would 'run the risk of entirely disabling herself for the discharge of those other duties which can not be neglected'.

Battle had now been entered, and for decades each successive government tried to encourage the Queen to let the people see her. In 1865 Lord Palmerston died, but his Liberal government carried on under Earl Russell as Prime Minister. The next year, after much cajoling, Russell managed to persuade her to open Parliament for the first time since Albert's death. She was anxious to let him know that her concession was not to become a precedent:

> The Queen *must say* that she does feel *very bitterly* the want of feeling of those who *ask* the Queen to go to open Parliament. That the public should wish to see her she fully understands, and has *no* wish to prevent – quite the contrary; but why this wish should be of so *unreasonable* and unfeeling a nature, as to *long* to *witness* the spectacle of a poor, broken-hearted widow, nervous and shrinking, dragged in *deep mourning*, ALONE *in* STATE as a *Show*, where she used to go supported by her husband, to be gazed at, without delicacy of feeling, is a thing *she cannot* understand. . . . She *will* do it *this time.* . . . Were the Queen a woman possessed of strong nerves, she would not mind going through this painful exhibition, but her nerves . . . are terribly and *increasingly* shaken. . . . It is hard, when she works and slaves away all day and till late at night, not to be spared at least such trials.

She had opened Parliament twenty-one times before Albert's death; in the forty years afterwards she did so only nine times, and on each occasion she insisted on all sorts of conditions to limit the ceremony. She would not wear her crown or robes, though the latter were draped across the throne. Her speech was read by the Lord Chancellor, and Prince Albert's chair was always present as a mute testimony to what she had lost.

By the late 1860s the Queen was relaxing her own rule about public appearances. In 1868 she gave a 'breakfast party' at Buckingham Palace – the precursor of the twentieth-century garden party – and in the next year she opened Blackfriars Bridge in London. But the complaints still grew. Lord Amberley, Russell's son, noted: 'Everybody is abusing the Queen very much for not being in London or Windsor and so delaying events so much. No respect or loyalty seems left in the way people allow themselves to talk . . . saying things like: "What do we pay her for if she will not do her work." '

Her 'work' was the one thing that she did do, and most assiduously. It ranged from drafting or correcting the most minute despatch to considering decisions involving war and peace. All documents received her careful attention: 'Mr

Gordon', she noted on a Foreign Office telegram, 'says *King* Frederick of Wurttemberg is dead – he must surely mean *Prince Frederick* who has been long ill – the King's name is Charles.' The Foreign Secretary, Lord Clarendon, who was highly critical about the Queen's public withdrawal, praised her 'enlightened judgement upon all foreign questions'. His papers in the Bodleian Library show the range of her involvement in foreign relations. For example, in 1868–9 there is extensive correspondence covering Turkey and Greece, French designs on Belgium, Hanover, a visit of the Prince of Wales to Greece, a protest from the Queen of Spain, the opening of the Suez Canal (members of the Royal Family, she decided, should not attend the ceremony), plans by the King of Prussia to declare himself Emperor of Germany, torture in Greece (the official despatch was not 'unequivocal' enough in its condemnation, she said), and a fund to help British victims of a fire in Constantinople. Her lifelines were the telegraph and the daily messenger services between Whitehall and Osborne, Windsor and Balmoral.

One other topic began to be the subject of much speculation and gossip. *Leaves from the Journal* had introduced 'our faithful Highland servant', John Brown, to the reading public. He is first mentioned in her Journal in 1849. By 1858 he had become 'my special servant; and there can't be a nicer, better or handier one. . . . Really,' she adds, 'there is nothing like these Highlanders for handiness.' Brown's initial attraction was two-fold. He happened to be a very good servant, loyal and hard-working. Secondly, he was a Scotsman, whose direct speech appealed to Victoria as a relief from courtly manners and political speeches. Brown had a way of saying exactly what she wanted to hear. For example, after his first visit to the Mausoleum for the service on 14 December 1865 (particularly poignant as Uncle Leopold had died only a few days before), Brown said, 'while tears rolled down his cheeks':

> I didn't like to see ye at Frogmore this morning; I felt for ye; to see ye coming there with your daughters and your husband lying there. . . . I know so well what your feeling must be – ye who had been so happy. There is no more pleasure for you, poor Queen, and I feel for ye but what can I do though for ye? I could die for ye.

When the Queen described this to Vicky, she mentioned a sermon she had been reading which spoke of the deep bond that could exist between master and servant. This is the real key to her relationship with John Brown: he was a loyal servant who knew that the worst thing to say was that her grief would pass.

Throughout the 1860s, Brown's influence and notoriety grew. He was almost always on the box when the Queen went out in her carriage. She felt safer when he was there even before he saved her from yet another assassination attempt. Brown also was the frequent bearer of the notes by which Victoria conducted almost all her business – official, Household and family. She never liked confronting people directly, so if she had a request to make, a rebuke to issue or praise to confer, a note was despatched. If the note did not please the recipient, the curt bearer often made yet another enemy. The Queen's sons particularly disliked Brown. The 'sailor prince', Alfred, was the worst offender in his mother's eyes for refusing to shake hands with Brown: to the Queen this was an example of princely pride. After all, when she was a child Mamma had made her be polite to servants and she herself had always adhered to that rule. 'In our days,' she wrote to Vicky,

> when a prince can only maintain his position by his character – pride is most dangerous. And then besides I do feel so strongly that we are before God all alike, and that in the twinkling of an eye, the highest may find themselves at the feet of the poorest and lowest. I have seen the noblest, most refined, high-bred feelings in the humblest and most unlearned and this is most necessary a Prince should feel.

Some people began to titter about 'Mrs Brown', and their relationship has provided scope for the salacious ever since. The Queen, however, had found a servant and a friend and, as she put it, 'The Queen will not be dictated to, or *made* to *alter* what she has found to answer for her comfort.' Brown's worst fault was his drinking, but this the Queen overlooked. Undoubtedly the Queen did at times behave foolishly, by writing and speaking of her affection for her 'friend and servant'. Ironically, the scandal of Sir John Conroy had in many ways now found an echo from the Highlands.

One other important aspect of her friendship with Brown was that he brought the Queen into contact with ordinary people. She had come increasingly to look with disfavour upon much of the aristocracy while remaining a strong believer in the importance of aristocratic leadership. She especially deprecated those members of the aristocracy whom she believed led Bertie and her other sons astray. As she wrote from Osborne to Vicky at the end of 1867:

> The young men are so ignorant, luxurious and self-indulgent – and the young women so fast, frivolous and imprudent that the danger [of a Revolution] really is very great, and they ought to be warned. The lower classes are becoming so well-informed, are so intelligent, and earn their bread and riches so deservedly – that they cannot and ought not to be kept back – to be abused by the wretched, ignorant, high-born beings who live only to kill time.

Victoria's views on social problems were among many which she shared with Charles Dickens when he came to Buckingham Palace in March 1870. They also had a mutual interest in photographs: when she heard that he had acquired a large collection of photographs of the recent war in America she let it be known she would like him to bring them to the Palace. She and Dickens spoke of 'the division of classes in England, which he hoped would get better in time'. Fortunately her rather short summary of their hour-long conversation is supplemented by an account that Dickens gave to his manager, whom he met afterwards. Since court etiquette dictated that no one could sit in the presence of the Queen, Dickens stood and talked while she leaned on a sofa. (One wonders if it was the same room in which she had once defended his works to Lord Melbourne.) She spoke about a whole host of subjects from the cost of meat and bread to his impressions of Irish revolutionary sentiment in America. Before he left she presented him with an autographed copy of *Leaves*, which she confessed she felt somewhat shy at giving to the best-known writer of the age. She asked, in return, that Dickens send her an autographed set of all his works, and she said she would like it that very afternoon. The Queen's eagerness was sadly justified, when Dickens died only a few weeks later.

When Prince Albert died the Queen believed her sorrow would remain the same. Yet by 1867 she was forced to admit to Vicky that there was an

> easing of that violent grief, those paroxysms of despair and yearning and longing and of daily, nightly longing to die which for the first three years never left me, and which were a rending asunder of heart and body and soul – the power of realising that married life seems gone.

Now she could look 'on adored Papa, who is ever mingled with every event, every pleasure, every pain as an Angel – no longer an earthly being'. She missed him most when it came to family questions, particularly the marriages of their children.

In 1869 she decided that the time had come to end the custom that royalty could only marry someone of their own rank. Princess Louise wanted to marry a commoner, the Marquess of Lorne, a Liberal MP and heir to the Duke of Argyll. The Prince of Wales opposed it, but the Queen allowed the marriage to take place. She had been alarmed by the temporary rift in the family caused by the outbreak of war between Denmark and Prussia: Bertie and his wife naturally took the Danish side, while Vicky naturally supported the German side, as did the Queen herself. Matters were even worse in 1866 when Alice's husband was on one side and Vicky's on the other in the Prussian war against Austria. Victoria realised that foreign marriages were not popular and did little to promote better feeling between nations. Allowing Louise to marry a British commoner would 'strengthen the *hold* of the Royal family, besides infusing new and healthy blood'.

Her fears of further war and consequent family division were justified in 1870 when the Franco-Prussian War broke out. Once again, Bertie was thought to oppose the 'German element'. The Queen did her best to secure peace and then to alleviate the horrors of war. She had grown increasingly suspicious of Napoleon III, but when he surrendered to the Prussians and his Empire fell to the mob of Paris, Victoria was full of sympathy. After Empress Eugénie fled to England, the Queen told her with great kindness, 'You no longer have the sovereignty of power but you have still a higher sovereignty, that of misfortune.' The disputes and suspicions of the last decade were forgotten when Napoleon III arrived in England to begin his exile. Victoria did all she could to make the Emperor comfortable in his few remaining years, and she would always treat Eugénie as a 'sister' and sovereign.

The death of General Grey, her private secretary, in 1870 was a great loss. The Queen admitted that he had his 'crochets and a difficult temper', but even so he was 'honest, clever, kind hearted and agreeable'. She insisted on going up to London to view his body and to console his widow. Part of the General's 'difficult temper' was caused by the Queen's continuing withdrawal from public life. Grey had come to believe that the Cabinet must make an official protest to her, as he wrote in 1869 to Lord Clarendon, the Foreign Secretary:

I cannot help repeating to you what I have frequently pressed, without the slightest effect upon Lord Derby, Dişraeli, Gladstone, Granville etc. that the *Govt alone* can interfere with any effect to save the Queen – I will not go so far as to say the *Monarchy* from the consequence of the course she is pursuing ... every day now I am getting paragraphs and articles [three words illegible] of the newspapers sent to me on the ... Queen's *absenteeism*.

The government were unwilling to confront the Queen. In 1868 Gladstone had become Liberal Prime Minister, and he was seriously worried that the constitutional position of the monarchy was being weakened. The proclamation of yet another republic in France stirred republican sentiment in England. When he was on his way to Balmoral to see her Gladstone noticed advertisements for a scurrilous pamphlet, *What Does She Do with It?*, which expressed the view that the Queen was hoarding the money that Parliament had voted for her ceremonial duties. Several of her children were becoming alarmed about both her seclusion and the attacks upon it.

Gladstone believed that the Queen's continuous moaning about her health was the 'subtlest working of the selfish principle in a fine character'. Yet in 1871 her complaints for once were not excuses. She was now over fifty and was suffering from a severe abscess on one arm. Her health was worse than at any time since she had come to the throne, and she lost two stones in weight in the autumn of 1871. Naturally wild rumours flew about. Disraeli did not help matters when, in an effort to defend her, he said she was too 'physically and morally incapacitated' for public appearances. Some radical newspapers interpreted this to mean that 'the Queen is crazy'. It was two months before the Queen's health began to improve, but her seclusion was still under attack.

Two events now intervened to support the Queen's power and influence. On the very day of Grey's death Victoria appointed Henry Ponsonby as his successor. He was married to Grey's niece (the Mary Bulteel who had accompanied Victoria on her incognito ride round Paris in 1855) and he served the Queen loyally and faithfully for the next quarter of a century. Not only did he assist with her correspondence, but he would move about London seeing ministers. Whenever a government came to power or fell, Ponsonby would arrive with messages and letters. With his discretion and common sense he helped to carry on Albert's mission to preserve the monarchy as an indispensable part of political life. Like Grey, Ponsonby was a Liberal which made it easier for him to cope with the ruffled feathers of Liberal politicians who were outraged to see the Queen's views became more conservative with time as their own grew more radical. Ponsonby's tact with politicians softened the rough edges and made government business easier for everyone.

The attacks on the Queen stopped when another tragedy theatened both her family and the nation. Just after the Prince of Wales celebrated his thirtieth birthday, in December 1871, he became seriously ill. Soon it was obvious that he had the disease which the Queen most dreaded: typhoid. His life was despaired of, and she made the sad rail journey to his country house at Sandringham in Norfolk. The doctors thought it unwise to let him know his mother had come. On the 'dreadful anniversary', 14 December, exactly ten years since he had knelt at his father's deathbed, the Prince opened his eyes and saw his mother: 'So kind of you to come; it is the kindest thing you could do.' The amazing coincidence of the Prince's recovery on the anniversary of his father's death made all criticism of the Queen seem churlish. A wave of loyalty swept across the land, washing away republican mutterings. On the last day of 1871 – at the end of the most difficult decade of her life – Queen Victoria wrote:

> Could hardly believe it was the last day in the old year, which has really been a most trying one. ... But I thank God for His great mercy, for amidst all danger, trials, and sufferings, He has always protected us and brought us through the 'fiery furnace'.

SIX

YOU HAVE IT, MADAM

On 27 February 1872 the streets of London were thronged with over a million people. It was one of those rare days when the Queen was in London, and she had come to attend a thanksgiving service at St Paul's Cathedral for the recovery of the Prince of Wales. 'The deafening cheers never ceased the whole way.... We seemed to be passing through a sea of people,' she wrote. The Queen and the Prince walked arm in arm, partly so that she could give him the support he needed, for he was still weak. When they returned to Buckingham Palace he went to Marlborough House to rest while Victoria went on to the balcony with Beatrice, Arthur, Leopold and Alfred. 'Felt tired by all the emotion', she wrote, 'but it is a day that can never be forgotten!'

Two days later Victoria went out in an open landau with Prince Arthur, Prince Leopold and Jane Churchill, her Lady in Waiting and close friend. After a drive through Hyde Park and Regent's Park, they returned to Buckingham Palace. At the garden entrance, the carriage stopped and John Brown jumped down to lower the step:

> Someone appeared at my side, whom I first imagined was a footman, going to lift off the wrapper. Then I perceived that it was someone unknown, peering above the carriage door, with an uplifted hand and a strange voice, at the same time the boys calling out and moving forward. Involuntarily, in a terrible fright, I threw myself over Jane C., calling out, 'Save me,' and heard a scuffle and voices! I soon recovered myself sufficiently to stand up and turn round, when I saw Brown holding a young man tightly, who was struggling, Arthur, the Equerries, etc., also near him ... the postilion, called out, 'There it is,' and looking down I then did see shining on the ground a small pistol. This filled us with horror. All were as white as sheets, Jane C. almost crying, and Leopold looked as if he were going to faint.

Her assailant, the 'wretched boy' O'Connor, had not loaded his pistol: his intention was to force the Queen to receive a paper about imprisoned Irish terrorists. 'It is to good Brown and to his wonderful presence of mind that I greatly owe my safety', she wrote, although the twenty-one-year-old Prince Arthur, who had seen the gun pointed at his mother's face, was about to tackle him when Brown, already on the ground, got to him first. When the Princess of Wales came for tea she said that 'she was glad she had not been in the carriage, and that it was no pleasure being a Queen, to which I most readily agreed'. This was the sixth attack on the Queen in her thirty-five years on the throne.

Queen Victoria's relative composure in the face of such attacks was founded in part on her deep belief in divine providence. 'What we do not understand now', she once told Empress Eugénie, 'we shall understand some day – in this life or the next. But we can be sure that the explanation will not be withheld.' Her views were simple: she believed strongly in the value of prayer, preferred simple, unadorned religious worship and had an eighteenth-century dislike of 'enthusiasm' or outward display. Even as a girl her mother wrote, 'She has Religion at her Heart.' In one of her periodic tiffs with her eldest daughter, who held more 'advanced' liberal and intellectual views, the Queen wrote, 'I think that a simple earnest belief is far more important than that knowledge which teaches you to begin to doubt the truth of many things which you have learnt to believe and respect.' Although she disliked those who make a living by doubting, she herself held traditional doctrines without rigidity and, as so often is the case, had no time for those whose hold was more tight. This led her to dislike both the Evangelical and High Church parties in the Church of England.

Her dislike of the High Church was intensified by her preference for the simple worship of rural Scotland. She firmly adhered to the old view that Protestantism lay at the foundation of England's greatness, and any attempt to be more 'catholic' met with a fierce rejoinder: 'The English Church should bethink itself of its dangers from *Papacy*.' One thing she never doubted was her position in the Established Church. Mary Ponsonby wrote that she treated her position 'exactly as she treated her headship of the army or the navy. It was a constitutional matter.... To have asked how it coincided with her personal inner convictions would have seemed to her like asking her if she had ever served as a soldier or a sailor.'

Much of 1873 was spent in negotiations with the Archbishop of Canterbury and the Prime Minister to get them to act on a bill to 'put down ritualism'. This was eventually passed in 1874 and proved a total disaster when conscientious priests languished in gaol. This year also saw the Queen involved in even more complicated negotiations with the imperial court of Russia over a marriage treaty between Tsar Alexander II's daughter, Marie Alexandrovna, and Victoria's second son, Prince Alfred. It is not surprising that the Queen, with her deep hatred of Russia, should oppose the match. Eventually she had to give in, but she could only be pressed so far. Princess Alice thought it a good idea for her mother to travel to Cologne where she could meet the Tsarina (who once referred to Victoria as 'that crazy old hag'). This was too much, and the Queen wrote to her daughter:

Instead of urging my wishes on which the future happiness and well doing of Marie much depend, you have *entirely* taken the *Russian side*, as if you were a Russian, and not a British Princess. And I do *not* think, dear Child, that *you* should tell *me* who have been nearly *20 years longer* on the throne than the Emperor of Russia and am the Doyenne of Sovereigns and who am a Reigning Sovereign which the Empress is *not*, – *what I ought to do. I* think *I* know *that*. The proposal ... for *me* to be *at Cologne* ... was one of the *coolest* things *I* ever heard ... how could I who am not like any little Princess ready to run to the slightest call of the almighty Russians – have been *able in 24 hours* to be *ready* to travel....

In January 1874 the couple were married amidst the splendours of the Winter

Palace in St Petersburg, while at Osborne the Queen sat reading the marriage service from the Prayer Book. In the evening she watched the fireworks and attended a servants' ball. She did not get to bed until half-past one. Victoria had sent Arthur Stanley, Dean of Westminster, to St Petersburg to perform a second, Church of England, ceremony. In addition he and his wife, the former Lady Augusta Bruce, sent her long accounts of the ceremonies.

Only a few weeks later the Queen presided over another change of government. The Liberals, led by Gladstone, were defeated in a general election and the Tories, under Disraeli, formed a government. On 20 February Gladstone came to take leave of the Queen. They consoled one another about the unmanageable nature of the Liberal Party, and as the Queen gave him her hand to kiss she expressed 'every wish for his health'. When Disraeli knelt to kiss the same hand later that day, he said, 'I plight my troth to the kindest of Mistresses.' The Queen was charmed, and would remain charmed for the next six years. Gladstone, far more upright than Disraeli and just as loyal to the throne, respected the Queen and, despite all the difficulties which would plague their relationship, always liked her. He was too honest and unsophisticated to flatter her. Disraeli, however, set out to charm her as he did all women. Princess Helena's daughter, Marie Louise, remembered that when she sat next to Gladstone she thought him the cleverest man in England; when she sat next to Disraeli she thought herself the cleverest woman.

In his self-mocking way Disraeli explained his 'method' for working with the Queen: 'I never deny; I never contradict; I sometimes forget.' In addition, he told the poet Matthew Arnold, 'You have heard me called a flatterer, and it is true. Everyone likes flattery; and, when you come to royalty, you should lay it on with a trowel.' This was said tongue-in-cheek, because Victoria recognised flattery as well as anyone else; but, like the rest of mankind, she could suspend judgement when she was its object. Quite simply, she liked Disraeli, approved his policies and admired his commitment to her Empire. The 'flattery' was only the icing on the cake: another word for it might be chivalry, as in this 1875 thank-you note for a bunch of snowdrops:

> Mr Disraeli with his humble duty to your Majesty:
> Yesterday eve, there appeared ... a delicate-looking case, with a royal superscription ... he thought, at first, that your Majesty had graciously bestowed upon him the stars of your Majesty's orders. And, indeed, he was so impressed with this graceful illusion, that, having a banquet, where there were many stars and ribbons, he could not resist the temptation, by placing some snowdrops on his heart, of showing that he, too, was decorated by a gracious Sovereign.
> Then, in the middle of the night, it occurred to him, that it might all be an enchantment, and that, perhaps, it was a Faery gift and came from another monarch: Queen Titania, gathering flowers, with her Court, in a soft and sea-girt isle, and sending magic blossoms, which, they say, turn the heads of those who receive them.
> They certainly would turn Mr. Disraeli's, if his sense of duty to your Majesty did not exceed, he sincerely believes, his conceit.

Disraeli frequently moaned that the Queen bombarded him with telegrams and letters; in the event he probably received no more communications than any other Prime Minister. In 1875 he complained that 'The Faery [as he called Victoria] writes to me every day and telegraphs to me in the interval. I have heard twice from Osborne this morning.' Two years later he was still complaining: 'Yesterday we had 3 boxes and 5 telegrams (two of them cyphered) from Osborne.' She wrote on a wide range of topics. For example, on 21 May 1875 the Queen wrote a long letter

> about vivisection which she insists upon my stopping as well as the theft of ladies' jewels. I think she is the most artless person, in her style, I ever corresponded with. She wrote to me the other day on the slaughter of young seals, with a printed description of the horrors and sufferings of the parents which she cut out of a newspaper. I never read anything so harrowing.

Disraeli admitted, however, that he got the Board of Trade to introduce legislation which was adopted.

Queen Victoria's kindness to her Prime Minister was touching. She sent secretly for reports from his secretary about his health and, breaking with etiquette, she had him sit during audiences. She sent him a portrait of herself (which now hangs in his former country house, Hughenden) and asked for one in return. She showed her public support by visiting Hughenden, just as she had visited Melbourne's country house thirty years before. He was also given a bust of John Brown, and he was wise enough to say how much he looked forward to 'Mr Brown's' coming to Hughenden to fish. She sent him letters on his birthday – one was, he said, 'the kindest letter I almost ever received'. However, she never let their friendship affect business: it is true that his audiences went on for a long time, but before his arrival she sent him detailed lists of the questions she wanted answered. Some letters stretched to sixteen pages.

Disraeli's influence was never absolute. He was not much more successful than Liberal Prime Ministers in getting Victoria regularly to open Parliament. She enunciated her policy: if she decided to open Parliament, only the Prime Minister would be informed – no one else; no public announcement must be made; finally, no decision could be expected too far in advance. Ponsonby, in reporting the policy, did agree that it caused a 'little confusion' and in a secret postscript added, 'H.M. don't like positively giving any order so far beforehand.'

Victoria could also be jealous. In 1876 Disraeli was dining at Windsor with the Queen and Vicky's mother-in-law, the Empress Augusta of Germany. Disraeli recorded:

> Whenever 'Augoosta' had got involved in some metaphysical speculation with [Lord] Carnarvon, the Faery took refuge in confidential whispers in which she indulged in the freest remarks on men and things.... After dinner I was attached to Augoosta who threw out all her resources, philosophical, poetic, political – till the Faery was a little jealous, for she had originally told Lady Ely that some one 'was not to make his pretty speeches to Augoosta, who only wanted to *draw him to her*!!!!' However, all went off very well, and the Faery made a happy dart and had the last word.

Queen Victoria at Balmoral with John Brown, c. 1865. Photograph by Downey. In April 1865 the Queen told her eldest daughter that she had 'taken good J. Brown entirely and permanently as my personal servant for out of doors'

The Queen's eldest daughter, Victoria, the Princess Royal, at the time of her marriage to Prince Frederick William of Prussia in 1858. The liberal-minded Fritz only reigned as Emperor Frederick III of Germany for a few tragic months in 1888. This lithograph is by Carl Suessnapp

Above *Queen Victoria with English, German and Russian royalty at a family wedding in Coburg in April 1894. Kaiser Wilhelm II sits on one side of the Queen while his mother, the Empress Frederick (Vicky), sits on the other. Between the Kaiser and the Queen are the last Tsar of Russia, Nicholas II, and his fiancée, Princess Alix, one of Victoria's granddaughters, later to be murdered by the communists*

Left *The marriage of the Prince of Wales to Princess Alexandra of Denmark in St George's Chapel, Windsor, 10 March 1863. The Queen observes the wedding from St Katherine's Closet*

Above *The Queen arriving at High Wycombe Railway Station in December 1877 on her visit to Disraeli's nearby house, Hughenden. The Prime Minister escorts the Queen*

Right *Sir Henry Ponsonby, the Queen's Private Secretary. When he died in 1895, the Queen wrote to his widow: 'He was always so kind and so fair and just that I miss him terribly'*

Far right *Queen Victoria with her youngest child, Princess Beatrice. The Queen insisted that Beatrice remain with her always as companion and confidante. After the Queen's death, Princess Beatrice carried out her orders to destroy the originals of the Queen's Journal. Photograph by Melhuish*

XIII

XIV

Above *Queen Victoria at work at
Frogmore in the last years of her reign,
surrounded by the boxes in which she
sent and received official letters and
documents. Because of her hatred of hot
rooms, she often did her work in special
tents. Her Indian servant and secretary,
the Munshi, attends her*

Left *One of the few photographs of
Queen Victoria showing her smiling.
This one was taken by the photographer,
Charles Knight, on 15 February 1898.
Lady Ponsonby, Sir Henry's widow,
said 'Those who never saw the Queen's
smile can have little idea of the
marvellous way in which it brightened
and exhilarated the lines of the Queen's
features . . . a flash of kindly light
beaming from the eyes'*

Far left *Queen Victoria with one of her
dogs, Sharp. The tartan indicates that
the picture was taken at Balmoral*

The marble sarcophagus of Queen Victoria and Prince Albert, sculpted by Baron Marochetti, in the Mausoleum at Frogmore, near Windsor Castle

XVI

Disraeli's friendship for the Queen was not a pretence but part of his romantic view of English life and history which jostled with the cynical strain in his character. After some contretemps had upset Victoria in 1879 he admitted to Lady Ely, one of the Queen's Ladies, 'I love the Queen – perhaps the only person in this world left to me that I do love.'

When the Queen and Disraeli discussed politics in their extended audiences, foreign relations predominated. The balance of power in Europe had been disturbed by the formation of a united Germany under the leadership of Bismarck, whom the Queen disliked both for his Prussian militarism and for his persecution of the Crown Prince, Vicky's husband, whose idealistic liberalism he despised. There was also the problem of the Ottoman Empire, where Moslem atrocities against Christians in the Balkans, and Russian attempts to secure control over European Turkey, plagued the Foreign Office. But the issue on which Queen and Prime Minister were as one was that of the Suez Canal. When the Egyptian ruler decided to sell his shares in the Canal privately to French financiers to pay his debts, Disraeli convinced the Cabinet to buy them with the help of the Rothschilds. Throughout, Victoria had given him good advice as well as encouragement. When she received the news of his success on 24 November 1875 she wrote, 'An immense thing. It is entirely Mr. Disraeli's doing ... my support had been a great help. It is of course a great step, and may have far-reaching consequences' – as indeed it did. In his letter to the Queen he said, 'It is just settled: you have it, Madam. The French Government has been out-generaled.'

The British government had thus acquired a substantial interest in the Canal and guaranteed quicker access to India, a country for which Victoria's love grew yearly. In 1873 the Queen first began sounding out opinion on a change in her title to reflect her concern for India. Only an empress could take precedence over the native princes and rulers. The title was increasingly heard there and she wondered if it could be formalised by a simple Order in Council, thereby avoiding Parliament. During the manoeuvring over the Canal Victoria raised the question once again. Disraeli disliked having two problems to cope with at once, for the Liberals under Gladstone were fighting the Canal scheme, to the Queen's fury. He gave in, however: 'The Empress-Queen demands her Imperial Crown.'

In 1876, when the Queen agreed to open Parliament, her speech included a reference to an India Titles Bill, whose passage would prove a much harder task than either Victoria or Disraeli had imagined. Many people were confused and thought she meant to give up the title of Queen and become Empress. Still others, who held the old Whig view, feared that the monarchy might be assuming too much power behind a new title. The legislation as introduced by Disraeli was badly drawn up and his delivery confusing: he was frequently offhand in matters of great complexity. He did not make it clear that the new title would be used in India, not in Britain. To stem the newspapers' misrepresentations the Queen ordered Theodore Martin, Albert's biographer, to canvass leading journals and inform them that

The Queen will be always called 'the Queen,' and her children 'their Royal Highnesses,' and *no* difference whatever is to be made except OFFICIALLY ADDING after *Queen* of Great Britain, '*Empress of India,*' the name which is best understood in the East. . . . Mr. Martin will easily believe that the Queen and her Government will *not* yield to *mere* clamour and intimidation! . . . *Never* yield to clamour and misrepresentation – if a thing is right and well considered. The Prince and Queen always have acted on this principle.

Three days later the bill got its second reading in the Commons with a majority of 105. Gladstone's fierce opposition caused Victoria to place a very black mark indeed against him.

On 1 January 1877 the Viceroy of India, surrounded by native princes, British officials and troops of the Indian Army, proclaimed the new title at a Durbar, or ceremonial audience. When the Viceroy had finished, a maharajah shouted spontaneously, 'Shah-in-Shah Padshah, be happy! The Princes of India bless you and pray that your sovereignty and powers may remain steadfast for ever.' Back in England it was announced that the new title would not be used in the United Kingdom or in the colonies except in Army commissions, because officers could serve in the Indian Army where the oath was to the Empress, not to the Queen. Because the new title belonged to the Queen personally, even if she did not use it outside India, foreign treaties and communications with foreign heads of state would be in the name of 'Victoria RI' – Victoria Regina et Imperatrix. In the event, however, within a few years the Queen was habitually signing herself 'Victoria RI'.

In 1878 the Queen's fear of Russia increased because of events in the Balkans. Disraeli's government advocated neutrality when the stories of Turkish atrocities against Christians became known in the West. Gladstone, with all the ardour of a knight errant, threw himself into a public campaign to force the government to act. The Queen was horrified: she distrusted 'extra-parliamentary' crusades which were got up to force the hand of those to whom she had entrusted the government. In addition the reports, she believed, were exaggerated. The civilised powers could bring diplomatic pressure to bear on Turkish officials; intervention would only rekindle Russia's imperial ambitions not just on the Ottoman Empire but on India; worst of all, the horrors of war would be unleashed. She was appalled that Gladstone could work with such agitators. For their part the campaigners could not abide the thought of Christian Britain standing by while fellow Christians were massacred. It was not, perhaps, the Queen's finest hour nor Britain's. Diplomatically there remains much to be said for Victoria's position, but for once it was Gladstone who had captured the heights of the moral summit which she had always believed was a crown possession.

In the midst of this crisis, personal tragedy struck the Queen once more when Princess Alice's children came down with diphtheria. Victoria wrote ominously, 'What an anxiety! It is like '61, when the poor Portuguese Royal Family [Coburg relations of Prince Albert] were struck down . . . and my beloved Albert too!' On 16 November she heard that Alice's daughter, known as May, had died. Worse was to follow. On the fated 14 December, seventeen years to the day since her father's death, Alice, who had caught the disease while nursing her children, died.

'This terrible day come round again!' began the Journal for that day. 'Slept tolerably, but woke very often, constantly seeing darling Alice before me. When I woke in the morning, was not for a moment aware of all our terrible anxiety.' As always on the 14th she went to pray in the Blue Room at Windsor where Albert had died. Then she went to her sitting room for breakfast. Here she met Brown, who handed her a telegram from the Grand Duke announcing Alice's death. At first Victoria did not take it in. Alice, who had supported her after Albert's death, 'this dear, talented, distinguished, tender-hearted, noble-minded, sweet child', was the first of her children to die.

Soon Victoria had to turn from her own grief to comfort her friend the Empress Eugénie. In 1879, six years after Napoleon III's death, the twenty-three-year-old Prince Imperial, his only son, volunteered to join a special British force to put down a Zulu uprising in South Africa. Victoria, who was very fond of the young Prince, had reluctantly given him permission. In June news arrived of his death. The Bonapartist hope had fallen before the spears of 'African savages' – partly, it seemed, because a British officer had abandoned him in the field. Victoria was plagued by the thought that he '*was not* sufficiently cared *for* or *kept from avoidable danger*'. She visited the Empress on the day of the funeral and arranged for three of her sons, the Prince of Wales, Prince Leopold and Prince Arthur, to be pall-bearers. When the Commons refused to support a proposed monument in Westminster Abbey the Queen erected one in St George's Chapel, Windsor. It stands in the south-west corner of the nave, a moving memorial of Victoria's loyalty as a friend.

In the spring of 1880 Disraeli's administration was defeated in a general election. The Queen hoped that she could avoid sending for Gladstone, whose 'Little England' foreign policy she detested. She feared that a Liberal government would not preserve a strong foreign policy nor maintain sufficient military strength. An added horror was the growth of radicalism in the Liberal Party. As always she expressed her concern in a personal lament, this time to Disraeli:

> There are times when people should have no hearts or feelings; for *what* can be more cruel than for a female Sovereign no longer young, severely tried – without a husband or any *one* person on whose help (when her valued Minister leaves her) she can securely rest – to have to take those people who have done all they could to vilify and weaken her Govt.? *Can* she have confidence in them?

Her fear of the radicals was well founded. Their attacks on the monarchy had benefited from the public outcry over her withdrawal from public ceremonial in the seventies. MPs like Sir Charles Dilke and Joseph Chamberlain were outright republicans. The MP for Northampton, Charles Bradlaugh, was a confessed atheist: how could he honestly take the oath to God by which he sealed his loyalty to her? When Ponsonby, himself a Liberal, put it to the Queen that Gladstone, even with his most difficult followers, was better in government than outside, and that he was also personally loyal to her, she turned on the poor man:

> He says 'Mr. Gladstone is *loyal* & *devoted to the Queen*'!!!
> He is *neither*; for *no one* CAN *be*, who spares no means – contrary to anything the

Queen & she thinks her Predecessors ever witnessed or experienced – to *vilify* – *attack* – accuse of *every* species of iniquity a Minister who had most difficult times & questions to deal with – & who showed a most unpardonable & disgraceful spite & personal hatred to Lord Beaconsfield who has restored England to the position she had lost under Mr. Gladstone's Govt.

Is this *patriotism* & devotion to the *sovereign?* . . .

Such conduct is *unheard of* & the *only* excuse is – that he is not quite *sane*.

Disraeli's final audience, on 27 April, was final only in his capacity as Prime Minister. The Queen continued to invite him to Windsor: in May, when he sat next to her at dinner, she turned to him and confided, 'I feel so happy that I think what has happened is only a horrid dream.' The 'horrid dream' would last for five years. Disraeli only survived his defeat by a year, and on his death Victoria sent flowers and messages to his friends. Four days after the funeral she went to Hughenden for a last visit, determined to follow the exact path along which his body had been carried to the parish church for interment. The vault, which is entered from outside the east end of the church, was opened so that she could lay her own wreath on the coffin. She used her own money to erect a memorial tablet inside the chancel, just above the seat Disraeli normally occupied. At the top are his arms as Earl of Beaconsfield; beneath is his profile and at the bottom is inscribed, 'To the dear and honored memory of Benjamin, Earl of Beaconsfield, this memorial is placed by his grateful Sovereign and Friend, Victoria R.I. "Kings love him that speaketh right," Proverbs, XVI. 13. February 27, 1882.' She would erect no memorial to Gladstone.

The year after Disraeli's death the Queen was involved in a head-on collision with Gladstone, who, to placate the radicals in his party, proposed Dilke for the Cabinet. The Queen objected and then gave in. Her stand, however, brought a partial victory: in a public speech Dilke declared that his republicanism had become 'theoretical' and did not apply to a country like Great Britain with such an excellent system of constitutional monarchy. When Gladstone wrote to the theoretical republican he reminded him of two of the Queen's leading attributes, 'the first her high good manners, and the second her love of truth'. He was the 'more desirous to do her justice, because, while she conducts all intercourse with me in absolute and perfect courtesy, I am convinced, from a hundred tokens, that she looks forward to the day of my retirement as a day, if not of jubilee, yet of relief.' He added that he had just received a telegram from the Queen in which she insisted that Dilke's recantation be seen not as a 'bargain, but as a free tender on your own part'. When, in 1883, Dilke did good work on the Royal Commission investigating the housing of the poor, the Queen joined others in praising him; when he was involved in a sordid divorce case, she refused to receive him at court.

In March 1883 Victoria missed the bottom step as she was coming down the stairs at Windsor and fell heavily, injuring her knee. She had to be lifted in and out of her carriage by Brown; twelve days later, Prince Leopold came in to tell her that her beloved Brown had died during the night. While a sigh of relief went up from courtiers, politicians and royal offspring, Victoria was crushed. He had, after all, attended her for over thirty years; if he was arrogant and overbearing to others, to her he was loyal, honest and devoted. If his uneducated views were made out to be worth more than they were, that was her fault, not his. She wrote to her friend, the German Empress:

> I miss my faithful, kind friend and constant companion more and more at every turn, especially just now, when I so greatly need his care and his strong arm. I enclose a photograph of him, but will send more later, as I think you would like to have them. . . . What you say about my peculiar isolation, due to my lofty station with its heavy burdens, and how, for that very reason, the loss of so loyal and esteemed a friend as my never to be forgotten and quite irreplaceable Brown, is doubly, or rather I might say, a thousand times, heavier, is only too true.

The language the Queen used here and elsewhere when writing about Brown was no more exaggerated than her manner of writing about any subject. She was a very emotional woman who in private wrote and spoke as she felt, and who felt deeply. If she erred, it was in making too much of a servant who had become a friend; we err more in making too much of their friendship.

Partially inspired, perhaps, by Brown's death she brought out the second volume of selections from her Journal, *More Leaves from the Journal of A Life in the Highlands*, in 1884. It was certainly dedicated to 'my loyal Highlanders and especially to the memory of my devoted personal attendant and faithful friend John Brown'. Not surprisingly, some eyebrows were raised at this public display of private emotions. Worse was to follow: the Queen decided she would prepare a memoir of Brown for private publication. She first asked Theodore Martin for his help, but he managed to decline this invidious task. Then she approached Dr J. Cameron Lees, a well-known Scottish minister, to undertake the work. In the meantime she showed the manuscript to Henry Ponsonby and Lord Rowton, who had been Disraeli's private secretary; they were horrified.

A conspiracy arose to stop the Queen. On 6 March Randall Davidson, the new Dean of Windsor, wrote to thank Victoria for a copy of *More Leaves*. Perhaps on Ponsonby's suggestion, he bravely took his courage in both hands and queried the idea of a memoir. He wondered if everyone would appreciate her confidences: '. . . I should be deceiving Your Majesty were I not to admit that there are, especially among the humbler classes, some (perhaps it would be true to say *many*) who do not shew themselves worthy of these confidences.' He advised her, in his round-about way, to reconsider any 'further publication'.

Two days later Honoria Stopford, a Lady in Waiting who was a close friend of the Queen and a fellow conspirator, wrote to Davidson, 'I am anxious to see you. . . . I have had a hard fight I assure you the last 48 hours, but I *believe* I have conquered, for which *I thank GOD!*' Her thanks were premature. The Queen was furious with Davidson and ordered him to withdraw his remarks. He apologised for any pain he had caused, but would not withdraw his advice. Instead he offered to resign his deanery. She pouted for a fortnight and refused to speak to him; then he was forgiven and the subject was not mentioned again. She had not, however, given up, for in June Dr Lees wrote to Davidson in some despair. He had, he said, agreed to write the proposed memoir to keep it from falling into 'worse hands'. 'The Queen', he added, 'is *determined "that it shall be done"*. You know what that means. She has pressed me to do it – as a Scotchman & a Highlander!'

About the same time Davidson had been sent a copy of a scurrilous American pamphlet by 'Kenward Philp' called *John Brown's Legs; or, Leaves from a Journal in the Lowlands*. On the cover was a drawing of a man's legs in a kilt. It was a very well-done lampoon by someone who either knew a fair amount about the House-hold or had guessed remarkably accurately. It begins, 'This little volume, with its simple record of the never-to-be-forgotten legs of him who bore many a burden (sometimes as heavy as 160 lbs., which is the writer's weight . . .)'. Some selections give its tone:

May 2. Oh! How I feel this morning!
Have just returned from poor, dear Brown's room.
I found him suffering from a dreadful malady termed 'mumps'.
What a sight.

September 15. Louise has just been here and is fearfully dejected.
Brown had comforted her, as he has done me many a time.

February 20. Have ordered Brown to have a cock-tail mixed by my imported American bartender and brought to me at seven o'clock every morning.

December 2. Bertie has just arrived, and knowing his hatred of Brown, a scene is sure to occur. . . . The prince has knocked Brown down and is dancing on the poor creature.

Dr Lees later heard that the Queen had decided to 'postpone' the memoir of Brown, and according to Henry Ponsonby's son the manuscript was destroyed.

Brown's death proved only the precursor to a greater tragedy in March 1884, when Prince Leopold died of a haemorrhage of the brain: he was just short of his thirty-first birthday. He had always been Victoria's most difficult child; his haemophilia had caused him to be over-protected and spoilt, and this in turn made him wilful, especially as he was clever and bookish. Only two years before, Leopold had married a German princess, Helena of Waldeck, whom the Queen at first pronounced 'so well & quietly brought up'. However, when Helena began to resent the Queen's strict control of Leopold's life and her dictatorial manner over all her children, there were scenes.

Victoria's resilient spirits and her enquiring mind ensured that all was not gloom and despair. Her inveterate curiosity was evident when she gave a new tricycle to Leopold's wife following his death; she decided, although in her sixty-fifth year, to try out the new machine herself. *The Rambler*, a penny weekly devoted to 'out-door life' described what happened:

Her Majesty herself unable to resist the temptation, mounted in private and took a turn round her beautiful domain at Osborne. Naturally no photograph of this most interesting occurence was allowed to be taken. . . . Her Majesty decided that her first essay on the fickle wheel should not be made in sight of any of her liege subjects . . . she declared herself very pleased with the pleasure and exhilaration to be derived from the exercise.

The Queen refused to countenance anything but skirts for lady cyclists. 'Of bloomers she has a very great abhorrence.'

The terrors of cycling were as nothing compared with those of coping with Gladstone's 'Little England' policy. Egypt was proving a running sore for Britain. In 1882 a British force was sent out to restore order and among the officers was Prince Arthur, Duke of Connaught since 1874, who had made the Army his career. As always, Victoria followed military expeditions with great care, and after one engagement telegraphed to the Prince to ask after the wounded 'in my name'. But the troubles in Egypt continued and reached a terrible climax when General Gordon met his death at the hands of the fanatical Moslem Mahdi at Khartoum in 1885. The force despatched by Gladstone to relieve Gordon arrived too late to save him. Like most of her subjects, Victoria regarded Gordon as a martyr for the Christian faith. Henry Ponsonby's wife and two daughters were sitting in their Osborne home after breakfast on the day the news arrived. They heard voices in the hall: suddenly the door opened and the Queen stood there, unannounced and unattended. She burst out, 'Khartoum has fallen. Gordon is dead.'

The Queen was so furious that she telegraphed *en clair* – that is, not in cypher – to Gladstone and two other ministers: 'These news from Khartoum are frightful, and to think that all this might have been prevented and many precious lives saved by earlier action is too frightful.' It was as serious and as public a reprimand as any government could receive, but Gladstone did not resign. The Cabinet knew that the Queen only said what most people thought, so resignation would have meant electoral defeat. When the election did come later that year the Liberals were defeated and the Conservatives under Lord Salisbury took office. Victoria regarded Gordon's Bible, sent her by his sister, as a relic and had it placed under glass at Windsor as a shrine. She never forgave Gladstone for his tardy action in failing to rescue Gordon.

For most of this same year, the Queen was engaged in a war of her own. In July 1885 Princess Beatrice, her Baby or Benjamina, was married in a private ceremony in Whippingham parish church on the Isle of Wight. The prospect of any of her children marrying always aroused in Victoria a welter of emotions. Years before, in 1871, on the occasion of Princess Louise's marriage, Sir William Harcourt had had a conversation with the Queen. He said he thought that all women were better married. 'I entirely differ from you, Sir William,' the Queen replied. 'I think no woman should marry except under exceptional circumstances.' There was an element of seriousness in the Queen's banter: children, especially girls, were born to serve their parents. Many years later the Queen was talking to Lady Lytton, a Lady in Waiting, who mentioned her son's kindness and praised him for it. 'Oh, you must not say that,' Victoria said. 'Children ought never to think that they can do enough for their parents.'

Victoria felt this most strongly about Beatrice. After having 'lost' all her other daughters, she decided that 'Baby' must always remain with her as confidante and secretary. In her late twenties, however, the Princess had fallen in love with Prince Henry of Battenberg. European royalty looked down on his family because it had originated in a morganatic marriage entered into by a member of the Hesse family.

Ironically, Victoria had always taken a sympathetic interest in the Battenbergs (from whom the Mountbattens descend) and disregarded their origins. However, in matters concerning the ordering of her family or Household the Queen's tyranny was at its greatest. When, therefore, she heard of the romance she was so furious that she refused to speak to her daughter, and for seven months they communicated only by note. When, eventually, Victoria gave in she did so on her own terms: 'Baby' could marry, but the couple must live with the Queen and Prince Henry must resign his commission in the Prussian Army. Peace was restored: Victoria had not lost a daughter, and had gained a son. She wrote to Lady Hertford a month after the marriage, '... my dear child, with her most amiable young husband, who is as kind as he is handsome, are with me comfortably established under my roof, which is always to be their home.... She is quite unchanged towards me and quietly happy.'

With Princess Beatrice's marriage the Queen's Household settled into a routine that lasted till her death. It revolved, naturally, round the Queen and her work. Despite being what she herself called 'rather a portly elderly lady', the Queen remained an indefatigable worker. Theodore Martin told his friend Arthur Munby about

> seeing her in her room surrounded by the despatch boxes which come to her twice a day from London: for, it seems, she adheres to her husband's rule, & reads & understands a matter before she passes it: so that ... from 7.30 a.m. when she gets up, to 12 at night or 12.30, when she goes to bed, she is continually at work, except the hours of meals & exercise, and half an hour after dinner, when someone reads to her.

When Lady Waterford crossed over to the Isle of Wight in 1890 she sat between two great bags, 'as big as large arm-chairs', which formed only one of the two deliveries made every day. As always there were the reports from the Cabinet, and accounts of debates in both Houses of Parliament.

The Queen's work would have been impossible without the assistance of Henry Ponsonby, who literally wore himself out in her service. His widow would say later: 'The watchword of the lives of her private secretaries was devotion to the will of the Queen.' Yet there were disputes between them. On at least one occasion Victoria asked Ponsonby's wife to tell him that when 'the Queen makes a remark he must not say "It is absurd"'. Arguments, however, were always followed by reconciliations. The one thing Victoria disliked more than being contradicted was not having people speak the truth to her. Ponsonby's own method for dealing with the Queen was fairly simple:

> When she insists that 2 and 2 make 5 I say that I cannot help thinking they make 4. She replies there may be some truth in what I say, but she knows they make 5. Thereupon I drop the discussion. It is of no consequence and I leave it there, knowing the fact. But X—— goes on with it, brings proofs, arguments and former sayings of her own. No one likes this. No one can stand admitting they are wrong ... and the Queen can't abide it. Consequently she won't give in, says X—— is unkind and there is trouble.

However volatile her temperament, common sense ultimately prevailed in most things – but not in all. One case where it did not was that of the Queen's Indian servant – the Munshi. Abdul Karim appeared on the scene in Jubilee Year, 1887. Victoria was taken with the young Indian and decided it would be nice to have an Indian waiter, to bring the Empire into the dining room. Soon he was teaching her Hindustani to add to her stock of German, French and Italian. Indian dishes began to appear at lunch and members of the Household complained about the smell of curry in Windsor Castle. Karim soon began assuming a position of some importance. Like Brown, he was asked to convey private messages and reprimands. The number of his 'wives' seemed to increase as relatives flocked to Britain. The Queen pressed ministers to advance him and his ever-growing 'family'. Rumours had it that he was shown confidential papers on India: he was certainly given some routine matters to deal with and in 1897 was created the Queen's Indian Secretary with a department under him. Photographs of him as a waiter were ordered destroyed. There were stories that he was a fraud.

Ponsonby's son, 'Fritz', was serving on the Viceroy of India's staff and the Queen ordered him to investigate the Munshi's background. He reported that his father was not a physician, as he had claimed, but a chemist in the gaol in Agra. The Queen dismissed these discoveries as 'colour prejudice'. In 1897, the House-hold refused to have him dine at their table while on holiday in France. Victoria went into a rage and swept everything off her desk. The Prime Minister, Lord Salisbury, was brought in to settle the dispute and he won the Queen over to the Household's view. The French, he reminded her, were such 'odd' people that they would not understand Karim's unique position. After the Queen's death the Munshi and his by now large department were sent packing by King Edward VII.

The court was described by some of its members as 'dull' and in some ways it was, certainly to younger members. Food played an important role for the 'portly elderly lady'. Victoria hated mutton, of which she had had so much as a child, and she disliked cold meat. She relished afternoon tea, a drink she preferred to coffee. The following is only one of four identical deliveries of pastries sent every week to Balmoral, Windsor or Osborne by Queen's Messenger from Buckingham Palace:

> one box of biscuits, one box of drop tablets, one box of pralines, sixteen chocolate sponges, twelve plain sponges, sixteen fondant biscuits, one box of wafers containing two or three dozen fancy shapes, one-and-a-half dozen flat finger biscuits, one sponge cake, one princess cake

and, for good measure, 'one rice cake'. Popular biographies still maintained that the Queen's appetite was 'never at any time a very large one' – except, that is, at mealtimes.

For breakfast Victoria normally had eggs on toast or porridge, dry toast and some fancy bread, although fish was always available. One of the Duke of Windsor's earliest memories was of his great-grandmother having breakfast outdoors, something she always enjoyed:

> What fascinated me most ... was her habit of taking breakfast in little revolving huts

mounted on turn-tables, so that they could be faced away from the wind. If the weather was fine, a small low-slung carriage, drawn by a pony led by a kilted attendant, would be at the front door. In this, with a relation or a lady-in-waiting walking alongside, she would ride slowly to one or another of the shelters, where her 'Kitmutgars' – Indian servants . . . would serve her breakfast, which always began with a bowl of steaming hot porridge. Later she would call for her Private Secretary and begin the business of the day.

Dinner, even in the somewhat relaxed atmosphere of Balmoral, was a more serious affair. Sometimes Victoria would dine only with her family, sometimes with the Household, and sometimes with guests. Occasionally there were Ladies' Dinners, which were greatly enjoyed: conversation was much easier. Frequently guests were invited, but this made no difference: dinner was limited to exactly thirty minutes and the service was so efficient that slow eaters, like Mr Gladstone, never had time to finish before the Queen rose. One suspects this did not particularly bother her. When Reginald Brett, who became Viscount Esher and was Secretary to the Office of Works from 1895 to 1902, dined at Windsor he

arrived at 8.45. . . . Shown into the corridor where we waited. . . . After a while at a sign from a page we moved to the southern end of the Corridor. . . . The Queen walked in supported by her youngest Indian – a handsome youth. She bowed to the company. . . . We went straight in to dinner. Previously we had been shown our places. . . . Gold plate, and beautiful Sevres. Indian servants behind the Queen. A Highlander to pour out the wine. The Queen ate everything. No 'courses'. Dinner is served straight on, and when you finish one dish you get the next, without a pause for breath. Everyone talked as at any other dinner, only in subdued tones. The Queen was in excellent humour. After dinner the Queen rose, and we stood back against the wall. She went out and we followed. Immediately to the left of the doorway in the Corridor was placed a chair, and in front . . . a little table. There the Queen seated herself. We stood in a circle at a considerable distance away from her. Coffee was brought and liqueurs. The Queen sipped her coffee while a page held the saucer on a small waiter.

Enormous quantities of wine were consumed not only by the royal table but by the Household and servants. Much was also used in cooking. One Liberal minister records that in 1885 between 80 and 120 bottles of wine a day were used at Windsor. The Queen herself was never a large drinker, but she did sometimes like a nightcap and enjoyed 'a small portion of Scotch whisky' bottled expressly for her. With her whisky she mixed Apollinaris, soda or Lithia water. Gladstone was astonished when he saw her add some whisky to her claret at Balmoral. Those with more orthodox tastes could enjoy wines from one of the greatest cellars in Europe, much of which had been laid down by her uncle, George IV.

The amount of food consumed in royal palaces staggers the twentieth-century imagination but one must remember the vast numbers of servants who had to be fed. When Gabriel Tschumi left Lausanne to follow his sister into the royal service and began work in the kitchens at Buckingham Palace he was amazed to learn that delivery vans would regularly unload 250 shoulders of lamb at a time. In addition there were pheasants, partridges, quail, plovers, woodcock and snipe from the royal estates and fruit and vegetables from the gardens at Windsor. In one year the Royal Household consumed, or at least had delivered, 1673 dozen dessert apples; 1500 dozen and twenty pecks of pears (a peck being a quarter of a bushel); 1250 pounds of grapes; 520 dozen peaches; 239 pineapples (averaging 8 pounds in weight); 1250 pounds of cherries; 400 melons; 2700 pounds of strawberries; 2000 pounds of currants; 1900 pounds of gooseberries and 220 dozen nectarines. At Windsor there were 250 varieties of apples and pears and 12 acres of potato beds, along with 5 miles of peas and 2220 yards of asparagus beds. All were grown by the Queen's 230 gardeners.

The food was delivered to the royal chef, who was helped by eighteen assistant chefs. The kitchen staff came to forty-five, not including the Indians who alone made the curries. Certain old customs were preserved at the royal table. For instance, plum pudding was always served before the roast beef as in George IV's time. At dinner, there was always a side table of cold meats, which few ever had the time or appetite to taste. Those who did were not popular with the servants, for this was just one of their many perks.

If the meals were enjoyable, though somewhat rushed, the 'stands' afterwards were neither. After dinner and until the Queen retired at eleven, guests were required to stand. For those suffering from corns or worse, these were sheer torture. Once, to secure a moment's respite, the Countess of Antrim, a Lady in Waiting, leaned against a chair for support. Unfortunately she chose the Queen's chair and got a tap from the royal fan as a warning. The rule that guests stood even when the Queen sat down (unless she invited them to sit) dated from the seventeenth century, but it was Victoria who invented the zoning of her drawing room. She occupied one zone, the Royal Family a second and 'others' a third. People came from their zone to hers only when invited to be presented. Everyone else was expected to stand in silence or to speak in subdued tones. The Royal Family's zone was in front of the fire on the hearthrug, absorbing what little heat was allowed in any of the Queen's residences. Occasionally people who had not been properly instructed in court etiquette violated the rule: when Sir Edward Bulwer-Lytton first came to Windsor he strolled round the room so casually that the Queen whispered in some agitation, 'If you don't do something to attract his attention, in another minute he'll be – on the rug!'

On the 'dull' nights when there were no guests there was some conversation while the Queen and her Ladies sewed or crocheted. Smoking was never allowed in the presence, but late in the evenings the gentlemen might escape to smoke in one of the special rooms set aside. The Queen liked to be read to by one of her daughters or Ladies. After Prince Albert's death she largely gave up the more intellectual works he had pressed on her; although she surprised one Archbishop of Canterbury by telling him that she was not only reading but enjoying his archdiocesan *Charges*, she was just as much at home with *The Female Jesuit*, a popular exposé of ritualist practices. Mr Gladstone was horrified when he discovered this. Mrs Oliphant, herself a novelist of some fame and a biographer of the Queen, claimed that 'the Queen cannot be called a connoisseur' of literature. Ironically, Victoria always listed Mrs Oliphant as one of her favourite writers.

Others included Sir Walter Scott, Jane Austen, Charles Kingsley, Dickens, Thackeray, the Brontës, Robert Louis Stevenson, Rudyard Kipling, H. Rider Haggard, Disraeli, Edna Lyall and, of course, Tennyson. She had read a little Trollope, but Albert found him lacking in romance. Wherever she went six huge cases of books followed her, and regular deliveries of books in English, French and German arrived from Mudie's lending library for herself and the Household.

On the nights which were not 'dull' there were amateur theatricals, singing or command performances by invited companies and orchestras. The Queen's excellent singing voice remained with her until her last years; Princess Beatrice, an accomplished pianist, frequently accompanied her mother. On one occasion in the early 1890s Victoria told Alick Yorke, a member of the Household, that they would sing a duet. She produced the score of Gilbert and Sullivan's *Patience* and selected the duet, 'Prithee, pretty maiden, will you marry me?' 'Now Mr Yorke,' she commanded, 'you begin', and in her turn she replied in her silvery voice, 'Gentle Sir, although to marry I'm inclined . . .'. Later she added, as she often did, 'You know, Mr Yorke, I was taught singing by Mendelssohn.'

Sometimes there was an impromptu dance as in 1891, when the Queen was seventy-two. She danced with her son-in-law, Prince Henry, and despite her rheumatic limbs – her 'tiresome arms and legs', she called them – she amazed everyone with her 'light airy steps in the old courtly fashion'. 'No limp or stick', Henry Ponsonby recorded, 'but every figure carefully and prettily danced.'

Amateur theatricals were an annual feature of court life. These productions were elaborate affairs and Victoria, who never lost her love of the theatre, relished supervising the rehearsals. Inappropriate lines were either altered or removed on her orders. In 1889 the Household put on a French play, *L'Homme Blasé*; the Queen decided it was not proper for Princess Beatrice to say the line, 'I had nothing to offer as dowry but my virtue', because her companion replied, 'Ah, little enough!' If someone forgot their lines their mistake was quickly covered by the applause of footmen stationed at the back of the audience for that purpose.

Professional companies were frequently commanded to appear. When George Alexander's company performed their play *Liberty Hall* at Balmoral, a stage was erected in the ballroom. After the court had assembled the Queen entered on the arm of the ubiquitous Munshi, preceded by the Lord Chamberlain walking backwards. She sat in an armchair at the front of the audience; beside her was a table on which stood a tumbler and a copy of the play. During the performance no one laughed or applauded until the Queen had done so; to the actors this gave a 'strange air of unreality to the performance'. Luckily Victoria could and frequently did laugh easily and vigorously.

After the performance the Queen received the actors in the drawing room, something that would never have been allowed in the more rigid courts of Vienna, Berlin or St Petersburg. Kinsey Peile recalled what happened to a fellow actor in George Alexander's company:

E.M. Robson had to make his bow just before me. He was in a terrible state of nerves. . . . When he advanced and stood in front of the Queen, she had just begun to speak . . .

when he, with a quick little bow, remembering what the equerry had told him, got out of the way ... and disappeared. The Queen burst out laughing, but she wasn't going to be denied her chat. She called after him: 'Come back, Mr. Robson, come back'.... By this time Robson had entirely effaced himself and ... Her Majesty said to an equerry: 'Bring him back.' She was still laughing heartily, so we waited until the official had chased him and placed him trembling before her. She complimented him on his acting and ... after this she dismissed him with a kind little nod and a smile.

After the Queen had retired for the evening, to carry on with her boxes, the company was invited to supper with the Royal Family and Household. Before leaving they were offered some lemonade along with the other guests. As a memento the Queen sent George Alexander a silver and enamel cigar box, while his wife was given a parasol with a crystal handle set with diamonds. Poor Mr Robson was delighted when he received a red enamel pen set with diamonds.

Music still ranked as one of Queen Victoria's greatest loves, but the 'musical evenings' which were highlights of court life could be difficult for the performers. As one pianist said of a concert given at Windsor, 'Queen Victoria inspired a feeling of awe and fright which seemed to communicate itself to everybody about her and paralyse those who did not perceive that behind that austere and stern expression there was lurking a very beautiful smile.' The same pianist, Landon Ronald, was asked to play at Balmoral where he found the atmosphere much more relaxed. The problem now was cold: which was worse, he asked himself, 'to die of fright or to die of cold'?

Occasionally an opera company or an orchestra would be commanded to perform. The Queen still loved the music of the Romantic period, especially Italian opera, but she also liked to keep up with new composers like Gounod, Leoncavallo or Wagner. She once invited Henry Wood and his Queen's Hall Orchestra to perform at Windsor. The evening was devoted mainly to Wagner and Tchaikovsky. The Queen chose the *Ride of the Valkyries* as an encore and afterwards Henry Wood was presented. 'Thank you very much, Mr Wood', were Victoria's first words. 'I knew Richard Wagner quite well, and I enjoyed the Good Friday Music so much. Unfortunately, I am too old to travel to Bayreuth now, but I do hope you will come again and play me some more *Parsifal*.' The Queen then looked at the young conductor rather closely and went on, 'Tell me, Mr Wood, are you *quite* English? Your appearance is – er – rather *un-English*.' Wood assured her that he was a Londoner of British stock. Victoria, suitably reassured, then presented him with a baton inscribed with a crown and the initials VRI.

The final element in the Queen's Household in the late 1880s and 1890s comprised the children of courtiers and her own expanding ranks of grandchildren. Whilst she still disliked babies, she now enjoyed the company of young children and no longer seemed to mind adolescents. Like many people she found her grandchildren easier to get on with than her children. She like to have grand-daughters, in particular Alice's children, to stay with her and she devoted considerable time to arranging suitable marriages for them. Victoria was particularly charming to young children. When the Hon. Miss Marie Adeane, a Maid of

Honour, returned to court as the Hon. Mrs Marie Mallet, a Lady in Waiting, she brought her twenty-three-month-old son, Victor, for the Queen to see:

> I curtsied and kissed the Queen's hand and H.M. kissed me and then I said to Victor 'What do you say? This is the Queen', he promptly kissed her hand and answered clearly 'Good morning Queen' – charmed at once by the Queen's beaming smile and great gentleness of voice and manner – then turning H.M. said 'I have got a present for him' and there on a little low table was a miniature landau drawn by a pair of grey horses, gaily painted and lined with blue satin – Victor's eyes grew large and murmuring 'Gee-gees' he ran to the table.... Victor whose eyes had been roving round the room suddenly pointed to a picture by Landseer of the Prince Consort's favourite greyhound ... and murmured 'Bootiful dog' – the Queen was enchanted.... After more talk ... the Queen touched her electric bell and the audience was at an end; then I said to Victor 'What do you say for the beautiful present'. 'Thank-oo kind Queen' was the immediate reply.

The sorrows and political worries that stand out in this period were but two strands in the total pattern of the Queen's life. Her work gave a meaning to her life; her family and their families, her Household, the joys of music and the theatre and the laughter of children made Victoria essentially a happy woman when, in 1887, the fiftieth anniversary of her accession arrived.

SEVEN

WHAT AN EMPIRE!
WHAT A QUEEN!

On Sunday, 20 June 1887 Queen Victoria sat in the gardens of Buckingham Palace with her Journal before her. 'The day has come', she wrote – the fiftieth anniversary of her accession. The day before Lord Salisbury had told her that the 'state of excitement and preparation in London was quite marvellous'. The only worry facing the government was how to cope with the large numbers of people who would pour into London. For the Household, however, the problems caused by visiting royalties were producing a sizeable headache.

Inevitably Victoria, with her passion for orderliness, had become involved. She visited Westminster Abbey on 11 May to make sure there was 'room for everybody and everything'. Then she went to see Lord Salisbury, and afterwards drove to Earls Court for a rare evening out, to see 'a very extraordinary and interesting sight – a performance of Buffalo Bill's "Wild West" '.

The Lord Chamberlain told the wife of the French Ambassador that 'the Queen was consulted *on every point*, as she knew more about etiquette and court ceremonies that anyone else. One day he had 42 telegrams from her.' Even by Victoria's standards this was an extraordinary number. One of the most troublesome visitors was Queen Kapiolani of Hawaii, who demanded and got a full sovereign's escort as well as an invitation to dinner at Buckingham Palace. Here, gossip had it, the 'Black Queen', as she was known in London, turned to Victoria and said, 'Your Majesty, I am a blood relative of yours.'

'How so?' was the Queen's astonished answer.

'Why', said Queen Kapiolani, 'my grandfather ate your Captain Cook.'

Parliament had voted £17,000 for the service of thanksgiving in Westminster Abbey on 21 June. In the Abbey itself workmen had provided accommodation for nine thousand guests by erecting tiers of stands. Space, however, was somewhat restricted, as Lady Monkswell discovered when she arrived:

We climbed into our places rather unceremoniously, several kind peers giving me a hand over the benches. Our 19 inches of seat was not really so very uncomfortable, tho' there were no backs. Just exactly in front of me sat Lady Burdett-Coutts in a splendid gown covered with silver braid & pearls: she was most kind to me & implored me whenever we stood up – as we did on the slightest provocation, we got so bored with waiting – to hold on to her shoulder.... Next to her was a very old & funny Lord Crewe, who was not at all satisfied with his seat & groaned & climbed about *upon his knees* across the benches. He was so extremely aged that I feel sure the effort would have killed him if Lady B-C. had not held his stick, while Bob [Lord Monkswell] caught hold of his cocked hat & very high feather.

The authorities feared an attack by Irish terrorists and Lady Monkswell found that 'to encourage us, just inside the Abbey was an array of pails of water & sand, hand grenades [i.e. fire extinguishers], rugs & all manner of things to put out fire'. Long before the day the Abbey had been closed and constables assigned to stand guard.

The procession to the Abbey was a magnificent affair but the thing which impressed many people, so the Archbishop of Canterbury wrote in his diary, was the crowd's 'perfect good behaviour throughout the streets'. He went on, 'The number of little children, and of babes in their mothers' arms in the multitudes, impressed greatly the ... Americans in general, as well as the foreigners.' Helen McKenny, the daughter of the minister of City Road Methodist Chapel, got up early for a good view:

> We had breakfast at 6 o'clock and were waiting on time trembling almost with vague fears of the great crush and possible danger and *dynamite*.... At last, after first seeing many brilliant equipages, the Royal guests began to appear. The Indian Princes, Persian, Siamese, Japanese Princes and the Queen of Hawaii, all very brilliant, their gold embroidered robes being studded with diamonds. After them followed a grand procession of Kings and Queens, the like of which I suppose has never been seen in the world, all come to pay their homage to our Sovereign Lady! ... Presently the Princesses passed.... Then the great sight. The nine Princes, sons, sons-in-law, and grandsons, riding before the Queen. The Crown Prince of Germany was greatly cheered and the Prince of Wales tremendously.... Then the Queen's carriage ... and the dear Queen, the centre of everyone's regard, looking very nice. The Princess of Wales sitting opposite to her looked more beautiful than ever.... What a day! What a City! What an Empire! What a Queen!

Inside the Abbey a complicated system of flags had been set up to alert the organist, Frederick Bridges, of the latest royal arrival so that he could begin the right march. The writer Augustus Hare was in the congregation and so near the Queen as she took her place that he could see 'every play of her expression':

> At last a blaze of trumpets announced the Queen's procession. It was headed by canons, the Bishop of London, the two Archbishops in most gorgeous copes.... Then – alone – serene – pale (not red) – beautifully dressed in something between a cap and bonnet of white lace and diamonds, but *most* becoming to her – perfectly self-possessed, full of the most gracious sweetness, lovely and lovable – the Queen! All the princesses in the choir, with the Queen of the Belgians at their head, curtseyed low as she took her place upon the throne, from which the long robe of state trailed so that it looked part of her dress.

Outside, the crowds had settled down to their picnic lunches. Ambulances raced back and forth carrying the injured to hospital, while placards for *The Echo* told of casualties; as always the costers in their yellow coats pushed their barrows with goods for sale.

The climax of the service came with the singing of the Te Deum. 'The Queen', noted Hare, 'did not shed a tear, and held a book all the time, but once sat down as if it was too much for her, and often looked round at the Crown Princess – who stood nearest.... with a look of "*What* this is to us!" Princess Beatrice ... cried the whole time.' For the Queen it must have been one of the most poignant moments of her life, a mixture of triumph and bitter-sweet memories:

> I sat *alone* (oh! without my beloved husband, for whom this would have been such a proud day!) where I sat forty-nine years ago and received the homage of the Princes and Peers.... The service was very well done and arranged. The *Te Deum*, by my darling Albert, sounded beautiful, and the anthem, by Dr Bridge, was fine, especially the way in which the National Anthem and dear Albert's Chorale were worked in.

When the last strains of Stainer's Amen had died away a great silence fell over the Abbey and a ray of sunshine shot through the stained glass to fall at the Queen's feet. The Prince of Wales came forward to pay homage, and after he had kissed her hand she kissed him twice most affectionately. Then came her other sons and sons-in-law, but when the Duke of Connaught came forward emotion overcame Victoria and, Hare wrote,

> she embraced him fervently, and then fearing that the last two princes might be hurt, she called them back, and kissed them too, and so all the princes who came in order.... Meantime the Crown Princess stood by the step of the throne ... and I think the most touching part of the whole was when she bent low to kiss her mother's hand and was folded in a close embrace, and so all the daughters and the grand-daughters.... Then the Queen went away, bowing all down the choir, and the flood of her youthful descendants ebbed after her.

To mark the Jubilee the Queen issued a proclamation granting a free pardon to all men who had deserted the Army if they reported back for service. There were, of course, official photographs, one of which became known as 'that grinning' photograph because it showed her smiling. 'Her daughters', wrote Reginald Brett, 'were indignant at its sale in the streets and wished her to have it stopped. All they could get her to say was: "Well, really I think it is *very like*. I have *no* illusions about my personal appearance."'

Sir Lyon Playfair, the Liberal MP and scientist, reflected on changes since 1837 and wrote to Henry Ponsonby:

> I tried to form an index of the progress of Civilisation during the Queen's reign.... The price of rags as indicating the demand for paper has always appeared to me the best index of progress and the following facts are striking: In 1837 each head of the population consumed $1\frac{1}{4}$ lb. of paper: in 1887 no less than 12 lbs. Measured by this index England is now at the head of all nations.... In 1837 each person ... spent 1/11 on books and newspapers annually; in 1887 ... 9s. In 1837 each person sent 9 letters ... in 1887 this had increased to 38.... Another index of well doing is the consumption of soap, because 'Cleanliness is next to Godliness'. This however has not increased so much as I could have wished: $1837 - 7\frac{3}{4}$ lbs. per head of soap; 1887 - 10 lbs.

Throughout the celebrations the Queen had shared with her eldest daughter a secret that was gnawing at her heart, the state of her husband's, the Prussian Crown Prince's, health. His presence, graciousness, bearing and civility had been universally praised, but comments were also made about his habitually speaking in a whisper. For some time the Queen had been involved in seeking medical help for the cancer of the throat that was slowly taking his life, but nothing seemed to work. When, on 9 March 1888, Fritz finally succeeded to the imperial throne it seemed that at last a liberal-minded ruler would guide Germany towards enlightened rule. But it was not to be and the new Emperor's health declined rapidly: he died on 15 June 1888, and with him died the hopes for a curb on Prussian militarism.

'I cannot, cannot realise the dreadful truth – the awful misfortune!' wrote Victoria. 'It is too, too dreadful! My poor dear Vicky. God help her! I went in directly and sent endless telegrams. . . . None of my own sons could be a greater loss. . . . My poor child's whole future gone, ruined, which they had prepared themselves for for nearly thirty years!' All the hopes which Victoria had held in 1858, all the advice poured forth in those endless letters since then, all the plans which Albert had so carefully laid were now in ruins, and her unpredictable eldest grandson ruled as Kaiser Wilhelm II. It was a tragedy the full extent of which would not be realised until August 1914. Victoria wrote to Fritz's mother a letter of consolation which contained an amazing admission: 'The tragedy for my poor child is too ghastly – much worse even than mine in 1861.' Time and tragedy had at last brought perspective to her own sorrow. Her real distress is seen in her incorrect signature: 'V.I.R.'

In 1890 the Queen celebrated her seventy-second birthday. Although rheumatism and overweight could make movement difficult, she still had amazing reserves of strength: vigilance was required by her Household to anticipate when the reserves would give out. A few weeks after her birthday she happily scaled a tall ladder to mount a horse 'which pranced along quite gaily'. On the other hand, the same year she visited the New Gallery in Regent Street to see an exhibition devoted to the Stuart period. The gallery director's wife, Mrs J. Comyns Carr, had little inkling how much work and discretion went into a brief royal visit:

Shortly before the Queen's arrival a gentleman-in-waiting . . . drove up in a four-wheeler with a bath-chair perched *perilously* on the roof. 'Can you arrange to have this concealed somewhere on the premises? Her Majesty would not like it if it were known that she needed a bath-chair – but, all the same, I know from experience that she's pretty sure to want it.'

The gallery was closed to the public but Mrs Carr found a good vantage point from which to watch the Queen as,

accompanied by my husband, she made her slow and critical tour. . . . Of course, I could not hear the conversation, but my husband told me afterwards of Her Majesty's very caustic remarks on the appearance and characteristics of ladies who had been notorious beauties at her early Courts. My erstwhile maid, who hitherto had had but little occasion to see royalty at close quarters, was evidently disappointed in the personal appearance of her sovereign. . ., 'So that's the Queen. Who'd have thought she'd look so much like an old apple-woman?' And, indeed, Her Majesty, who by this time had had recourse to the bath-chair ... did not present so imposing an appearance as I had seen her do on more formal occasions.

As with most of us, in the pursuit of pleasure the Queen appeared to have little difficulty in calling upon her reserves of strength. No alteration was allowed in her annual progress from Osborne to Windsor to the Riviera to Balmoral and back to Windsor. In 1891, for example, she stayed at her favourite hotel, the Grand, in Grasse. She came with her customary retinue of princesses, Ladies, secretaries, dressers, maids and Indians. She was registered as the Countess of Balmoral, a ruse which – although everyone knew perfectly well who she was – indicated a private visit and saved her from some of the social obligations she would otherwise have faced. As usual, daily reports were sent back to England by special reporters and *The Times* paid £50 a week for its reports. Much of the preparation for this visit was undertaken by Alice de Rothschild, an acquaintance of the Queen who had a villa in Grasse. The Queen respected her skills and began calling her 'The All-Powerful', a play on the German title for the Kaiser, the 'All-Highest'.

Most days saw the Queen venture forth in her open carriage or donkey-chair, utterly oblivious of the dust storms produced by the Mistral. One of these trips was recalled by Lady Battersea, who was staying in Grasse with her Rothschild cousins:

We had had a delicious morning, with air like crystal; part of it I spent on the mountain side, *panting* after H.M.'s donkey chair. Off goes the donkey at a good firm pace, led by the groom ... H.M. in a grey shawl, with a mushroom hat, a large white sunshade, sits comfortably installed ... then come the two Princesses close behind, walking like troopers; the two Scottish servants not quite so active; beside them romps the collie 'Roy,' Lady Churchill and I close up the procession, and the little pug belonging to Princess Beatrice toddles last of all. The Queen never stops, but goes steadily on.

In 1891 the Queen's visit to Grasse coincided with its colourful Battle of Flowers. Victoria watched it from her hotel balcony and 'enjoyed herself immensely', as Alice de Rothschild wrote:

we handed her the flowers ... for throwing at the passers by, and she was much amused when one of the small bouquets came flying up from below and hit her sunshade. The procession cheered as they passed and called out '*Vive la Reine*'.... One man on horseback held up a long box on the top of a pole. I proceeded to put a bouquet into it, upon which he remonstrated with me, saying: '*Je ne desire pas des fleurs, mais de la monnaie.*' This remark I had to repeat to Her Majesty who said: 'We must be better provided upon the return.' So a gold piece was given to the Queen, and when our friend came back we guided his long pole to Her Majesty's chair, though she said pathetically: 'I am afraid I can't reach him' but she managed to pop the money into the box.

The Queen, with her usual childlike enjoyment, insisted on throwing most of the flowers out at once and then, like Oliver Twist, she asked for more. Some of the men went down to the street, collected flowers and brought them back for a second throw. Lady Battersea laughed at this until hushed by Princess Louise.

The Queen, however, had heard her laughter and had enjoyed it: 'I like to hear her laugh.'

In addition to the drives there were walks in Alice de Rothschild's gardens, which were put at the Queen's disposal. Her respect for the Queen's privacy went beyond the call of duty; her cousin wrote that Alice's

> gymnastics when she chances to meet Her Majesty are really very funny. Yesterday both she and Amy, in trying to escape from the Queen ... ran as hard as they could and finally threw themselves flat down on the ground, whilst the other day Alice walked backwards, through her little wood for some yards, until the Queen was able to pass her.

Along with lessons in Hindustani from the oleaginous Munshi there were talks with Lady Battersea on comparisons between Hebrew and Hindustani. Visiting royalty had to be entertained, including the deposed Maharajah of the Punjab, Duleep Singh, who, in spite of illness, came over from Nice. The Queen had always taken a keen interest in this extraordinary man, who was the last Maharajah of the Punjab. He had been sent to England as a boy when the Punjab was annexed to the British Raj in 1849, and brought with him the famous Koh-i-noor diamond as a gift for the Queen. He remained in England and became a convert to Christianity. The Queen stood godmother to his first son and therefore, as was always the case with godchildren, the child was named after her – Victor; Albert was thrown in for good measure. Now Duleep Singh had come to apologise for his 'disloyal conduct' during recent years when he rejected Christianity and developed a hankering for an independent Punjab. The Queen forgave the sobbing Maharajah in one of her most characteristic utterances: 'I forget the past; it does not exist.'

Wherever she was, the boxes had to be attended to, especially as the Queen insisted on going abroad even though Parliament was still sitting. Nothing must interfere with her 'royal progress'. When, in the following year, the government asked if she might delay her departure for France long enough to confer some knighthoods Ponsonby wrote, 'I am afraid that the Knights Expectant will have to remain expectant for H.M. declines to knight them before she goes abroad.'

On 14 January 1892 the Queen suffered another family tragedy when the feckless Duke of Clarence, the Prince of Wales's heir, died from pneumonia. If his death would not prove a great loss to the monarchy, it still struck the Queen hard and she recorded her feelings of 'grief, horror, and distress' at the loss of a favourite grandson. Victoria gave over Windsor to the parents for the funeral and went to Osborne. Windsor, of course, had its disadvantages and in the midst of the greatest grief mankind can always find comic relief, as Sir Arthur Ellis, Equerry to the Prince of Wales, wrote to Ponsonby:

> We are fairly comfortable in this most conveniently built house – and most of our time is spent in a sort of game of 'post' or hide-and-seek, looking for and searching for each other – and being hunted by servants who get lost. We all admire various little economical thrifty dodges here. In the W.C.s – NEWSPAPER squares – there was one idea of sending them to Cowell [Master of the Household] in an unpaid envelope.... And with

a cup of tea – three lumps of loose sugar on the tray!! It is admirable – and we now see why you are so rich.

The nation's grief was widespread, and the personal grief of the Prince of Wales added another bond to the closeness that was growing between himself and his mother. In 1890 she had noted his birthday in her Journal: 'May God bless and preserve him! He has always been a very good affectionate son to me.' The barometric pressure of the 1860s had settled at last. Increasingly the Prince was consulted in political matters; although the Queen kept daily business very much in her own hands, the Prince began to play an important role as go-between in relations with ministers, especially Liberal ministers.

The family's grief was the greater because the Duke of Clarence had only recently become engaged to marry his cousin, Princess Mary of Teck (later Queen Mary). Within a short time, however, Clarence's younger brother, the Duke of York, asked Princess Mary to be his wife and they were married on 6 July 1893, not quite eighteen months after Clarence's death. On the morning of the wedding Victoria left Buckingham Palace for the Chapel Royal, in St James's Palace. With her was the bride's mother, the Duchess of Teck. No one had planned on her procession going to the Chapel by a shorter route than that taken by the rest of the Royal Family. As a result, she arrived there first, whereas protocol demands that the sovereign always arrives last. Victoria was delighted while everyone else was thrown into confusion. The Duchess took matters into her own hands and

> suggested that she should proceed to her place, and that the Queen should remain in a room on the left prepared for her use. Scarcely had Her Royal Highness advanced a few steps ... than Miss Thesiger, who was in attendance upon the Duchess, felt a pull at her dress, and at the same time heard a voice saying, 'I am going first.' Looking round, she saw Her Majesty ... and in this informal way the Queen entered the Chapel.

The Archbishop of Canterbury was entranced:

> I could scarcely believe my eyes when the Queen entered.... There she was, alone and began to walk up alone.... On she came, looking most pleasant, slightly amused, bowing most gracefully to either side as she came, her black silk almost covered with wonderful lace and a little crown with chains of diamonds on her head, walking lame and with a tallish stick. She looked Empire, gracious Empire ... and sat down ... looking so gallant and commanding, and kind too. Not a soul walked before her backwards or any other way. I wouldn't have missed the sight of her for the world.

Within a few minutes the Household arrived, breathless but too late. The Queen beamed with pleasure: for once she would see the show. The lace she wore was the wedding lace she had first worn in that same Chapel fifty-three years before. She never wore it again in public.

The sermon preached by Archbishop Benson was a tribute to the Queen's achievement, itself a legacy to the new couple:

> This is an age and this a people which, in spite of many outward changes, still, in its

heart of hearts, looks to the highest to do the common duties of all better than all. They desire to have before their eyes and to be sure in their hearts, that, amid all the splendour and care of a kingdom, there is about its central hearth all mutual honour and reverence, all sweetness of domestic life, the faith and worship of God, the quiet spirit which is in the sight of God of great price.... To Your union a glorious Empire and a strenuous, laborious People look to perpetuate among them the tradition that translates principle into life; that lets no responsibility seek the most desired ends by any but the purest ways. This is the tradition that can alone make society ... a blessing to itself.

The Queen thought it an 'excellent address' and was delighted with the new couple.

In the years following the celebrations of 1887 the position of the monarchy was greater than it had ever been. Victoria's personal popularity, too, now stood higher than ever before, even though she did nothing to court it. One of her greatest strengths in the last two decades of her reign derived from the fact that she had reigned so long. Of her last three Prime Ministers, Gladstone, Rosebery and Salisbury, only Gladstone had been involved in politics longer: he had first been returned to Parliament in 1832. Rosebery's mother had been a bridesmaid at the Queen's wedding, and Lord Salisbury did not enter the Commons until the Queen had reigned sixteen years. Henry Campbell-Bannerman, Secretary of State for War between 1892 and 1895, once told Ponsonby's son, Fritz, of a discussion he had with the Queen. He was trying to persuade her to withdraw her opposition to a proposal. She told him, 'I remember Lord Melbourne using the same arguments many years ago, but it was not true then and it is not true now.' Campbell-Bannerman added, 'I felt like a little boy talking to his grandmother.'

Lord Rosebery said that the Queen was 'an old lady with all the foibles and strengths of one'. This is true as far as it goes. Like many old ladies – and quite a few old gentlemen for that matter – she could be remarkably stubborn. She was used to having her own way and did not like being crossed. Sometimes she could be silly, as over the Munshi or when she once asked the Duke of York to change his name from George to Albert so that he could succeed his father as King Albert II: he refused. While this stubbornness only increased with age, its roots lay in one of her most positive characteristics. She had once told Sir Howard Elphinstone that '*most* of *evil* done in the world arises from the wish to do as others do and *not* to be laughed at'. Victoria had always possessed a singleness of purpose almost unique in its directness. Although she was never pompous, she found it simply impossible to believe that she could be wrong in a matter of principle. This independence gave her a strong position as a constitutional sovereign who kept her eye on the end of government – the good of her peoples – not on the political jobbing necessary to achieve that end. It was in this sense that she told her Lady in Waiting Marie Mallet that 'she has always *disliked* politics and does not consider them a woman's province but that the Prince Consort forced her to take an interest in them even to her disgust, and that since he died she has tried to keep up the interest for his sake'.

Until the very end of her life the Queen retained her remarkable eye for detail. Take, for example, an undated letter written by the Queen probably in 1894. As was normal with her 'business letters' it lacked addressee and signature, but her message is clear enough:

> There is a terrible mistake in the new coinage. The 'Imperatrix' is left out while Defender of the Faith is left.
> It *must* be corrected. —— [word illegible] for *all* State Proclamations Military & Civil the Queen is *Empress*, & all this is a shocking mistake. In all Treaties, in *all* Proclamations ... & in the Queen's '*style*' – She is always Empress of India. This must be put *right*....

The Chancellor of the Exchequer was brought in, and he then wrote to the Queen in January 1895 that 'On the *obverse* the addition of the title *Ind. Imp.* has been made.'

With her penchant for facts and her dislike of waffle, Victoria retained her ability to collect information. There were, as always, state papers, memoranda from her staff, Foreign Office despatches both going out and coming in, the letters from the Prime Minister after each Cabinet, and the nightly reports of debates in the Lords and Commons. Sir William Harcourt, when Leader of the House, was responsible for these reports. He asked the Queen if she wanted 'a general report of the evening', and if she liked gossip. She replied, 'Yes, anything there is to tell me.' She regularly invited ministers to stay with her to pick their brains. When Henry Ponsonby told Harcourt in 1894 that a carriage would meet him at West Cowes, he added, 'You are going to be invited to dine and sleep and I trust you will explain all doubtful questions which are put to me and on which I have no opinion.' Some ministers, like the Tory Lord Privy Seal, Lord Cross, were so delighted to be invited that they rattled away about Cabinet secrets even when not in their cups.

On foreign relations the Queen's expertise was based to a considerable degree on her own private network of correspondents. In 1892 Lord Rowton, who had been Disraeli's private secretary, described to Reginald Brett how the Queen

> selected all over Europe the most intelligent member of the royal family of every Court, and upon any question, domestic or foreign ... she obtains by letter an opinion.... So that the Queen really gets the best opinion from the most experienced foreign authorities who are 'in the know,' to use a slang term.

The papers of her ambassadors, like those of Sir Edmund Monson (Ambassador in Paris from 1896) and now in the Bodleian Library, Oxford, show the extent to which she gathered information from ambassadors as well as gave advice.

The climate of politics at home was changing in the late 1880s and the 1890s; radicalism was gaining strength within the Liberal Party and the Lords' rejection of various radical measures led to cries for its reform and even abolition. While the Queen was not opposed to reform she was totally opposed to any major change in the Constitution, which might leave the throne exposed as the only check on the Commons. The House of Lords was a 'necessity in a free country', for it held an 'independent body of men who have no need of being afraid of the clamour of a noisy set of constituents who represent no party but only a temporary excitement'. She put this more succinctly when she heard of a demand for the Bishop of Oxford to give up his episcopal palace at Cuddesdon: 'If you begin giving up they will go on grabbing till they get everything.' In 1894 she asked the Liberal Prime Minister, Lord Rosebery, and his Cabinet to bear in mind that

> 57 years ago the Constitution was delivered into her keeping and that right or wrong she has her views as to the fulfilment of that trust. She cannot but think Lord Rosebery will feel that *his* position is not the only difficult one in these democratic days.

After the general election of 1892 had unseated Lord Salisbury's Conservative government, the Queen had no choice but to call Mr Gladstone to form a new government. The announcement in the Court Circular for 15 August 1892 betrayed her own feelings: 'Lord Salisbury tendered his resignation, which Her Majesty accepted with great regret.' Liberals, like Sir William Harcourt's son Lewis, (usually known as Loulou) asked, 'I wonder if tomorrow there will be a statement that "Her Majesty received Mr Gladstone with great regret"?' She was more fulsome in a letter to Lord Lansdowne, Viceroy of India:

> The Queen-Empress can hardly trust herself to say what she feels and thinks on the subject. Apart from the pain of parting from some great personal friends and people whom she can trust and rely on, the danger to the country, to Europe, to her vast Empire, which is involved in having all these great interests entrusted to the shaking hand of an old, wild, and incomprehensible man of $82\frac{1}{2}$, is very great! It is a terrible trial, but, thank God, the country is sound, and it cannot last.

On the day of the Court Circular's announcement Mr Gladstone arrived at Osborne to become Prime Minister for the fourth time. The Queen might have reflected on one of the mottoes inscribed at the Mausoleum at Frogmore, taken from Isaiah 32, 8: 'The liberal deviseth liberal things and by liberal things shall he stand.' The prophet might have added that what stood might also fall. The Queen noted that Gladstone was 'greatly altered and changed, not only much aged and walking rather bent with a stick, but altogether'. Of course, he could have said the same about her. She found 'his face shrunk, deadly pale with a weird look in his eyes, a feeble expression about the mouth, and the voice altered'. Gladstone was so nervous that he forgot to kiss hands; the Queen did not remind him. He stayed for dinner as one of the other guests, Ponsonby's daughter, recalled:

> We all waited in the drawing-room till, at 8.30, she swept in. He was most obviously nervous, fumbling over his stick. Not so the Queen ... with the utmost '*savoir faire*' and '*grace d'état*' she walked in, shook hands, and added with a smile: 'You and I, Mr Gladstone, are lamer than we used to be!' Then we all followed her into the dining-room....
>
> I sat next to Mr Gladstone and he talked to me loudly and eagerly all the time, though guests usually spoke in hushed tones ... I glanced nervously at the Queen's piercing eye, but she said nothing. He went on openly to a glorification of the policy he advocated for Ireland. I looked at the lovely Belfast linen table-cloth, in which were woven the Rose, Thistle and Shamrock, with the motto '*Quis separabit?*' just in front of us.

After dinner the Queen came straight over to Ponsonby's daughter and asked, 'What did Mr Gladstone talk to you about?'

'Home Rule, ma'am!'

She shrugged her shoulders and said: 'I know! He always will!'

When the Queen saw Gladstone she did not discuss 'politics' but 'the arrangements for the government'. This shows both her weakness and her strength. Because she felt the Home Rule agitation unnecessary and Home Rule dangerous, she simply refused to discuss it. Etiquette forbade Gladstone's introducing a topic, so the issue that dominated politics was not mentioned. This meant that she could only react once policy had been decided, not advise as it was being formulated. In discussing the 'arrangements', that is the members of the new government, the Queen was able to influence politics, especially as here she and Gladstone agreed. One of the leading radical MPs in the Liberal Party was the notorious journalist Henry Labouchere. It was known in society that before he married his wife Labouchere had hired her from her husband for £1500 a year. The Queen was adamantly opposed to receiving him as a minister because of his immoral life as well as his attacks on her and the monarchy. Gladstone was happy to accede to her wishes as the reason why he could not have Labouchere in his administration – something he did not want anyway; the Queen could then take the blame for his exclusion from office.

Labouchere now prattled on to his fellow radicals about being a martyr and was determined on revenge. He told Loulou Harcourt,

I mean to go for the Queen as the cause of my exclusion and challenge the old man [Gladstone] . . . they can't prove I ever said anything personally against the Royal Family except that the Heir apparent [the Prince of Wales] was the associate of swindlers and prostitutes. . . . I shall talk about a voracious old woman who has been rattling the money box ever since she came to the throne.

The Queen also used her influence and that of the Prince of Wales to make sure that Lord Rosebery would be the new Foreign Secretary. Again Gladstone agreed. The Queen's desire was to have someone who would be a steadying influence, especially where she most distrusted the Liberals, in foreign relations. Rosebery would also emerge as the obvious successor to Gladstone, which would make the Queen's task easier if she should have to make such a choice on the happy day of Gladstone's final departure. On 18 August the new government came to Osborne to receive their seals of office. The ferry carrying the new Liberal government passed the ferry carrying the former Conservative ministers away; the Liberals took off their hats and waved.

After a lunch which both Harcourt and Rosebery found 'bad and very insufficient' the Privy Councillors proceeded into the drawing room, where the Queen was sitting at a round table with her son the Duke of Connaught on one side and her son-in-law the Marquess of Lorne, himself a former Liberal MP, on the other. When all were assembled it was discovered that the Lord President and the Clerk of the Council were missing, so for five minutes 'the line of new ministers stood facing the Queen in absolute silence'. Harcourt 'never saw people so uncomfortable'. Then the new Privy Councillors were shown in to kneel round the table to take the oath; afterwards each minister came up to receive his seal and to kiss hands. Not a word was spoken. Three ministers were granted audiences, and when Harcourt went in he said, 'I hope, Madam, you will feel that our desire is to make matters as easy and as little troublesome to you as we can possibly do.' The Queen bowed, said nothing and then asked, 'How is Lady Harcourt? Terrible weather, is it not? and so oppressive.'

The audience was over. On the way back to Portsmouth the government ferry had to go through a great thunderstorm which Loulou Harcourt recorded as 'ominous', as it proved to be: Gladstone's ministry collapsed eighteen and a half months later after the Lords had thrown out his second Home Rule bill.

In 1893 the wife of the departing French Ambassador, Madame Waddington, had a final audience of the Queen at Buckingham Palace. Presumably she did not know that only a few days before the Queen had had a furious exchange with Gladstone. She was outraged, as she had often been in the past with Gladstone, because she felt he had not kept her adequately and fully informed of government plans. In this case they centred on a government bill which she saw as a precursor to disestablishing the Church. Perhaps Madame Waddington was mischievous or foolhardy, as her letter to a sister shows:

> I found myself in the Royal presence. It was a small, ordinary room, rather like a sort of waiting-room, no traces of habitation, nothing pretty or interesting. The Queen was standing, very simply dressed in black (her travelling dress she said, she was starting at once for Windsor) before a writing-table ... covered with books and papers. She was most kind, made me sit down on the sofa next to her, and said she was afraid she had kept me waiting, but that she had been kept by a visit from Mr Gladstone – she then paused a moment, so I made a perfectly banal remark, 'what a wonderful man, such an extraordinary intelligence,' to which she replied, 'He is very deaf.'

On 2 March 1894 Gladstone resigned as Prime Minister because of age and because the rest of the Cabinet did not want to tackle the House of Lords on the issue of their 'reform'. His relations with the Queen had gone from bad to worse. He told his wife about their meetings: 'A painful sense of unreality pervades these conversations and the public announcement of our audience hoodwinks the public.' Even so he and Mrs Gladstone were invited to stay at Windsor. The day after his resignation he had his final audience. 'When I came into the room and came near to take the seat she has now for some time courteously commanded' he wrote:

> I did think she was going to 'break down.' If I was not mistaken, at any rate she rallied herself, as I thought by a prompt effort, and remained ... at her ease. Then came the conversation, which may be called neither here nor there.... There was the question of eyes and ears, of German *versus* English oculists, she believing in the German as decidedly superior. Some reference to my wife, with whom she had had an interview and had ended it affectionately, – and various nothings.... I saw no sign of embarrassment or preoccupation.

Victoria did not offer him a peerage because she knew he would reject it, and she adamantly refused to offer him the Garter as this was a purely personal honour. Gladstone saved his anger for Ponsonby, a sympathetic listener who had tried to pour some secretarial oil on to troubled waters. The only gift the Queen, normally a generous woman, sent the man who had served her four times as Prime Minister was a print of herself. Two years later he still remembered the snub: 'For I cannot reckon as anything what appeared to be a twopenny-halfpenny scrap, photographic or other, sent . . . by the hand of a footman.'

Such behaviour was uncharacteristic. On a personal level the Queen was extremely kind to those who served her, even when she violently disliked their views. In 1895 Henry Asquith was still in the Queen's disfavour for his support of Gladstone in the disestablishment wrangle. Nevertheless when his wife, Margot, lost their first child Victoria wrote:

> The Queen, after hearing . . . the very distressing details of Mrs. Asquith's confinement, cannot refrain from writing Mr. Asquith a line to express her deep sympathy for him, for he must have suffered terribly.
> The sight of such suffering is dreadful to witness.
> The Queen hopes Mrs. Asquith continues to improve. The loss of the poor child is a great aggravation of their trouble.

The Queen did not ask for Gladstone's 'advice' about his successor and chose Lord Rosebery, as she had intended back in 1892, hoping that he would 'act as a check & drag' should radical proposals about the Church or the Lords re-emerge. Victoria had a somewhat easier time with him, although she did refuse to sanction the word 'disestablishment' in the Queen's Speech. She also warned him about a weakness which could – and would – harm his career:

> What she would however wish to say, speaking *very* openly to him, is that in his Speeches *out* of Parliament he should take a more serious tone, & be, if she may say so, less *jocular*; which is hardly befitting a Prime Minister. Ld. Rosebery is so clever that he may be carried away by a sense of humour, which is a little dangerous. It is as a sincere well wisher of Lord Rosebery that the Queen says this.

Even with her advice, Lord Rosebery's administration was short-lived and he submitted his resignation on 22 June 1895.

Six months before, on the morning of 6 January 1895, the Queen received a much more devastating blow when Sir Henry Ponsonby suffered a stroke that left him paralysed. For twenty-five years he had held one of the most important, if unrecognised, positions in the kingdom as intermediary, censor, secretary, adviser and confidant not only to the Queen but to her ministers, Household and family. He lingered until 21 November, when the Queen noted: 'It is indeed a merciful release, though, thank God! there never has been any real suffering. His loss is very great to me. . . . He had always carried out his work so admirably, was so even-tempered, kind, and dependable.'

Ponsonby had served the Queen with the utmost discretion. He had acted as a buffer to soften the impact of others on his mistress and of his mistress on others.

As often as not, Ponsonby's moderating influence worked, but his advice was not always followed. He admitted this in a characteristic letter written in 1892 to J. S. Sandars, Private Secretary to Arthur Balfour, at the time First Lord of the Treasury. At stake was the First Lord's query about a £3 expenditure:

> No I am sorry to say there is no change in the bad custom of giving £3 to living triplets. The parents must be poor – as it is a charity and not a reward for propagation. And the question arose about a Welch Minister. I said, you would not call a Minister, a man in indigent circumstances. But when H.M. heard he had 100 a yr. and 9 children She gave the £3.

Ponsonby's second son, Frederick, known as Fritz, now became Assistant Private Secretary while Sir Arthur Bigge succeeded as Private Secretary. Both men would live to serve the Queen's son and grandson. The Queen's admiration for Sir Henry was real, as was her sympathy for his widow, to whom she wrote one of her most beautiful letters of consolation. She said simply, 'I miss him terribly.' She also gave Lady Ponsonby a comfortable pension: Fritz Ponsonby later told his brother, 'Queen allowed Ma a thou to live on.'

In the month after Ponsonby's death Prince Henry of Battenberg, known as Liko in the family, volunteered for an expedition to the Gold Coast of West Africa to put down a local rebellion by the Ashanti tribesmen. In the ten years since his marriage to Princess Beatrice, Prince Henry had become indispensable to the Queen. Victoria enjoyed having a man near her and his good humour made him pleasant company: for his part, however, the Prince was increasingly bored with his role as courtier and aide-de-camp. Once in Africa he was made Military Secretary to the commanding officer. Although the expedition was successful and bloodless, soldiers knew that the west coast of Africa was not called 'the white man's grave' for nothing; malaria was rife and the Prince was stationed in the very centre of the jungle.

On 10 January a telegram arrived at Osborne: Prince Henry had succumbed to the fever and was being sent to a hospital ship. On the 14th Victoria and Beatrice heard that he was taking food and improving. Then on the 22nd another telegram arrived at Osborne which led the Queen to write in her Journal:

> A terrible blow has fallen on us all, especially on my poor darling Beatrice. Our dearly loved Liko has been taken from us. Can I write it? ... What will become of my poor child? All she said in a trembling voice, apparently quite stunned, was, 'The life is gone out of me'.... My heart aches for my darling child ... God in His mercy help us! It seems as though the years '61 and '62 had returned.... My grief is great, and I am quite unnerved.

On his deathbed the Prince told the chaplain to 'tell the Princess from me that I came here not to win glory, but from a sense of duty ... serving the Queen and the country of my adoption'. His death was a real tragedy for the Queen. She wrote, 'The sunbeam in our Home is *gone*.' Prince Henry was interred in a chapel at Whippingham parish church, in whose churchyard Sir Henry Ponsonby had been buried only two months before. Etiquette had changed so much since Prince Albert's death that both the Queen and Princess Beatrice could follow the coffin in their carriage. To commemorate Prince Henry and his devotion to duty, on 21 April the Queen instituted the Royal Victorian Order to reward 'personal service to the Sovereign and her successors'; it remains in the personal gift of the sovereign. It is ironic that, now she was a widow, Princess Beatrice spent the longest time she ever had away from her mother when she went alone to the South of France to recuperate.

That same year, 1895, the general election had brought back the Conservatives under Lord Salisbury. Once again the Queen had a government which she fully trusted, and in this situation her task was to encourage her ministers when necessary. In 1896 the government brought in a far-reaching bill to reorganise state education in England and Wales. It was a subject in which Queen Victoria took a deep interest, especially as the bill would help working-class children. The Liberals, to pay off their debt to the Nonconformists who opposed the extra aid to Church schools, fiercely obstructed the bill. On 19 June the Cabinet decided to drop the bill and Salisbury telegraphed the news to the Queen at Balmoral, confirming the decision with another telegram the next day. Victoria, who had encouraged the government to carry through the complicated measure despite the opposition, now acted to check what she thought was a panic decision. She reminded her government of other considerations. It was bad for a strong government, newly elected, to give in so readily to parliamentary obstruction on an important measure. She fired off two telegrams to London: one was sent at 5.30 p.m. and arrived at 7 p.m., although with some faulty deciphering:

I must earnestly beg you to call another Cabinet & lay before it my views before any announcement is made as to the decision regarding the bill. I deprecate in the highest degree a step which I amider [consider] may be disastrous to the Govt. especially when at this time with so many foreign difficulties I feel more than ever the necessity of preserving a bold front.

As commanded, the Cabinet met again on 22 June, but again decided to drop the bill. Salisbury told the Queen that the opposition's 'unexampled obstruction' combined with the 'exceptionally complicated' nature of the subject left them with no other choice. The Queen was 'very much grieved at the way in which the Government have dropped it and cannot make out why they make such an open profession of weakness'.

While the government in London set about making good the damage brought about by their dropping the education bill, the Queen at Balmoral was doing some diplomatic work. In late September the Tsar and Tsarina of Russia arrived for a private visit. The Queen was delighted to see one of her favourite granddaughters, Alicky, Princess Alice's daughter. She was also happy to meet their first baby: the passing years had brought Victoria a more favourable view of infancy. Victoria took the opportunity to have a political talk with the Tsar for, no matter how much she personally liked Nicholas II, her long-standing hatred of Russia was as strong as ever. Personal feelings were put aside when it came to questions of

Indian security and Russian aims in the Ottoman Empire. After leaving Britain the Tsar was to visit Paris, and Victoria asked him to have a private word with French officials to see if they could lessen anti-British effusions in the French press.

Before the Tsar's departure, the Queen sent for Lord Salisbury to join them. He was only the latest minister to dread going to Balmoral because of the cold, and his secretary wrote to Arthur Bigge:

> I am sure you will forgive my mentioning it; but it is most necessary that Lord Salisbury's room should be very warm: a minimum temperature of 60 is the climate to which he is habituated and a cold room is really dangerous to him. I am ashamed to bother you about so trifling a matter; but it is not so trifling as it seems.

An added difficulty for the Prime Minister was his increasing deafness. The Household was amused when the Prime Minister sat in one room while the Queen sat in another, shouting to each other across the corridor: their every word was overheard.

During the visit the Duke and Duchess of York joined the party and brought their two sons, Edward, known to the family as David (the future Edward VIII), and Albert (the future George VI). 'David', the Queen wrote, 'is a most attractive little boy, and so forward and clever. He always tries at luncheon time to pull me up out of my chair, saying "Get up, Gangan," and then to one of the Indian servants, "Man pull it," which makes us laugh very much.'

Despite all the warmth and love with which her family and Household surrounded her, the Queen's spirits had suffered severely since the Jubilee. She told Sir William Harcourt on 2 October 1896, 'Alas! within the last nine years and a half the Queen has had great sorrows. She has lost three dearly beloved sons-in-law and a dear grandson, all in the prime of life – besides very many kind devoted friends who were with her in '87.' Her infirmities were growing. The year before, the Empress Frederick told Lord Wolseley that her mother 'cannot move her legs now, and can only read through a *magnifying* glass, and cannot recognise any one across the table'.

Yet 1897 would bring Victoria a second Jubilee and with it a wave of affection and respect from the whole Empire that would help her to face the final years of her life in a golden and prolonged sunset. Her own spirits, of course, were still her greatest source of strength. It was not long after Prince Henry's death that the following exchange with the evangelical Lady Errol is supposed to have taken place during one of Victoria's afternoon drives. The Queen was 'very silent' and Lady Errol thought it time to make a little conversation. So she said, 'Oh, Your Majesty, think of when we shall see our dear ones again in Heaven!'

'Yes,' said the Queen.

Undeterred, Lady Errol added, 'We will all meet in Abraham's bosom.'

'I will *not* meet Abraham,' said Queen Victoria.

EIGHT

A SOLDIER'S DAUGHTER

'It was like a triumphal entry', the Queen wrote about her arrival in London for the Diamond Jubilee celebrations of 1897. The crowds formed 'one mass of beaming faces' and the cheering never stopped from Paddington to Buckingham Palace. The day she added, was 'very fine and very hot'.

Preparations for the celebrations had begun the year before. The first question was what to call them: never before had a British sovereign reigned for sixty years. The Home Secretary, recalling the Jubilee of 1887 and his schoolboy Latin, toyed with 'Jubilissimee' but admitted, it 'would not, I think, take on'. He then suggested 'The Queen's Year' or 'The Queen's Commemoration'. Victoria ended the quandary by choosing her own title – the 'Diamond Jubilee'. She also ordered that, unlike 1887, no foreign monarchs should be invited, to simplify the arrangements. She was supported by the Colonial Secretary, Joseph Chamberlain, anxious to promote imperial unity. He suggested inviting the prime ministers from the larger colonies, an idea which the Queen accepted. The Diamond Jubilee would be a festival of Empire.

The other question was about the nature of the celebration. It was proposed to have a Thanksgiving Service in St Paul's Cathedral. However, the state of the Queen's health made this impossible: she could not walk up the aisle. Letters flew between the Queen and Downing Street. The Prime Minister's secretary wrote that one idea – driving the Queen's carriage into the Cathedral itself – 'might shock the people'. Perhaps her horses could be unhitched and her carriage 'drawn in procession up the aisle'? It would, he said, be a 'magnificent spectacle, and would afford the Queen the minimum of discomfort'. Luckily this absurd plan was dropped. All agreed that the celebrations would centre not on the service but on a grand procession through London with a Te Deum at the cathedral steps, where the Queen's carriage would halt. The Queen insisted on a short service – 'about a quarter of an hour – or at all events well under 20 minutes' – for she dreaded sitting in a carriage surrounded by mounted men for longer than that.

As soon as one problem was solved, another arose. How reliable was the elderly Archbishop of Canterbury, Frederick Temple? Then there were the horses. Could they be depended on to stand still for twenty minutes? Of the eight which would pull the carriage, two were difficult. One would simply lie down out of laziness; the remedy here was found to be the discreet application of a pin at the right moment. The other horse would not stand still unless bribed with sugar; the answer here was even simpler.

Once the plans for the Diamond Jubilee were released, the public's enthusiasm rose. One enterprising firm pulled down an entire shop in St Paul's Churchyard to erect temporary seating. *Punch* showed a bewildered colonial visitor asking if the forms being set up were to enable contractors to pull down St Paul's itself. Many were worried about the Queen's health, and one well-wisher wrote to her suggesting that a 'puppet Queen should be in the carriage for the Jubilee Procession to save the Queen from fatigue'.

The actual anniversary of the accession, 20 June, fell on a Sunday, and on the Queen's command Thanksgiving Services were held throughout the Empire. Victoria had travelled down from Balmoral a few days before, and as the royal train came south overnight crowds gathered in towns and fields along the route. As the carriage carrying the sleeping Queen passed, men removed their hats in silent tribute. On the Sunday Victoria attended St George's Chapel, Windsor, and confided in her Journal, 'How well I remember this day sixty years ago, when I was called from my bed by dear Mamma to receive the news of my accession!'

On the following day the Queen left Windsor for London. That night she attended a banquet, and on the urging of the Princess of Wales came out of mourning for the first time since 1861. She wore a magnificent white dress 'of which the whole front was embroidered in gold ... specially worked in India, diamonds in my cap, and a diamond necklace, etc'. Twenty-four extra chefs had been imported from France to help out. The menu, which ran to fourteen courses, featured *Rosettes de saumon au rubis*, a 'salmon dish served cold with claret jelly'.

As the Queen enjoyed her salmon the House of Commons met to adopt a congratulatory address. The House of Lords had done so that afternoon. As the First Lord of the Treasury rose to move the address, MPs removed their hats as a sign of respect. Sir William Harcourt seconded the motion. Unfortunately there were discordant notes, and when the House divided there were forty-four Irish MPs against the motion.

Now came the excitement of Tuesday the 22nd, described by Victoria as a 'never-to-be-forgotten day'. The procession had already started as she finished breakfast. Before leaving Buckingham Palace she touched an electric button 'by which I started a message which was telegraphed throughout the whole Empire ... "From my heart I thank my beloved people, May God bless them!"' The Queen rode in an open state landau drawn by eight cream horses, including the two difficult ones. Opposite her were the Princess of Wales and Princess Helena. The procession wound its way to St Paul's, and as she went through the City she noticed one house in whose windows she saw the survivors of the Charge of the Light Brigade.

At St Paul's the steps were crowded with clergymen, over one hundred bishops, massed choirs, bands and the Gentlemen-at-Arms. As she had ordered, the service was short: the Te Deum was followed by the Lord's Prayer, 'most beautifully chanted', a special Jubilee prayer, the Old Hundredth, a benediction and the National Anthem. Then everything stopped. The Queen's carriage stood waiting for the seventeen coaches carrying the Princesses to start. Suddenly the rough old Archbishop called out for 'Three Cheers for the Queen!' and the cries echoed round St Paul's, down Ludgate Hill and along the Strand. Tears sprang to the Queen's eyes.

The great procession now moved off over London Bridge, along the Borough Road and then back again over the Thames via Westminster Bridge, past the Palace of Westminster, down Whitehall, through Horse Guards and back to Buckingham Palace. The Queen, who had set off at 11.15, finally returned at 1.45, having covered six miles. As she entered the gates of the Palace forecourt, ecstatic shouts once again caused the tears to roll down her cheeks. This only produced more cheering and she was heard to say, over and over again, 'How kind they are to me! How kind they are!' Lady Radnor, watching her enter the Palace, was amazed at how fresh she was. All that the Queen could say to the Lord Chamberlain as he led her to her room was, 'Splendid, Lord Lathom, *splendid*!'

Never before had the reality of Empire been brought home to the nation: the Empire was not a theory; it was people. The parliamentary correspondent Henry Lucy saw both the setting out and the coming back of the procession. 'There was', he wrote,

> no doubt as to the main attraction of the pageant – of course apart from the Queen. The Life Guards, the Hussars ... and the Lancers were splendid.... These we have with us always.... What was new, what touched the heart of the people ... was the spectacle of the detachments drawn from the uttermost ends of the earth ... all subjects of the Queen, all, it seemed, as they rode by, born soldiers, elate with pride at their visible ... incorporation with the might and majesty of the Empire. Here were troops from Canada and New South Wales, from Victoria, from New Zealand, from Queensland, from the Cape of Good Hope, from South Australia, from Tasmania, from Natal, and not least in popular esteem, a compact little body of the Rhodesian Horse. Later came horsemen from far-off India ... Colonists and Indian troops wore their native uniform, adding generously to the life and colour of the fast-shifting scene. The enthusiasm never flagged. From west to extreme east and back again, Colonists and Native troops rode through incessant ovation.

Throughout Jubilee Week the Queen rode about London in triumph. In one of these rides Princess Helena's daughter, Marie Louise, accompanied her. As they drove through cheering crowds the twenty-five-year-old Princess asked, 'Oh Grandmama, does not this make you very proud?'

Victoria replied, 'No, dear child, very humble.'

The popular image of Queen Victoria largely dates from the Diamond Jubilee. Her photographs show her as venerable, indomitable and humourless. This is the image which many wished to see, but to some at the time, and certainly to succeeding generations, her glum expression was not endearing. In her biography of the Queen Mrs Oliphant, who knew Victoria, tackled this question. Why, she asked, did the Queen always look 'cross'? 'This arises', she answered, 'solely from the conformation of the face, unnoticed in her prime, which, giving a certain projection to the lower jaw throws into the close shut mouth an air almost of discontent and dissatisfaction.' She added that this was a 'false' impression.

The Jubilee actually did something to correct this picture. The radical journalist W. T. Steed wrote to Sir Alfred Milner in South Africa:

> I wish that you had been here at Jubilee time. It has been a great week and everything

has passed off superbly. We were all astonished at the Queen. None of her photographs have done her justice and she is certainly immensely improved both in power and benevolence of expression since she was in the Abbey ten years ago.

Sir William Harcourt, when writing to Sir Arthur Bigge about a garden party for MPs, reminded him that: 'It is everything that people who are not accustomed to see The Queen should have such opportunities of realising the innate charm and simpleness' of her character. 'I am sure among some people', he added, 'she is looked upon as more or less a Myth! But we know better, don't we?'

The Diamond Jubilee marked the apogee of Victoria's reign. Whatever Harcourt or Bigge might feel, she was still a myth to many people. Helene Vacaresco, a Maid of Honour to the Queen of Romania who stayed in Windsor Castle, saw from her windows, which looked out towards the Queen's private apartments, the light of the Queen's lamp 'glowing late into the night'. She thought of the 'frail little old lady working there and holding in her hands the threads of ... her vast Empire, it fills me with something like awe'. The Queen filled others with something much more than awe – fear, as Fritz Ponsonby once observed when the composer Hubert Parry came to be knighted:

What a ripper he is. He told me he had had a private rehearsal & had split his breeches in trying to kneel down in his velvet pants. Some of the others who came to be decorated were chattering with fear & one of them kept on repeating his name to me, he was so frightened.

Later on that summer the Duke and Duchess of York visited Ireland on behalf of the Queen. The visit was a great success and they recalled 'the great kindness & hospitality we received from everyone in all parts of the country'. Victoria was delighted, but confided to the Lord Lieutenant that 'It was the same on the occasion of our three visits there, but alas! it did not produce a lasting effect.' This same summer saw the Lambeth Conference of Anglican Bishops, and a delegation called on the Queen; her demeanour hid her basic dislike of episcopacy. Later, when out for her afternoon drive, she burst out to her Lady in Waiting that the bishops were 'very ugly' and went on, according to Princess Marie Louise:

'I do not like bishops!' Edith Lytton nearly fell out of the carriage ... 'Oh, but your dear Majesty likes *some* bishops – for instance, the Bishop of Winchester [Randall Davidson] ... 'Yes,' said Her gracious Majesty, 'I like the man but not the Bishop!'

Victoria had now passed her seventy-eighth birthday. She endured with little complaint the burdens of increasing age. Her appetite was good (too good, some said) and she still slept well. Every day she still took her afternoon carriage ride. Her knees, however, were very stiff and a plank covered in green baize was run from the door to her carriage to save her the steps. One of the Indian servants supported her up the ramp. She refused to take an afternoon nap, but quite frequently fell asleep in the carriage: her Ladies in Waiting and the outriders had the delicate task of making sure that she woke up before passing a crowd. One afternoon, following the daily outing, Princess Marie Louise was summoned by a page. The Queen had had an accident:

> I leapt out to the corridor and found her half sitting and half lying in a little passage. 'My dear, I have had a terrible accident.' 'Good heavens, what?' I said. Apparently the horses had shied and nearly upset the carriage and, in Grandmama's words, 'Dear Frankie Clark lifted me out of the carriage and, would you believe it, all my petticoats came undone!'

The complaint which worried Victoria most was her declining eyesight, which was due partly to cataracts and partly to nerves. In 1896 a German oculist had dilated the pupils and dispersed the film by using belladonna. This treatment gave only temporary respite, however, and the Queen steadfastly refused to undergo surgery. She could still read during the day but was forbidden to do so at night: for several years documents had been read to her. Her writing grew even worse, and letters to ministers were often handed round the office to see if anyone could make out what she had written.

Telephones had been installed at Windsor in 1896, but the Queen insisted on using messengers to carry her letters along the draughty corridors of the Castle. She also disliked motor cars, and in the summer of 1900 an order appeared banning them from Hyde Park. Society was outraged and the Lord Chamberlain made enquiries about the ban on behalf of the Commissioner of Works. He discovered 'that the reason for the order is that the Queen refuses to drive in the park if motors are allowed to enter it in the afternoon'. 'Of course this settles the matter', he added in a spirit of rebellion, 'as none of us would wish our convenience to be considered where H.M.'s pleasure is concerned.' Insult was added to injury because, of course, the Queen was seldom if ever actually in Hyde Park.

Despite her advancing years the Queen was still able to get through a massive amount of work. Some of it was, to observers, unnecessary. Before his death Sir Henry Ponsonby tried, as others had before him, to reduce the number of signatures required from the Queen but, he lamented, 'The number ... increase [sic] and ... I have only succeeded in reducing one in 3 years.' She still insisted on signing officers' commissions: after all, they were her offficers. Her main political work still centred on foreign relations. She worked well with the Foreign Secretary, Lord Salisbury, who was also Prime Minister. It was the area where she could do most good, especially when she used her own intelligence network or made private efforts as with the Tsar in 1896. Sometimes she acted on her own: in 1896 she sent Theodore Martin on a secret mission to London to ask Fleet Street to curtail the current campaign against the German Emperor. He wrote on 13 July that he was 'now able to assure her Majesty that all the leading Journals will adopt a quite altered tone towards the Emperor ... & the German people'.

To cope with her work she increasingly depended on a loyal band of helpers made up of her daughters, granddaughters and Ladies – 'the petticoats', as the Kaiser called them. The most important were Princess Beatrice, Princess Helena and her daughter Victoria, known as Thora or Tora. The chief assistant was Princess Beatrice, whom Gladstone referred to as the 'manageress general'; he understood that she was 'omnipotent'. Beatrice certainly knew how to deal with an old lady's whims; it was she who would have her mother reminded that it was time to go to bed.

The Queen still occasionally attended Drawing Rooms where presentations were made. Sometimes these had their own moments of light relief. She noted on 10 May 1898 that the Drawing Room was 'a very full one. I remained an hour.' Her published Journal entry does not record the following incident, which Lady Monkswell heard from a Secretary at the United States Embassy:

> Old Lady Esher who is over 80 made the Queen such a low curtsey that she could not rise up again but simply sat on the floor with her feet sticking out in front of her. The Queen was so disturbed by this catastrophe that her spectacles tumbled off, & it was some minutes before the Lord in Waiting & other officials collected sufficient presence of mind to rush & pick up poor old Lady Esher.

Six hundred miles away other amusing stories circulated. One minister summoned to preach at Crathie church prayed fervently, if not discreetly, that 'as the Queen became an auld woman she might put on the new man, and in all righteous causes stand before her people like a he-goat upon the mountains'. Victoria's reaction can be imagined. So, too, can her response to a letter she received in 1899 from a well-wisher who had heard of her stiff knees. The writer suggested that she wear 'a tight leather jacket, and have a little balloon easily puffed out, attached to it, which would drag her about easily'.

In 1898 the vicar of Portsea, Cosmo Gordon Lang (later Archbishop of Canterbury), came to Osborne to preach for the first time before the Queen. Although in Victoria's eyes he gained by being a Scotsman, he lost points by being a High Churchman. Like others he was entranced by the Queen's 'charming smile' and her 'soft, gentle, and very delightful laugh, a sort of gurgle of pleasure'. When he was presented she enquired about his parish and he told her of his sixteen curates who shared the vicarage.

'Don't you think you ought to marry?' she asked. 'A wife would be so great a help.'

Lang replied tactfully, not wishing to mention celibacy, 'I fear I cannot afford one: my curates cost too much.'

'But surely a wife would be worth more than one or two curates?'

'No doubt, ma'am', he said, 'but there is this difference: if a curate proves ... unsatisfactory I can get rid of him. A wife is a fixture.'

The Queen answered, laughing, 'I can see you have a very poor idea of matrimony.'

Bad manners still infuriated her. On 9 March 1899 the American Ambassador, Joseph Choate, dined at Windsor. Gossip had it that the Choates were 'very difficult people with no idea of how to behave in polite society'. The meal got off to a bad start because Choate did not know or did not obey the rule that a guest did not speak to the Queen unless he were seated next to her or unless she spoke to him. As usual the meal proceeded quickly, and this evening Victoria was not in a talkative mood so there were periods of silence. She spoke only to Princess

Beatrice, and the other guests spoke to each other only in subdued tones. Lady Wolseley described it as a 'very whispery evening'. To relieve the tension the Ambassador leaned across Princess Beatrice: 'Queen Victoria!' he said. He was met with silence.

'Queen Victoria,' he tried again, 'I was just telling your daughter that she looks fine tonight.'

This time he got a bow and a freezing stare. No one at the table spoke another word.

Within a few days the Queen was off for her now annual visit to Nice. While there she visited a zoo owned by a Comtesse of somewhat dubious status, who presented her with a newly laid ostrich egg. The Comtesse had written her name on the egg, 'Just as if she had laid it herself!' said Victoria. Then she turned to Princess Beatrice and demanded to know why there were no ostrich eggs at Windsor: 'We *have* an ostrich,' she added in triumph.

'Yes, mama,' the 'manageress general' replied, 'a male one.'

The Queen enjoyed rides about the countryside and listening to selections from a new opera by Leoncavallo played by the composer himself. While in Nice she stayed at the Excelsior Hotel in Cimiez, which rises on the hills just north of the city. There she could look out on the Bay of Angels, which Nice faces, the Roman baths and amphitheatre to her left, and behind her the Alps. Round her were the hills covered in mimosa, pine trees, oleander and cypresses. A few days before leaving she wrote, understandably, 'Alas! my last charming drive in this paradise of nature, which I grieve to leave as I get more attached to it every year. I shall mind returning to the sunless north, but I am so grateful for all I have enjoyed here.' (In 1912 the grateful owner of the Excelsior, now the Excelsior Regina, erected a beautiful statue of the Queen in the grounds of the hotel. Although the building is now used for offices the statue remains, framed by pine and palm trees.) On her return to the 'sunless north' she would have appreciated the current joke about an imaginary African prince who was presented to her. She is supposed to have asked him if he did not worship the sun. 'Yes,' the prince says, 'and so would you, if you were to see Him.'

Back in Britain the Queen celebrated her eightieth birthday on 24 May: she talked to Marie Mallet about her life and told her that it was not 'trouble and sorrow' but 'joy and peace'. Marie was touched by her confidences and delighted that the Queen, despite her heavy burdens, 'enjoys life with the best of us and in the best and highest way'. To the young woman 'these little Sunday evening talks with the greatest of Queens, who before God, is the humblest of women' were a privilege without equal. That night the Queen wrote in her Journal,

I must express one word of deep gratitude to God for having preserved me so long to my dear children, all my friends, and the whole nation, which has come forward with the greatest affection and loyalty; I am deeply touched. May God still mercifully preserve me to work for the good of my country!

He did preserve her, but it was to face a crisis greater than any she had faced since the dark days of the Crimea, as the troubles so long brewing in South Africa finally erupted into war.

As with all the Queen's feelings, her hatred of war was straightforward and, to sophisticated minds, almost simplistic in its directness. In November 1898 Arthur Balfour had been staying at Balmoral. 'She has the utmost horror of war', he wrote, 'on the simple but sufficient ground that you cannot have war without a great many people being killed. No better reason can be given for this laudable sentiment, but she expresses it with singular naïveté.' To Victoria it was a question of personal responsibility: they were her soldiers, not Mr Balfour's. During a colonial dispute with France that same year she wrote: 'not a stone should be left unturned to prevent war, for I felt what an awful responsibility to God and man it would be were we to go to war, and what a sacrifice of thousands of lives!'

Victoria, however, shared the general anger at the Boers' treatment of British settlers, and in September 1899 orders were given to mobilise a force for South Africa. She took the expanse and work of the Empire very much to heart. If not in her own words, then in the words of the song that young soldiers like Winston Churchill sang in India, she was the

> Great White Mother, far across the sea,
> Ruler of the Empire may she ever be.
> Long may she reign, glorious and free,
> In the Great White Motherland.

While the Queen still had the same will to work, she no longer had the same energy. In October, while talking to the Secretary of State for Scotland, she fell asleep twice, much to his consternation. 'On awakening, Her Majesty excused herself with great candour on the score of her long drive, which was more than calculated to produce the effect on an old lady of eighty who insists on dining at 9.15.' Victoria nonetheless threw herself into the war effort: she had once told Lord Rosebery: 'I have always had a special feeling for the Army.' She had special large-scale maps of South Africa prepared and insisted on locating every farmstead where skirmishes had occurred. Fritz Ponsonby complained that 'The Queen has suddenly developed a culte for me & sends for me to talk over things & read things to her ... I have been to her almost every day.... One has to be certain of one's facts as she asks so many difficult questions.' She was also difficult in not allowing him to go to South Africa.

Between 10 and 15 December 1899, in a week that became known as Black Week, British forces suffered a series of humiliating reverses in attempts to relieve Ladysmith and Mafeking. On 12 December the Queen gave an audience to Arthur Balfour, whose mission was to reassure her, but she cut him short: 'Please understand that there is no one depressed in *this* house: we are not interested in the possibilities of defeat; they do not exist.' The next week Cosmo Gordon Lang saw her again and described her as '*Britannia at bay!*'

The Queen had no doubts as to the justice of Britain's position. 'It was not only necessary,' she told Lang, 'it was just. It must, it shall be fought out to the end. These brave fellows shall not be allowed to suffer in vain.' As she stamped her foot she added, 'I will hear of no complaints against my generals till the war is over. They have my confidence. They will do their utmost.' She then turned her batteries on to the Boers' leader, President Kruger. 'That man's parade of religion annoys me. I don't think much of a religion which is used to justify such self-aggrandisement and wilfulness and corrupt government.' Having warmed to her subject she dragged Gladstone, who had died the year before, into her tirade: 'What I most dislike about President Kruger is the way he brings his politics into his religion and his religion into his politics. I am bound to say that in Mr Gladstone also I disliked this mixture of politics and religion, which is of course quite intolerable.'

The war's second year brought better news but no lessening of the Queen's interest. Hundreds of telegrams from generals poured in each week. When they were not clear, she would fire off another telegram to get the precise information she always wanted. On 9 February, for example, on seeing a telegram from General Buller, she telegraphed to the Commander-in-Chief, Lord Wolseley, to ask his interpretation of the message. He telegraphed back that he thought Buller meant that 'he finds a direct advance from the position he had won was too difficult & that he would consequently try to move in some other direction'. Another of her concerns was over hospital conditions. Sir Arthur Bigge told her that, in obedience to her command, 5818 feather pillows had been sent to Cape Town hospitals and 1450 to hospitals in Britain. The lessons of the Crimea had not been forgotten.

The losses sustained by British and colonial troops hurt the Queen deeply, and she wrote to one granddaughter that 'my heart bleeds most truly and deeply for the many losses ... I assure you it makes me quite miserable.' When Lord Esher dined with the Queen a month after this he saw her turn quite pale as a telegram was brought to her at her table: 'She said it made her ill to open telegrams about the war.' However bad the news, she rallied quickly. When the inevitable critics and armchair generals began their cries for enquiries the Queen urged on the government 'the necessity of resisting these unpatriotic & unjust criticisms of our ... conduct of the War'. She agreed that 'the War Office is greatly at fault', but insisted that if there were an enquiry it should come after the war; an enquiry now would produce 'great harm'. The next month she exploded to Balfour, 'The conduct of the Opposition is very despicable & unpatriotic.'

Victoria found coping with generals much easier than politicians. It was during Black Week that Princess Marie Louise was staying with the Queen. Victoria turned to Marie Louise's sister, Thora, and asked her to tell Sir Arthur Bigge to 'clear the line as I wish to telegraph to the troops'. Thora returned to say that Bigge humbly reminded Her Majesty that 'it is only customary for the Sovereign to telegraph to the troops if they win a victory, and this is not a victory'. The Queen retorted, 'And since when have I not been proud of my troops whether in success or defeat? Clear the line.' The line was cleared and the message sent. Fifty years later Princess Marie Louise, now an old woman herself, met a retired officer who had been in South Africa and said, 'I can assure you, ma'am, that it bucked us up no end.' Victoria also paid a special three-week visit to Ireland to thank the people for their contribution to the war. As a permanent memorial to Irish heroism she created a new regiment, the Irish Guards.

The Queen's last great social occasion was on 11 July, when she attended a garden party at Buckingham Palace for five thousand guests. Although she was 'dreadfully hot and rather tired' when it was over, she knew it had been a success. She was taken twice round the grounds at a snail's pace in her small pony-chair and then went to a private tent for tea. Perhaps it was on this occasion that an American visitor saw her spread an immense napkin over herself before she tackled the ices, jellies, fruit, sandwiches, pastries, cakes and ice creams set before her.

A fortnight later Marie Mallet found the Queen 'certainly less vigorous' and having trouble with her digestion. If she would 'follow a diet and live on Benger's Food and chicken all would be well but she clings to roast beef and ices! And what can you then expect?' Her physician had suggested Benger's, a special preparation for invalids. The Queen liked it but 'now to his horror, instead of substituting it for other foods she adds it to her already copious meals.... She is very sleepy in the evenings and goes to bed earlier although not early enough.'

In May Victoria had noted, 'I am very tired and long for rest and quiet.' She would have neither in the nine months of life left her. There were difficulties involved in creating the new Commonwealth of Australia; in Peking the Boxer Rebellion and a massacre of Europeans left the Queen 'quite miserable, horror-struck'. Almost as troubling were the reports that the Kaiser was planning to intervene in China; his capacity for trouble was unlimited in both personal and diplomatic relations. When he had last visited Windsor in 1899 Fritz Ponsonby told his brother that the Emperor 'was full of barlooneries & royal jokes. All the others were terrified of him except of course the Queen who did exactly the same as if he were not here'.

The year 1900 also brought the Queen a dreadful succession of tragedies and crises which undermined her spirits. In April, an anarchist in Brussels tried to shoot the Prince and Princess of Wales. The scourge of terrorism was stalking Europe. On 30 July Victoria was 'horrified' on coming in for breakfast to hear that the 'good kind King of Italy had been shot at and killed last night'. The court was plunged into yet another period of mourning, which cause Marie Mallet to moan, 'We never escape jet for long.'

The following day brought far worse news. Victoria's second son, Prince Alfred, Duke of Saxe-Coburg since 1893, had died in his sleep. 'Oh, God! my poor darling Affie gone too. My third grown-up child, besides three very dear sons-in-law. It is hard at eighty-one! ... It is a horrible year, nothing but sadness and horrors of one kind and another.' Later on in the day the Queen sent for Marie Mallet, who kissed her hand and 'knelt down to take it in mine and so we remained for a full five minutes, trying to be calm enough to speak. The Queen cried so gently and seemed so patient and resigned in her great sorrow.'

On 26 August Prince Albert would have celebrated his eighty-first birthday. Inevitably her thoughts turned to him and previous birthdays:

This ever dear day has returned again without my beloved Albert being with me, who on this day, eighty-one years ago, came into the world as a blessing to so many, leaving an imperishable name behind him! How I remember the happy day it used to be, and preparing presents for him, which he would like! I thought much of the birthday spent at the dear lovely Rosenau in '45, when I so enjoyed being there, and where now his poor dear son [Prince Alfred], of whom he was so proud, has breathed his last. Another birthday we spent ten years later at St. Cloud ... now gone, when the Emperor and Empress were so kind to us and dear Albert was not well. His last birthday of all he spent at the Viceregal Lodge, and we went on to Killarney. All, all is engraven on my mind and in my heart.

This autumn Cosmo Gordon Lang paid his last visit to Osborne. He mentioned a sailor on one of the royal yachts who had drowned, leaving a destitute wife in his parish. The next morning Lang was summoned to the Queen's private room where he found her at her desk, working. 'I want to give you something from me to help the poor sailor's widow,' she said, and took a bundle of keys from her girdle as if she were an ordinary housekeeper. She went to a cupboard which contained an odd assortment of papers and parcels but mainly toys used for grandchildren's presents. There was also a small tin box which she opened with difficulty. She carefully took out five sovereigns and handed them to Lang. 'Please give these to that poor woman. But', she added with a smile, 'you mustn't tell Sir Fleetwood Edwards [Comptroller of the Privy Purse].'

October brought the Queen yet more sorrows. On the 29th a telegram announced the death of Prince Christian, Princess Helena's son, who was serving in South Africa and due home for leave in three weeks. Again the Queen turned to Marie Mallet, not as a sovereign but as a 'sorrowing woman who clings to human sympathy and hungers for all that can be given on such occasion'. Lord James of Hereford, the Minister in Attendance, worried that the Queen has 'lost much flesh and had shrunk so as to appear about one-half of the person she had been. Her spirits, too, had apparently left her', when Lord George Hamilton succeeded him in November he was 'shocked to note the marked declension in her vitality. . . . There were unmistakable symptoms of an impending physical breakdown.' For the first time he felt that the Queen's work was proving too much for her.

As the weeks wore on Victoria began talking to Princess Thora about illness and even death, something she did not normally do. Her health now declined steadily. For the first time in her life she had serious trouble sleeping, not getting to sleep until late and therefore waking late the next morning. This threw out her schedule, to her great frustration. She was now suffering from back pain as well as rheumatism and her enormous appetite, which in the summer allowed her to finish a large dinner followed by chocolate ice, apricots and iced water, had vanished. Her afternoon tea now consisted of arrowroot and milk. The Household, like its mistress, was slowly running down. There were complaints about the servants: on one occasion the Queen only ordered one dish for dinner, noodles, but the cooks forgot about it and she had nothing to eat. In addition the footmen smelt of whisky, were slow in answering the bell and began adopting a supercilious manner.

The Queen's face was frequently marked by pain, but she would not give up.

'After the Prince Consort's death', she confided to Marie Mallet, 'I wished to die, but *now* I wish to live and do what I can for my country and those I love.' It was a remark she frequently made. On 12 November she presided over a Privy Council to swear in new ministers – Lord Salisbury's government had recently been returned to power after a general election. She amazed Almeric Fitzroy, the new Clerk to the Council: her memory 'guided us through the mazes of a somewhat intricate transaction whereon official records were dumb, and the recollections of ministers a blank'. On 30 November she reviewed 240 Canadian troops on their way home from South Africa and entertained some of the officers to dinner. Afterwards an officer said with emotion, 'I could die for her!'

The Queen fulfilled her last public engagement on 12 December when she visited Windsor town hall to see a sale of Irish industrial products. On 14 December she made her thirty-ninth annual pilgrimage to the Mausoleum to mark Prince Albert's death, but she admitted afterwards that she felt 'very unwell'. On the 18th the court moved to Osborne. The journey exhausted the Queen and for five days she saw no one. Because of her difficulty in sleeping, she asked Thora to come to her bedroom to read to her; when Princess Beatrice heard of this she said that she, and not her niece, would go. Her reason was a simple one: the Queen had never allowed her daughters to see her in bed, or at least not since they were very small children. This was a chance not to be missed. The next day, however, the Queen, speaking quietly, told Thora, 'We must enter in the Diary please that Aunt Beatrice's reading roused me up thoroughly when I was going to sleep.'

The Journal for 1901 began on a sombre note: 'Another year begun, and I am feeling so weak and unwell that I enter upon it sadly.' Later in the day she drove to a soldiers' home where she spoke to some men back from South Africa. The following day she received Lord Roberts on his return from South Africa, where he had been Commander-in-Chief. During the audience she surprised him by conferring an earldom on him and by remaindering it to his daughter because his only son had been killed in the war. As a personal token of respect she also gave him the Garter. On 10 January she saw the Colonial Secretary, Joseph Chamberlain, who found her much better than he had expected and said that she showed 'not the slightest sign of failing intelligence'. They spoke mainly about the war and she told him, 'I am not anxious about the result.' Her main worry was about the continued call for an enquiry. The former Birmingham republican, now a Secretary of State, was the last minister whom Queen Victoria received. The first had been Lord Melbourne, who sixty-three years before had kissed the small hand of a young Queen of eighteen.

For even more years than that Victoria had been faithful to her Journal which recorded her triumphs and her defeats, her joys and her sorrows, her frustrations and her achievements. On almost 25,000 days, she had added to this record, a feat never equalled by any other sovereign and by few other people:

1 August 1832: We left Kensington Palace at 6 minutes past 7 ... $\frac{1}{2}$ past 8 p.m. .... Mamma is not well and is lying on the sofa in the next room. I was asleep in a minute in my own little bed which travels always with me.

20 June 1837: Lord Conyngham then acquainted me that my poor Uncle, the King, was no more ... and consequently I am *Queen*. ... Since it has pleased Providence to place me in this station, I shall do my utmost to fulfil my duty towards my country.

16 October 1861: Balmoral, I made some hasty sketches; and then Albert wrote on a bit of paper that we had lunched here, put it in the Selters-water bottle, and buried it there.

1 January 1862: With what a heavy broken heart I enter on a new year without him. ... Last year music woke us.

24 November 1874: Received a box from Mr. Disraeli, with the very important news that the Government has purchased the Viceroy of Egypt's shares in the Suez Canal. ... An immense thing. It is entirely Mr Disraeli's doing.

22 April 1897: Cimiez. At half past six the celebrated and famous actress Sarah Bernhardt ... performed a little piece for me in the drawing-room ... quite marvellous.

Now, on Sunday evening, 13 January 1901 – sixty-eight years, five months and thirteen days after that first entry – the Queen dictated her last entry:

Had a fair night, but was a little wakeful. Got up earlier and had some milk. Lenchen [Princess Helena] came and read some papers. Out before one, in the garden chair. Lenchen and Beatrice going with me. Rested a little, had some food, and took a short drive. ... Rested when I came in, and at five-thirty went down to the drawing-room, where a short service was held by Mr. Clement Smith, who performed it so well, and it was a great comfort to me. Rested again afterwards, then did some signing, and dictated to Lenchen.

Randall Davidson compiled a long memorandum about the Queen's last days, most of which has never been used; it is among his papers in Lambeth Palace Library and gives us a unique record. On Monday, 14 January she saw Lord Roberts for a second visit. She was anxious to have the latest war news now that he had had time to consult London. The 'petticoats' had been dreading this audience, fearing that it would prove too much for her, and had devised a scheme whereby they would send someone with a message to end the audience after twenty minutes. 'Do nothing of the kind,' Victoria retorted. 'I have a great deal to say to him which I *must* say and a great deal to hear from him. I shall want plenty of time, and I won't be interrupted.' Their meeting was a long one, and afterwards she was in good spirits. But on the following day she became confused during her afternoon drive and had great difficulty in keeping awake and in remembering things. She gave one last command when she ordered her Ambassador in Berlin to refuse an honour from the Kaiser in the celebrations to mark the Hohenzollern dynasty's bicentenary.

Although she knew her faculties were failing her, she was adamant that she would not lay down her burden. 'They will want me to give in and to have a Regency to do my work. But they are wrong. I won't. For I know they would be doing things in my name without telling me.' But from 15 January she conducted no further government business. There were no more letters, telegrams, audiences, papers to be read, ministers to be seen, mistakes to be corrected, commissions to be signed, or warnings to be given. She had worked for over 22,000 days but could work no more. This state of affairs could not carry on without a major government crisis: already judges could not go out on circuit because of the missing commissions; government business, especially foreign relations, were being held up and despatch boxes were piling up at Osborne.

On Thursday the 17th the Queen had difficulty in speaking, although it appears that she did not actually suffer a stroke; for the first time the Court Circular did not appear. As Bishop Davidson said, 'Dear old lady she is simply worn out after nearly 64 years of honest hard work for her people.' The Royal Family was summoned on the 18th and a bulletin was prepared because rumours were proliferating. It appeared on the 19th:

> The Queen has not lately been in her usual health, and is unable for the present to take her customary drives. The Queen during the past year has had a great strain upon her powers, which has rather told upon her Majesty's nervous system. It has, therefore, been thought advisable by her Majesty's physicians that the Queen should be kept perfectly quiet in the house, and should abstain for the present from transacting business.

At noon another bulletin referred to the Queen's 'great physical prostration', accompanied by 'symptoms that caused anxiety'.

On Sunday the 20th the Prince of Wales and the Kaiser, who had come over specially, arrived at Osborne. On the following day the Queen rallied and asked her doctor, 'Am I better at all?'

He said 'Yes', and she quickly asked for Turi, her little Pomeranian dog. When he arrived she held him for about an hour. No one was allowed near her for fear of exciting her. She said to a doctor, 'I don't want to die yet. There are several things I want to arrange.' A bulletin was published which announced that the Queen had 'slightly rallied', but this was done at the insistence of the Prince and in the face of the doctors' objections. The great fear now was that she would actually rally enough to lead, in Bishop Davidson's words, 'a sort of vegetable life'. The spectre of a regency rose again.

On the morning of the 22nd the doctors thought that the Queen's time had come and the family, some not fully dressed, quickly assembled in her bedroom. The Prince of Wales knelt on her right side and the Kaiser on her left. A nurse was behind her to hold up her pillows because she was having so much difficulty in breathing. She was quite conscious and alert, for when the Duke of Connaught said that Bishop Davidson was there she replied, 'Yes, of course; and is Mr Smith [the vicar of Whippingham] here too?' Even in her last hours she was considerate of others. A messenger was immediately sent to bring the Queen's vicar to her side. She uttered her last word when she opened her arms to the Prince of Wales and whispered what some heard as 'Bertie' and others as 'Albert'. He broke down in tears. Because of the emotional upset the doctors asked everyone to leave. As she slept, members of the Household were allowed in for a last look at their sovereign.

Later that afternoon Bishop Davidson was summoned to the Queen's bedroom. The Royal Family had again gathered and oxygen was being administered to help her breathe. As the Bishop and the vicar of Whippingham recited prayers and hymns, certain words would catch and hold her attention and she took particular note of the last verse of Cardinal Newman's great hymn, 'Lead, Kindly Light':

> So long Thy power hath blest me, sure it still will lead me on,
> O'er moor and fen, o'er crag and torrent, till the night is gone;
> And with the morn those Angel faces smile,
> Which I have loved long since, and lost awhile.

At six o'clock the doctors warned the family that the end was quickly approaching. Although her breathing was still laboured her mind was clearer than it had been all day. Her family came up to her one by one and named themselves. The Prince of Wales knelt beside her and the Kaiser stood near the head of her bed. At 6.25 one of the doctors told Bishop Davidson that the end was at hand. The Bishop recited the Commendatory Prayer from the Prayer Book and some verses of scripture. As he pronounced the blessing, 'The Lord bless thee, and keep thee: The Lord make his face shine upon thee, and be gracious unto thee: The Lord lift up his countenance upon thee, and give thee peace', the Queen opened her eyes quite wide and died quite peacefully. Princess Helena '*felt* & knew she saw beyond the Border Land – & had *seen* & *met* all *her loved ones*. In death she was so beautiful, such peace & joy on her dear face – a radiance from Heaven.'

The first to come out of the room was the new King. Osborne House had been sealed by the police to keep the journalists at bay while the official telegrams were prepared. The final bulletin read: 'Her Majesty the Queen breathed her last at 6.30 p.m., surrounded by her children and grandchildren.' As the notice was fixed to the locked gates the journalists raced to East Cowes, shouting as they ran, cycled or drove: 'The Queen is dead!' When the news reached London the theatres closed, and at 8.15 the Great Bell of St Paul's began tolling every minute for two hours. That evening at 10.15 a service was held in the Queen's bedroom; flowers had been placed round her body and the crucifix that had been above her bed now lay in her hands. The new King set off for London, leaving the Kaiser in charge of the arrangements. Everyone commented on the latter's unexpected tact and kindness.

The Queen had left specific instructions for her funeral. The service was to be at St George's Chapel, Windsor; it was to be in the day and not at night, as had been traditional; there was to be a minimum of ceremonial; the funeral must be 'white', by which she meant as little 'mourning' as possible – black was to be replaced with purple and white; Chopin, Beethoven and Scottish laments were to be played, but no Handel; the funeral must be 'military' in tone – there was to be no hearse, but a simple gun carriage as used for a private in her Army; the Royal Standard was to be placed 'partially' – not fully – over the pall on the coffin, and Princess Beatrice was to be her executrix: the 'manageress general' would carry on her work as normal.

Inevitably problems arose. The first was a command from the King for a Eucharist in his mother's bedroom. Davidson wondered if 'perhaps there was some mistake': he feared a backlash from extreme Protestants, and also perhaps wondered what the Queen herself would have said. The second problem arose when the undertaker's assistant arrived. Bishop Davidson was shocked to find him 'a rough, ordinary man' who had come without a coffin. Time was pressing. The Bishop called for the Kaiser's help. He ordered the assistant not to touch the Queen. 'If', Davidson wrote,

> the occasion had been a less grave & solemn one there wd. have been much that was humourous in the Emperor's harangue to the rather dull undertaker's assistant. 'It is always like this. When an ordinary humble person dies everything is arranged quite easily & with reverence & care. When a "personage" [dies] you fellows all lose your senses and make stupid mistakes. . . .' The man was simply terrified.

When the coffin did arrive the body was lifted into it by the King, who had returned from London on the 24th, assisted by the Kaiser and the Duke of Connaught. The Queen was dressed in white with a white widow's cap and veil, but not her wedding veil.

The dining room had been converted into a temporary chapel. A white pall with the royal arms in the corners was placed over the coffin and on this was laid the Queen's coronation robe and the crown, sceptre and orbs. With them lay her small crucifix.

The news of the Queen's death had gone quickly round the world. In France, hostility to Britain over the Boer War was laid aside for a while and *Le Figaro* said that, to her people, Victoria was 'more than a Queen, being, as it were, the head of all English families'. In the United States, President McKinley ordered the White House flag lowered to half-mast and spoke of the Queen as a 'Sovereign, whose noble life and beneficent influences have promoted peace and won the affection of the world'.

On 25 January Parliament met to receive the official notification of the Queen's death and to adopt messages of condolence. In the Lords the Prime Minister delivered a restrained speech, probably in order to avoid breaking down. In the Commons Arthur Balfour referred to the Queen's

> unostentatious patience which for sixty-three years, through sorrow, through suffering, in moments of weariness . . . had enabled her to carry on . . . her share in the government of this great Empire. For her there was no holiday, to her there was no intermission of toil.

Far away from Parliament, in the depths of Aylesbury Prison, Lady Battersea saw women convicts with small back bows pinned to their gowns. She discovered they had made their tokens of mourning from torn-off bits of their bootlaces.

On Friday, 1 February the coffin began its journey to London. Cosmo Gordon Lang saw it cross the Solent:

> Suddenly the silence was broken. A sound smote the heart. It was the sound of the guns from Osborne . . . telling that the Queen's body was being saluted by the Fleet. Then, through the long lines of battleships, stretching in a curve from Cowes to Portsmouth,

came the little yacht *Alberta* bearing the body ... preceded by six torpedo-destroyers moving black and silent, like dark messengers of death sent to summon the Queen. The *Alberta* – small, slight, but dignified, passing through the huge ironclads, seemed strangely like the Queen herself.... The sound was varied only by the strains of Chopin's Funeral March, played by each ship's band as the body passed. Then – the most moving thing of all – just as the *Alberta* entered the harbour, the sun set in a rich glow of tranquil glory.

The *Alberta* lay in the harbour overnight and the next morning Lang went on board to conduct a short service before the body was taken by train to London. Only the Royal Family and the Kaiser were there, and as Lang waited for the sailors to come for the coffin he saw the new King pause for a few minutes and kneel in silent prayer at his mother's feet; he was joined there by the Kaiser, who knelt beside him. As the train journeyed to London, Lady Lytton, who was attending the coffin, looked out of the window to see people kneeling on the ground as the Queen passed. For the first time in modern history, as the body was taken from Victoria to Paddington Station, London was able to take part in a sovereign's funeral. The streets were decorated in purple and white as she had wanted. Her coffin lay on a simple gun carriage: the greatest of Victorians would not have a Victorian funeral.

At Windsor, when the horses were being brought up to be harnessed to the gun carriage they began kicking and plunging: the wait in the cold had been too much for them. Prince Louis of Battenberg came to the rescue by suggesting that the sailors pull the gun carriage: thus was born a custom that has been adhered to at every Sovereign's funeral since. Inside St George's Chapel, where the candles 'glimmered like jewels in a dark casket', the congregation waited, wondering what had happened. 'At last', Almeric Fitzroy wrote, 'the west doors were flung open, and up the steep steps was borne the casket containing the dead Queen's body: the extreme shortness of it struck one with pathetic insistence; almost a child's coffin.' After the service the coffin was taken into the Albert Chapel where it lay in state until 4 February, the date of the interment at Frogmore.

When preparations were underway for the interment Lord Esher was horrified to discover that no one could find the recumbent marble figure of the Queen, carved by Marochetti forty years before, which was to cover her grave beside the Prince Consort. The Clerk of the Works had never even heard of it; some doubted if it had ever been carved. At last an 'old workman remembered that about 1865 the figure had been walled up in the stores at Windsor'. The wall was knocked down and the marble figure revealed.

On the 4th, when the procession arrived at the Mausoleum the military escort fell away and the Queen's Pipers played for the last time 'Flowers of the Forest' as the coffin was carried into the building. Both the coffin and its lead case had the following inscriptions fixed to them: '*Depositum Serenissimae Potentissimae et Excellentissimae Principis Victoriae Dei Gratia Britanniarum Reginae Fidei Defensoris Indiae Imperatricis Obiit XXII, Die Januarii Anno Domini MDCCCCI. Aetatis Suae LXXXII. Regnique Sui LXIV.*' 'Here lies the body of the most serene, powerful and excellent Prince, Victoria, by the Grace of God, of the British

Dominions, Queen, Defender of the Faith, Empress of India, who died on 22 January 1901 in the eighty-second year of her life and the sixty-fourth of her reign.'

As Bishop Davidson read the committal the Master of the Household, Lord Edward Pelham Clinton, sprinkled on the case earth that was said to have come from the Holy Land. After the final blessing the Royal Family was to process across the platform erected beside the sarcophagus for a final look at the grave. 'The King', wrote Davidson, 'came first alone, but, instead of simply walking by, he knelt down.' Then Queen Alexandra followed, leading her grandson, little Prince Edward of York, by the hand. As she knelt the boy became frightened, so 'the King took him gently and made him kneel beside him, and the three, in perfect silence, were there together – a sight not soon to be forgotten.' When they had passed on the rest of the Royal Family, the Kaiser and those of the Household invited to the service came and did likewise. As the mourners left the Mausoleum they found that the rain which had held off all day was falling and within a short time snow fell. The Queen had had her white funeral after all.

When Queen Victoria ordered the construction of the Mausoleum for Prince Albert she had had inscribed over the door, '*Vale desideratissime . . .*' – 'Farewell, most beloved! Here at last I will rest with thee; with thee in Christ I shall rise again.' But in those talks with Princess Thora Queen Victoria admitted, 'My dear, do you know, I sometimes feel that when I die I shall be a little, just a little, nervous about meeting Grandpapa for I have taken to doing a good many things that he would not quite approve of.'

☞HE ROYAL FAMILY

Between 1840 and 1857 Queen Victoria had nine children, of whom three died in her lifetime:

VICTORIA, 1840–1901
(Vicky), styled Princess Royal; married 1858 Prince Frederick (Fritz) of Prussia, heir to Prussian throne; became Empress of Germany 1888 and on Fritz's death that same year became known as Empress Frederick. Had nine children of whom three died young; her eldest son became the last German Kaiser, Wilhelm II; her daughter Sophie became Queen of Greece.

ALBERT EDWARD, 1841–1910
(Bertie), Prince of Wales; married 1863 Princess Alexandra of Denmark; succeeded 22 January 1901 not as Albert Edward I but as Edward VII. Had six children of whom two died young. His eldest son, the Duke of Clarence, died 1892, and his second son, George, Duke of York, succeeded him as George V. His third daughter, Maud, married a Danish prince, later King of Norway.

ALICE, 1843–78
Married 1862 Louis, later Grand Duke of Hesse; she died after nursing her children through diphtheria. Of her seven children two married into Imperial Russian Family – Elizabeth and Alexandra (Alicky), who married the last Tsar, Nicholas II; both were killed by the communists. Alice's eldest daughter, Victoria, married Prince Louis of Battenberg and from her descend the Mountbatten family, the Swedish Royal family and Prince Philip.

ALFRED, 1844–1900
(Affie), created Duke of Edinburgh 1866; married 1874 Grand Duchess Marie Alexandrovna, daughter of Tsar Alexander II of Russia; on death of Prince Albert's brother, his uncle Ernest, he succeeded by arrangement as Duke of Saxe-Coburg-Gotha. He died a year after his only son; of his five children one daughter, Marie, became Queen of Romania.

HELENA, 1846–1923
(Lenchen), married Prince Christian of Schleswig-Holstein; of her five children two daughters, Marie Louise and Helena Victoria (Thora) acted as secretaries to the Queen.

LOUISE, 1848–1939

(Louischen), married Marquess of Lorne, who succeeded as Duke of Argyll in 1900; he was for a time Governor General of Canada; she had no children.

ARTHUR, 1850–1942

Named after his godfather, the Duke of Wellington; created Duke of Connaught and Strathearn 1874; married Princess Louisa of Prussia, 1879; had three daughters one of whom, Margaret, became Queen of Sweden. Pursued a military career.

LEOPOLD, 1853–84

Suffered from haemophilia; created Duke of Albany 1881; married Princess Helena of Waldeck 1882. His son, born after his death, succeeded Prince Alfred as last reigning Duke of Saxe-Coburg-Gotha.

BEATRICE, 1857–1944

(Baby). Victoria's confidante; married 1885 Prince Henry of Battenberg; had four children; her one daughter, Victoria Eugenie, became Queen of Spain; the present King, Juan Carlos, is the great-grandson of Beatrice.

Queen Victoria had forty-one grandchildren, of whom thirty-one survived her.

$\mathscr{P}$RINCIPAL SOURCES BY CHAPTER

Books are cited in the chapter where first used. All books were published in London unless noted otherwise. Manuscript sources are listed under each chapter in which they are used, but their location is only given when first cited.

Queen Victoria's published writings, that is, her Journals and correspondence, which are used throughout this book, include the following: Viscount Esher (ed.), *The Girlhood of Queen Victoria*, 2 vols (1912); A.C. Benson and Viscount Esher (eds), *The Letters of Queen Victoria ... 1837–1861*, 3 vols (1907); G. E. Buckle (ed.), *The Letters of Queen Victoria Second Series ... 1862–1885*, 3 vols (1926–1928); G. E. Buckle (ed.), *The Letters of Queen Victoria Third Series ... 1886–1901*, 3 vols (1930–1932); Hector Bolitho (ed.), *Further Letters of Queen Victoria from the Archives of the House of Brandenburg–Prussia* (1938); Roger Fulford (ed.), *Private Correspondence of Queen Victoria and the Crown Princess of Prussia 1858–1885*, 5 vols (1964–1981); Arthur Helps (ed.), *Leaves From the Journal of Our Life in the Highlands, from 1848 to 1861* (1868); *More Leaves From the Journal of a Life in the Highlands, from 1862–1882* (1884); Richard Hough (ed.), *Advice to a Grand-daughter, Letters from Queen Victoria to Princess Victoria of Hesse* (1975).

Extensive selections from the Queen's Journals as well as notes by her were included in Theodore Martin, *The Life of His Royal Highness The Prince Consort*, 5 vols (1875–1880).

Chapter I

Mabell, Countess of Airlie, *Lady Palmerston* (1922); Duke of Argyll, *V. R. I.* (1902); Egerton Castle (ed.), *Jerningham Letters* (1896); Lionel Cust, *King Edward VII and His Court* (1930); Jane Ellice, 'Queen Victoria ... ' in *The Cornhill Magazine* (June 1897); W. G. FitzGerald, 'Personal Relics of the Queen' in *Strand Magazine* (June 1897); Mollie Gillen, *Royal Duke* (1976); Caroline Grosvenor and Charles Beilby (eds), *The First Lady Wharncliffe* (1927); Lord Holland (Lord Staverdale, ed.), *Further Memoirs of the Whig Party* (1905); Richard R. Holmes, *Queen Victoria 1819–1901* (1901 edn); Gervase Huxley, *Lady Elizabeth and the Grosvenors* (1965); Maud, Lady Leconfield and John Gore (eds), *Three Howard Sisters* (1955); Elizabeth Longford, *Victoria R.I.* (1964); Frances Low, *Queen Victoria's Dolls* (1894); Princess Marie Louise, *My Memories of Six Reigns* (1956); Peter Quennell (ed.), *Private Letters of Princess Lieven* (1937); Cecil Woodham-Smith, *Queen Victoria ... 1819–1861* (1972); E. A. Smith, *Whig Principles and Party Politics: Earl Fitzwilliam* (1975); Baron E. von Stockmar and F. Max Müller (eds), *Memoirs of Baron Stockmar* (1872); Dorothy Stuart, *The Daughters of George*

III (1939); Duke of Wellington, *Wellington and His Friends* (1965); Marquis of Zetland (ed.), *Letters of Disraeli to Lady Bradford and Lady Chesterfield* (1929).

Manuscript Collections

Broadlands MSS, Palmerston Correspondence with Lord Beauvale (Historical Manuscripts Commission); Bryn-y-pys MSS, Correspondence of the Duchess of Kent and Queen Victoria with the 3rd Duchess of Northumberland, D/BP/1104–6, 1110–14, 1134–47 (Clwyd Record Office); Archbishop Davidson Papers, Vol. XIX (Lambeth Palace Library); Archbishop Howley Papers, Vol. 1754 (Lambeth Palace Library); Liverpool Papers, BL Add. MSS 38303 (British Library); MS Engl. Misc. d 665: Archbishop Howley's Confirmation Address of 30 July 1835 (Bodleian Library); Miscellaneous Manuscripts: Duke of Kent's Correspondence, BL Add. MSS 43377 (British Library).

Chapter II

Annual Register (1840); Georgiana Blakiston, *Lord William Russell and His Wife* (1972); Edward Boykin (ed.), *Victoria, Albert, and Mrs Stevenson* (New York, 1957); Ralph Disraeli (ed.), *Home Letters by Lord Beaconsfield 1830–1852* (1928); Madeline House et al. (eds), *Letters of Charles Dickens* (1965–); Kurt Jagow (ed.), *Letters of the Prince Consort 1831–1861* (1938); R. R. James, *Rosebery* (1963); L. J. Jennings (ed.), *The Croker Papers* (1884); Shane Leslie (ed.), *Letters of Mrs Fitzherbert* (1940); Geraldine Macpherson, *Memoirs of Anna Jameson* (1878); Betty Miller (ed.), *Elizabeth Barrett to Miss Mitford* (1954); Charles Murray, 'Three Weeks at Court' in *The Cornhill Magazine* (January 1897); Alan Nevins (ed.), *The Diary of Philip Hone* (New York, 1927); Rowland Prothero, *Life and Correspondence of A. P. Stanley* (1893); G. N. Ray (ed.), *Letters and Private Papers of William Makepeace Thackeray* (1945–6); Thomas Sadler (ed.), *Diary, Reminiscences and Correspondence of Henry Crabb Robinson* (1872); *The Standard* (10 May 1839); Kay Staniland and Santina M. Levey, *Queen Victoria's Wedding Dress and Lace* (1983); Lytton Strachey and Roger Fulford (eds), *The Memoirs of Charles Greville* (1938); *The Sunday Times* (9 February 1840); Tom Taylor (ed.), *Autobiographical Recollections by Charles Leslie* (1860); William Toynbee (ed.), *The Diaries of William Charles Macready* (1912); Vera Watson, *A Queen at Home* (1952); Mrs Hugh Wyndham (ed.), *Correspondence of Sarah Spencer Lady Lyttelton* (1912).

Manuscript Collections

Bryn-y-pys MSS D/BP/1110 *passim*; Davidson Papers, Vol. XIX; Gladstone Papers, BL Add. MSS 44819 (British Library); Holland House Papers, BL Add MSS 51871–51872 (British Library).

Chapter III

Hector Bolitho (ed.), *The Prince Consort and His Brother. Two Hundred New Letters* (1933); Austen Chamberlain, *Down The Years* (1935, 2nd edn); A. G. Gardiner, *Life of Sir William Harcourt* (1923); Mrs Gaskell, *The Life of Charlotte Brontë* (1900 edn); Constantin de Grunwald (trans. Brigit Patmore), *Tsar Nicholas I* (1954); Arthur Helps (ed.), *The Principal Speeches ... of ... The Prince Consort* (1862); Edwin Hodder, *Life and Work of the ... Earl of Shaftesbury* (1886); Elizabeth Longford. 'Queen Victoria's Doctors' in Martin Gilbert (ed.), *A Century of Conflict* (1966); Desmond MacCarthy and Agatha Russell (eds), *Lady John Russell A Memoir* (1910); R. F. Mullen, 'The House of Lords and the Repeal of the Corn Laws' (Oxford D. Phil. thesis, 1974); Charles Murray, 'Ten Days at Court: The Emperor Nicholas's Visit' in *The Cornhill Magazine* (March 1897); J. H. Plumb, *Royal Heritage* (1977); Magdalen Ponsonby (ed.), *Mary Ponsonby A Memoir* (1927); Mary Ponsonby and Edmund Gosse, 'The Character of Queen Victoria' in *The Quarterly Review* (April 1901, CXCIII, 386); T. W. Reid, *Lyon Playfair* (1899); *The Sunday Times* (9 February 1845); Tyler Whittle, *Victoria and Albert at Home* (1980).

Manuscript Collections

Auckland Supplementary MSS, BL Add. MSS 45730 (British Library); Broadlands MSS, Melbourne's Correspondence with Palmerston; Dawson MSS, Lady A. M. Dawson's copies of correspondence between Queen Victoria and the Duchess of Kent, MS Eng. Lett. c 400 (Bodleian Library); Gladstone MSS, BL Add. MSS 44777; Liverpool MSS, BL Add. MSS 38303; Mendelssohn MSS, Letters in MS Deneke d 21 (Bodleian Library); Peel MSS, BL Add. MSS 40432, 40441, 40447, 40452, 40456 (British Library); Stevenson Family MSS, Correspondence with Secretary of State 1836–1840, Vols 42, 43 (Library of Congress).

Chapter IV

Anon, *The History of The Times* (Vols I and II, 1935, 1939); John Bailey (ed.), *The Diary of Lady Frederick Cavendish* (1927); Georgiana Baroness Bloomfield, *Reminiscences of Court and Diplomatic Life* (1883); A. M. Broadley, *The Boyhood of a Great King 1841–1858* (1906); Charles Bullock, *The Queen's Resolve: 'I Will be Good'* (n.d [1887]); Frances Bunsen, *A Memoir of Baron Bunsen* (1868); Lucy Cohen, *Lady de Rothschild and Her Daughters* (1935); Edward Cook, *The Life of Florence Nightingale* (1913); Julia Dallas (ed.), *George Mifflin Dallas Letters From London* (1870); George Douglas [8th Duke of Argyll] (ed. Dowager Countess of Argyll), *Autobiography and Memoirs* (1906); Mrs Steuart Erskine (ed.), *Twenty Years at Court from the Correspondence of ... Eleanor Stanley* (1916); Viscountess Enfield [later Countess of Strafford] (ed.), *Leaves from the Diary of Henry Greville* (1883–1905); Lord Edward Fitzmaurice, *The Life of ... Second Earl Granville* (1905); Comte Fleury, *Memoirs of the Empress Eugénie* (1920); Helmut and Alison Gernsheim, *Victoria R* (New York, 1959); Emile Jaegle, *Biographie de s.m. le reine de la Grande Bretagne* (Paris, 1858); Treasham Lever (ed.), *Correspondence of Lady Palmerston* (1957); Earl of Malmesbury, *Memoirs of an Ex-Minister* (1884); W. F. Monypenny and G. E. Buckle, *The Life of Benjamin Disraeli* (1929 edn); F. Max Müller, *Auld Lang Syne* (1898); *Notes and Queries* (1931, CLX, 193–4); C. E. Quarme, *A Narrative of the Visit of Queen Victoria to Lancaster in 1851* (1877); Jasper Ridley, *Napoleon III and Eugénie* (1979); E. E. P. Tisdall, *Queen Victoria's Private Life* (1961); G. O. Trevelyan, *Life and Letters of Lord Macaulay* (1876); Anthony Trollope, *Framley Parsonage* (1879 edn); Queen Victoria, *Leaves from a Journal ... of the Visit of The Emperor and Empress of The French ... and of the Visit of the Queen ... 1855* (1961); J. F. Vincent (ed.), *Journals of Lord Stanley 1849–1869* (1978); Count Vitzthum (ed. and trans. Henry Reeve), *St Petersburg and London* (1887); Reginald Wilberforce, *Life of Samuel Wilberforce* (1888 rev. edn).

Manuscript Collections

Aberdeen Papers, BL Add. MSS 43067; Archbishop Davidson Papers, Vol. XIX.

Chapter V

Anon [Princess Helena], *Alice Grand Duchess of Hesse* (1885); John Bailey and Hector Bolitho (eds), *Letters of Lady Augusta Stanley* (1927); A. Tilney Bassett (ed.), *Gladstone to his Wife* (1936); A. B. Cooke and J. R. Vincent (eds), *Lord Carlingford's Journal* (1971); A. I. Dasent, *John Thadeus Delane* (1908); George Dolby, *Charles Dickens As I Knew Him* (1885); Hope Dyson and Charles Tennyson (eds), *Dear and Honoured Lady The Correspondence Between Queen Victoria and Alfred Tennyson* (1969); Derek Hudson, *Munby* (1972); Sir Sidney Lee, *King Edward VII* (1925); Donald Macleod, *Memoir of Norman Macleod, D.D.* (1876); Mary Howard McClintock, *The Queen Thanks Sir Howard* (1945); Theodore Martin, *Queen Victoria As I Knew Her* (1901); R. F. Mullen, 'The Last Marriage of a Prince of Wales, 1863' in *History Today* (June 1981); Maurice Paléologue, *The Tragic Empress: Intimate Conversations with the Empress Eugénie* (1928); Arthur Ponsonby, *Henry Ponsonby* (1942); Agatha Ramm (ed.), *The Political Correspondence of Mr Gladstone and Lord Granville 1868–1876* (1952); Bertrand Russell and Patricia Russell (eds), *The Amberley Papers* (1966); F. Barham Zincke, *Last Winter in the United States* (1868).

Manuscript Collections

MS Acland d 1 (Bodleian Library); MS Clarendon Dep. 509 (2,3) (Bodleian Library); Disraeli Papers, Box 26 [A/X/A Sections 43,51] (Bodleian Library); Moran Papers (Library of Congress, Washington DC); Parrish Collection, Trollope MS: Letters to T. A. Trollope (Princeton University Library); MS Wilberforce c 13, d 22 (Bodleian Library).

Chapter VI

Anon, *The Private Life of the Queen* (1898); G. K. A. Bell, *Randall Davidson* (1952); E. F. Benson, *As We Were* (1930); Lady Burghclere (ed.), *Letters of the Duke of Wellington to Marchioness of Salisbury* (1927); Mrs Stewart Erskine, *Memoirs of Sir David Erskine* (1926); Maurice V. Brett (ed.), *Journals and Letters of Reginald Viscount Esher* (1934); Augustus J. C. Hare (ed. Malcolm Barnes), *In My Solitary Life* (1953); Mary Lutyens (ed.), *Lady Lytton's Court Diary* (1961); Marie Mallet (ed. Victor Mallet), *Life With Queen Victoria* (1968); Kinsey Peile, *Candied Peel* (1931); 'Kenward Philp', *John Brown's Legs; or, Leaves from a Journal in the Lowlands* (New York, 1884); Landon Ronald, *Myself and Others* (n.d.); Desmond MacCarthy and Agatha Russell (eds), *Lady John Russell* (1910); Gabriel Tschumi (ed Joan Powe), *Royal Chef* (1954); Walter Walsh, *The Religious Life ... of Queen Victoria* (1902); Duke of Windsor, *A King's Story* (1951); Sir Henry Wood, *My Life of Music* (1938).

Manuscript Collections

MS Acland d 1; Alison MS, MS Eng. Lett. d 420 (Bodleian Library); Davidson Papers, Vol. XIX; Dilke Papers, BL Add. MSS 43875 (British Library); Disraeli Papers, B/XIX/D/98; Harcourt Papers, MS Harcourt Dep. 690 (Bodleian Library); Liverpool Papers, BL Add. MSS 38303; Müller Papers, MS Müller Dep. d 155 (Bodleian Library); Royal Archives, RA S 27 (Windsor Castle); Tait Papers, Vol. 74 (Lambeth Palace Library); MS Eng. Lett. d 267 f 72 (Bodleian Library).

Chapter VII

Eve Adam (ed.), *Mrs J. Comyns Carr's Reminiscences* (n.d.); George Arthur (ed.), *The Letters of Lord and Lady Wolseley* (1922); Constance Battersea, *Reminiscences* (1922); A. C. Benson, *The Life of Edward White Benson* (1899); Frederick Bridge, *A Westminster Pilgrim* (n.d. [1919]); C. K. Cooke, *Princess Mary Adelaide* (1900); Marquess of Crewe, *Lord Rosebery* (1931); Helen G. McKenny (eds Alfred Binney and John A Vickers), *A City Road Diary* (1978); Mary, Lady Monkswell (ed. E. C. F. Collier), *A Victorian Diarist* (1944); John Morley, *Life of William Ewart Gladstone* (1903); J. E. B. Munson, 'The Unionist Coalition and Education, 1895–1902' in *The Historical Journal* (1977); Lord Newton, *Lord Lansdowne* (1929); Frederick Ponsonby (ed. Colin Welsh), *Recollection of Three Reigns* (1957); Rowland E. Prothero, *Prince Henry of Battenberg* (1897); Mary King Waddington (ed. Tompkins McIlvaine), *Letters of A Diplomat's Wife* (1903).

Manuscript Collections

Asquith Papers, MS Asquith 9 (Bodleian Library); Benson Papers, Dep. Benson 3/74 (Bodleian Library); Cabinet Papers, CAB 41/23/591 (Royal Archives); Gladstone Papers, BL Add. MSS 44791; Glynne-Gladstone Papers, MSS 780 (Clwyd Record Office); Harcourt Papers, MS Harcourt Dep. 694, 390; Maj. P. H. Lowe, MS Diary of The Ashanti Campaign, 1895–6, by courtesy of Mr R. B. Backhouse,

QC; Mallet Papers, by courtesy of Mr P. L. V. Mallet; Milner Papers, MS Milner Dep. 55 (Bodleian Library); Ponsonby Papers, MS Eng. Hist. c 651 (Bodleian Library); Salisbury Papers, Class H (Christ Church College, Oxford); Sandars Papers, MS Eng. Hist. c 713, 729 (Bodleian Library).

Chapter VIII

'An Eminent Literary Gentleman', *King Edward VII* (n.d.); *Annual Register for 1901*; Lord Askwith, *Lord James of Hereford* (1930); E. F. Benson, *Final Edition* (1940); G. F. Browne, *Recollections of a Bishop* (1915); Lady Gwendolen Cecil, *Life of Robert Marquis of Salisbury* (1922–32); Winston Churchill, *My Early Life* (1930); Blanche E. C. Dugdale, *Arthur James Balfour* (1939); Sir Almeric Fitzroy, *Memories* (n.d.); J. L. Garvin and Julian Amery, *Life of Joseph Chamberlain* (1932–1969); Viscount [Herbert] Gladstone, *After Thirty Years* (1928); Lord George Hamilton, *Parliamentary Reminiscences* (1922); J. G. Lockhart, *Cosmo Gordon Lang* (1949); Elizabeth Longford (ed.), *Louisa Lady in Waiting* (1979); Henry W. Lucy, *Diary of the Unionist Parliament 1895–1900* (Bristol, 1901); W. C. E. Newbolt, *Years That Are Past* (n.d.); Mrs [Margaret] Oliphant, *Queen Victoria* (1900); *Parliamentary Debates* (4th Ser., LXXXIX, 1901, 19–23); Helen, Countess Dowager of Radnor, *From a Great-Grandmother's Armchair* (n.d.).

Manuscript Collections

Chilston Papers, U 564 c 341/3 (Kent Record Office); Davidson Papers, Vol. XIX Item 101; Gladstone Papers, BL Add. MSS 44791; Harcourt Papers, MS Harcourt Dep. 694; Milner Papers, MS Milner Dep. 182, 349; Sir Edmund Monson Papers, MS Eng. Hist. c 595 (Bodleian Library); Ponsonby Papers, MS Eng. Hist. c 651; Sandars Papers, MS Eng. Hist. c 713; Zimmern Papers, MS Zimmern 10 (Bodleian Library).

$\mathscr{P}$ICTURE CREDITS

NDEX

NOTE: In the index VR denotes Queen Victoria and A denotes Prince Albert.